BRITISH RAIL SCENE

BRITISH RAIL SCENE

THE 1970S AND EARLY 1980S IN PHOTOGRAPHS

ANDY SPARKS

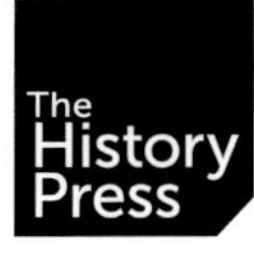

First published 2017

The History Press
97 St George's Place,
Cheltenham Gloucestershire, GL50 3QB
www.thehistorypress.co.uk

British Library Cataloguing in Publication Data.
A catalogue record for this book is available from the British
Library.

ISBN 978 0 7509 7013 6

Typesetting and origination by The History Press
Printed by TJ Books, Padstow, Cornwall

CONTENTS

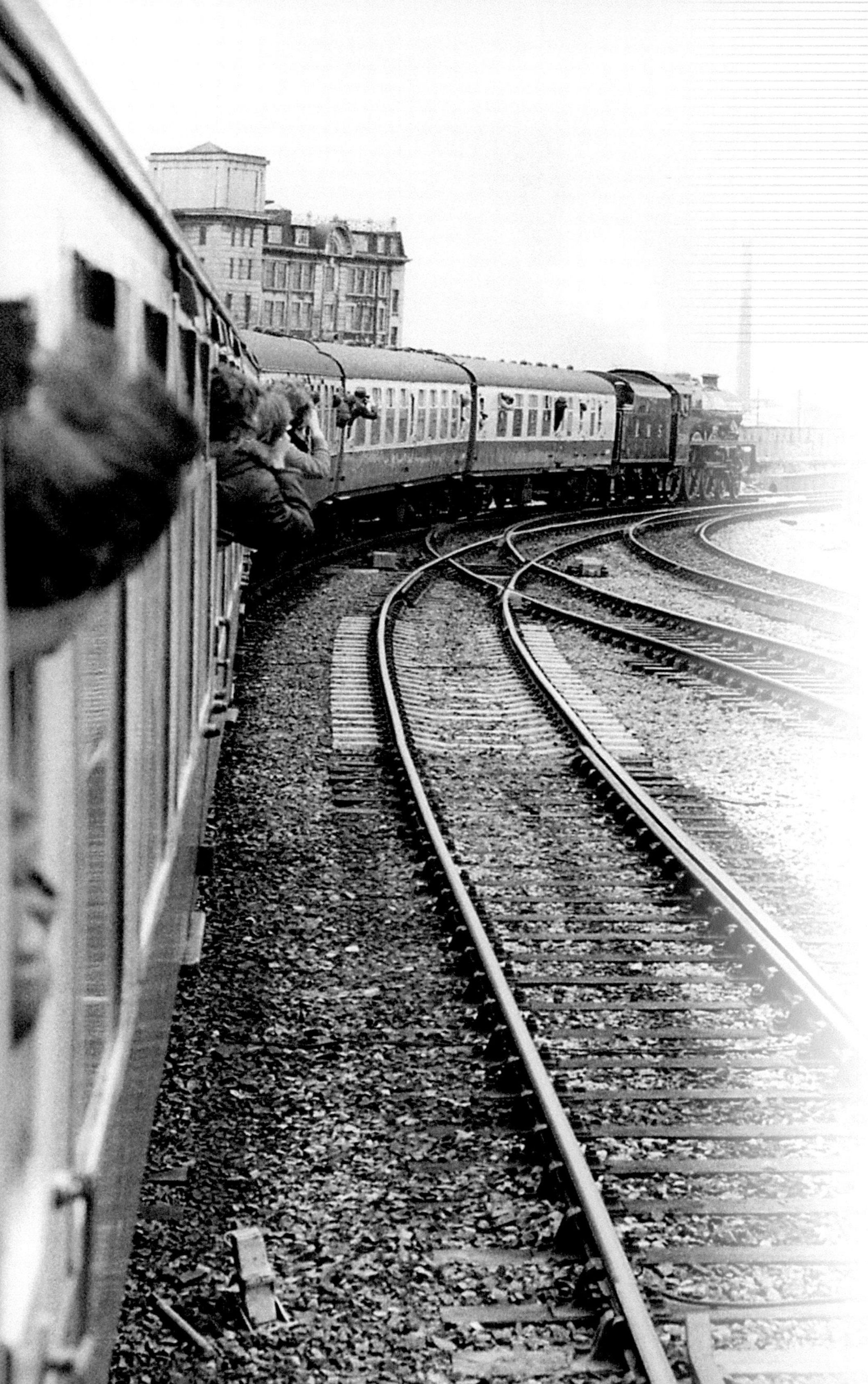

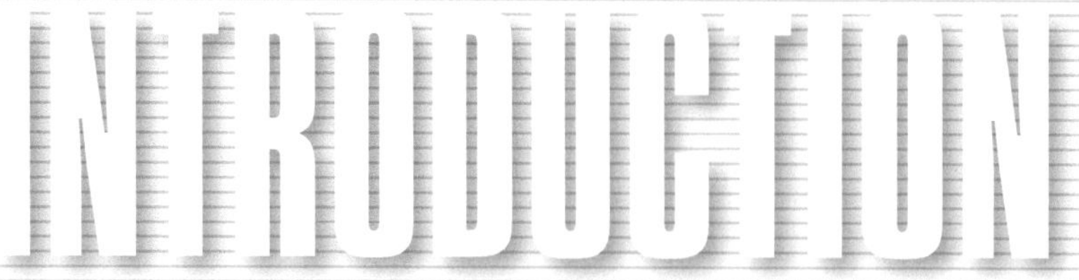

INTRODUCTION

Welcome to my third book of photographs and accompanying captions depicting the rail scene during the period 1972 to 1982. My first two books, *British Rail Northern Scene: A 1970s Railway Album* and *British Rail Northern Scene: Coast to Coast*, concentrated on the North West, North Wales and Yorkshire area. This book spreads the net, focusing on many areas of Britain. It is intended to give a glimpse into the nation's fascinating and rapidly changing railway environment during that ten-year period. In addition to rationalisation and modernisation, massive social, political and economic changes compounded their effect to make this period like no other. I knew the gritty steam age atmosphere of the old order was on borrowed time. I was on a quest to bag as many different images as possible, to help tell the story. Quite often, soon after I had taken a photograph, many aspects of it were swept away forever. The bright, squeaky clean and efficient new order, now synonymous with the modern railway network, was well under way.

My first attempts at railway photography date back to 1968 when steam was coming to an end. I was just 9 years old. My attempts were made possible, indirectly, by an elderly family friend who was clearing out some old Crested Ware ornaments. She said I could have them. They were nice, but I decided to swap them at the local junk shop for a Kodak 127 camera. I used my pocket money at the chemist a few doors down from the junk shop, where they loaded and unloaded the camera with film, and sent it away for processing. My photographs were poor, to say the least. I decided to give up my part-time career as a rail cameraman until I was a little older. In the meantime, I spent many a happy time out trainspotting. I also pored over timetables, books and magazines to gen up on railway facts and figures. In addition, I closely examined the photographs on every page. This was in a bid to help me develop a style and purpose if I returned to taking photographs of my all-consuming interest: railways.

My favourite photographer, by far, was and still is Colin T. Gifford. His style is fantastic, having an awesome ability to capture so much when triggering the camera shutter. On my travels I used to pass a second-hand camera shop, in Gorton – Mr Dodd's. He had a vast array of cameras on display, although most were far too expensive to ever dream of owning: Bronica, Canon, Minolta, Leica, Pentax and Rolleiflex, to name but a few. However, just before my 14th birthday, I spied a cheap little Russian camera sitting near the front of his vast display. It was nowhere near as sophisticated as a Russian 'Zenith', but I thought it would be a good way to recommence my railway photography endeavours. By this time, I felt ready to have another go and was about to embark on a mission to photograph as much of the changing rail scene as I could. My mum and dad bought me the camera, along with some Kodak Tri-X film. My quest immediately began.

My first port of call was the hyper-atmospheric and very busy Manchester Victoria station. This was followed by a train ride to steam-age Wigan Wallgate station. I soon wore the camera out, so for my 15th birthday my mum and dad bought me a brand-new bombproof Russian Leica lookalike. It was a Zorki 4 – a brilliant camera. Once I started work as an engineering trainee, the Zorki 4 was eclipsed by a Pentax SP1000, bought on twelve months' hire-purchase from Debenhams in Manchester.

My quest yielded thousands of photographs, some of which were sadly lost or destroyed. Fortunately, a large proportion survived as prints and/or negatives or unprocessed films. Astonishingly, when processed the films produced usable photographs twenty-five years after their use-by dates. Thanks to the wonders of modern-day science, technology and computerisation, I have been able to marshal and improve my photographs to create a series of themed chapters – enough to produce several books, if there is sufficient demand. It is surprising how each photograph jogs my memory. In most cases I can remember taking them. If my memory has played tricks on me, however, and the accompanying caption is wrong in some way, please forgive me. I hope you enjoy this book, which is meant to be informative, smile inducing, thought provoking, a little bit different and a wallow in nostalgia. It is something I hope will be dipped into time and time again.

Andy Sparks

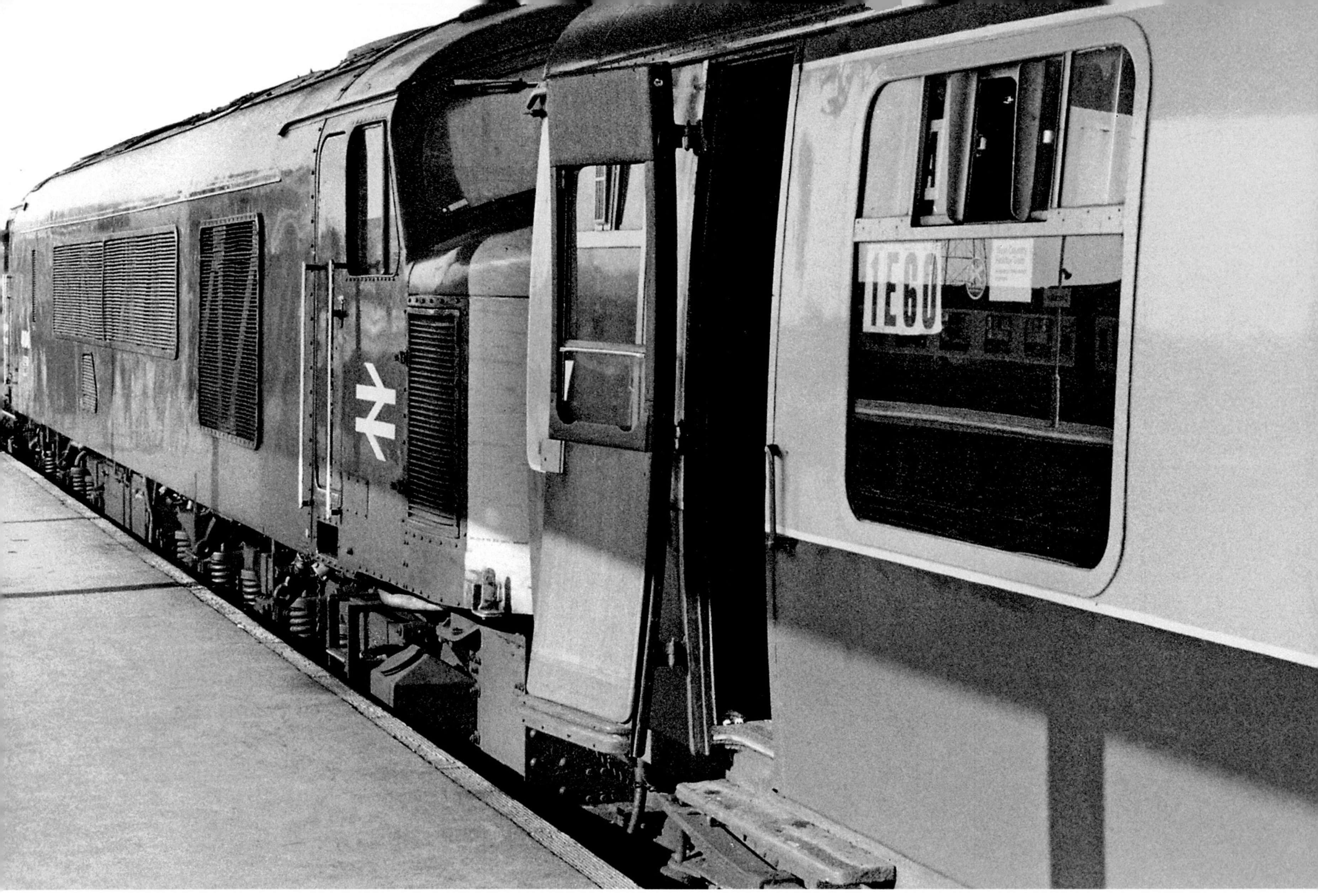

Can You Resist Wanting to Climb Aboard? Doncaster, August 1980.
If my memory banks are correct, I reckon this train has just arrived at Doncaster after hauling the well-filled Saturdays-only train from Paignton. How inviting the open door is. I wish I could climb aboard. The train is hauled by 46048, which only lasted another year in service. It was withdrawn on 13 September 1981 and then scrapped two years later at British Rail Engineering Ltd (BREL) Swindon. By 1980 loco and multiple-unit reporting number headcode displays had not been in use for several years. Despite this, they still appeared on coaching stock in the form of paper labels as seen in this shot. They are accompanied by a West Country holiday train paper-label sign. The photograph also features a red No Smoking sign. Nowadays smoking is not allowed on trains but back then it was, apart from where these little red signs appeared. You can also see one of Doncaster's black-on-white station signs in the coach window reflection.

READY TO DEPART

INTRODUCTION

A train journey of any length, from any station, is an event: the mild sense of excitement and anticipation just before departure has never left me, the multi-aspect signal changing to green or the semaphore being raised giving an indication of what is about to happen and the sight of the driver getting ready to get the train under way always adding to the sense of purpose.

Back in the days of first-generation diesel multiple units (DMUs), the guard's buzzer to indicate to the driver that it was okay to get the train under way was a sound I really liked. I can almost hear it as I write this introduction. Plus, of course, many trains still made use of the guard's green flag and whistle to indicate to the driver that the train was ready to depart.

The station environment and general railway paraphernalia added to the impeding theatre of a train departing, while the garbled station announcement emanating from an aged Tannoy speaker put the icing on cake.

The amount of times I have stood and watched a train waiting to depart, wishing I were on it, are countless. Loco-hauled or a multiple unit, express or suburban, made no difference. I still do it. As a young lad many of their destinations were dream locations to take photographs, see iconic locomotives and explore. On my 'if only' list were Doncaster, York, Carlisle, London, Glasgow and Torquay, to name but a few. Fortunately, my dreams did come true and I visited them all and many more besides, my trusty Pentax SP1000 or Zorki 4 camera always on my shoulder.

Get ready, this chapter, and the book, is about to get under way ...

Green Flag and a Shrill Whistle, Manchester Victoria, summer 1977.
This evocative and rather dreamy ready-to-depart shot was taken on Platform 11 at Manchester Victoria. You can almost hear the guard's whistle and see the flag being waved. The train is bound for Llandudno, hauled by an unidentified Class 40. I feel like jumping aboard. Sadly, it has long since departed.

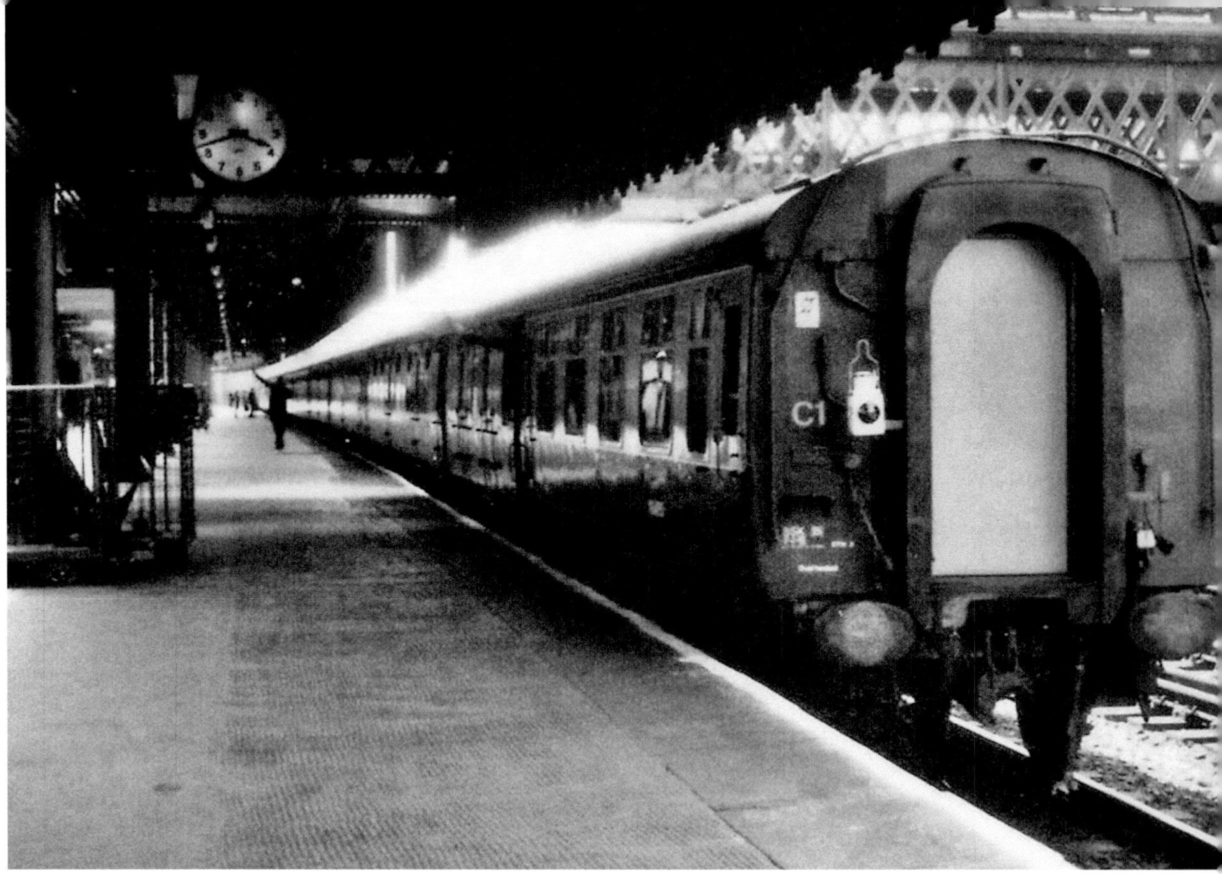

I Can't Take My Eyes Off It, Llandudno Junction, August 1975.
Being an avid train enthusiast, I find it unsurprising that this chap is fixated by the about-to-depart London Euston-bound Class 47-hauled train. The signal is up; the driver is about to release the brakes and bring on the power. Probably an eruption of aromatic fume-laden clag will accompany the event. After this the ten or eleven bogie coaches the 47 has in tow will rumble by at a gradually increasing speed. The man will no doubt watch the show until the last coach's tail lamp disappears into the distance. Surely anyone would find all this hard to resist? Next stop for the Holyhead–Euston train will be Colwyn Bay. The 47 will be replaced by an electric loco, probably a Class 86, at Crewe. It is likely the onlooker is waiting to board a Manchester Victoria or Conway Valley Line train. Then again, he might be spending the whole day sat on this strategically placed bench seat – and why not?

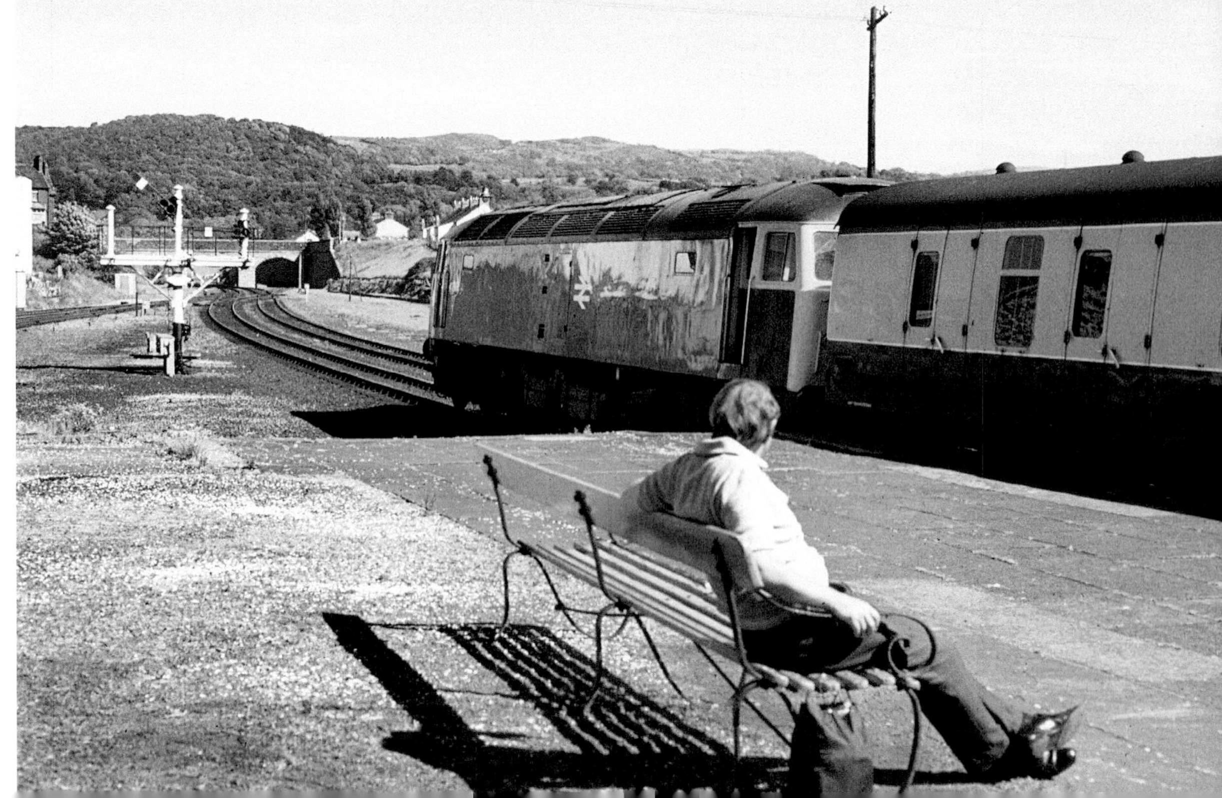

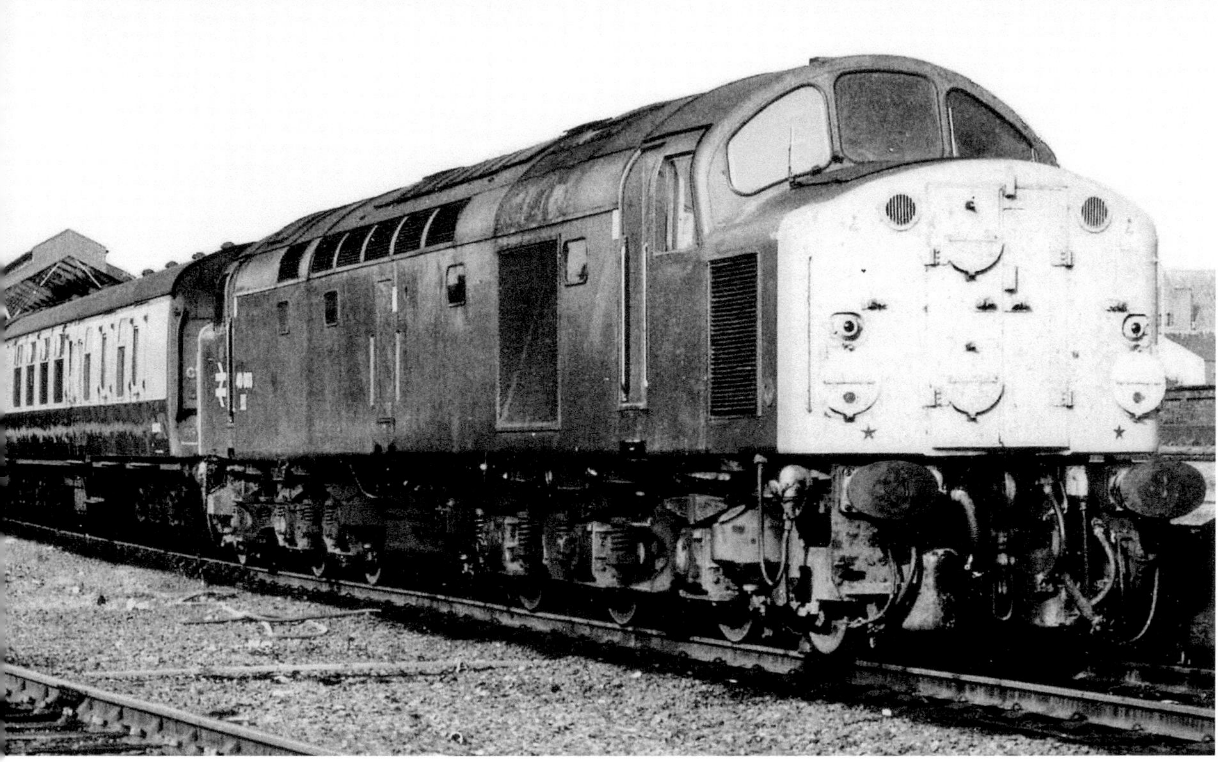

The Majesty of a Class 40, Llandudno, summer 1974.
I think this shot of a Class 40 waiting to depart from Llandudno goes some way to show the immensity and certain majesty of the class. I hope you agree. Summer days during the 1970s and '80s, Llandudno and Class 40s are synonymous with each other. It was often possible to see several 40-hauled trains, both timetabled and specials, at the same time in the station's lengthy bay platforms. The locos would lie silent until close to departure time, when they would be fired up ready for the return journey. Soon afterwards the station would be filled with a steady and purposeful whistling emanating from the locos' trusty power plants. This is the case with the loco in this photograph; listen carefully and you might just hear it.

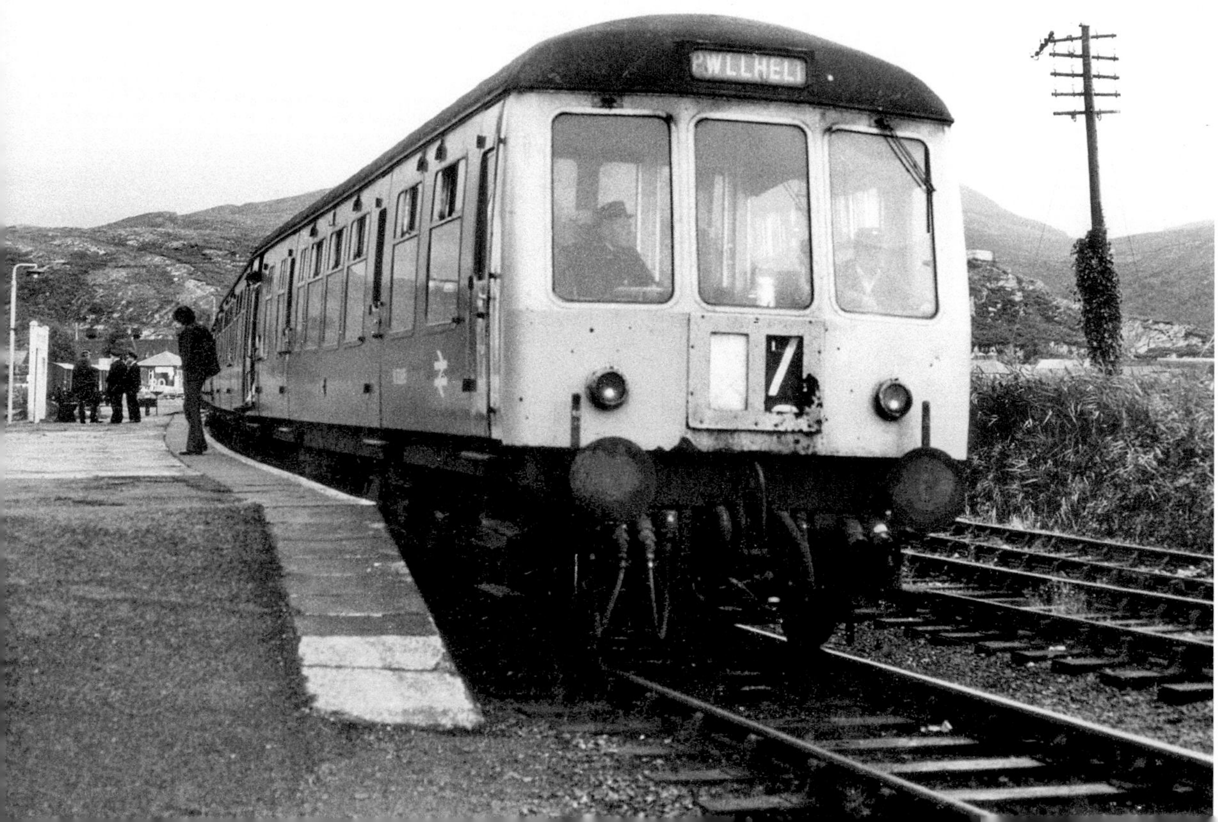

Pwllheli Bound, Porthmadog, 23 August 1977.
The platform has a few locals talking, plus the guard looking for any last-minute passengers. In the cab of the Class 108 two-car DMU are the driver and a fellow rail man, chatting while waiting for departure time. Could the other chap be a driver travelling up the line to make the return working, a friend or someone learning the route? You might be able to make out the driver's billycan, probably containing tea or coffee, behind the central cab window. No doubt this was a throw back to the days when the driver would have driven a steam loco along the route just ten or eleven years earlier. Anyway, the train is ready to depart with just a handful of passengers for a brisk run along the upper reaches of the Cambrian Coast Line to Pwllheli.

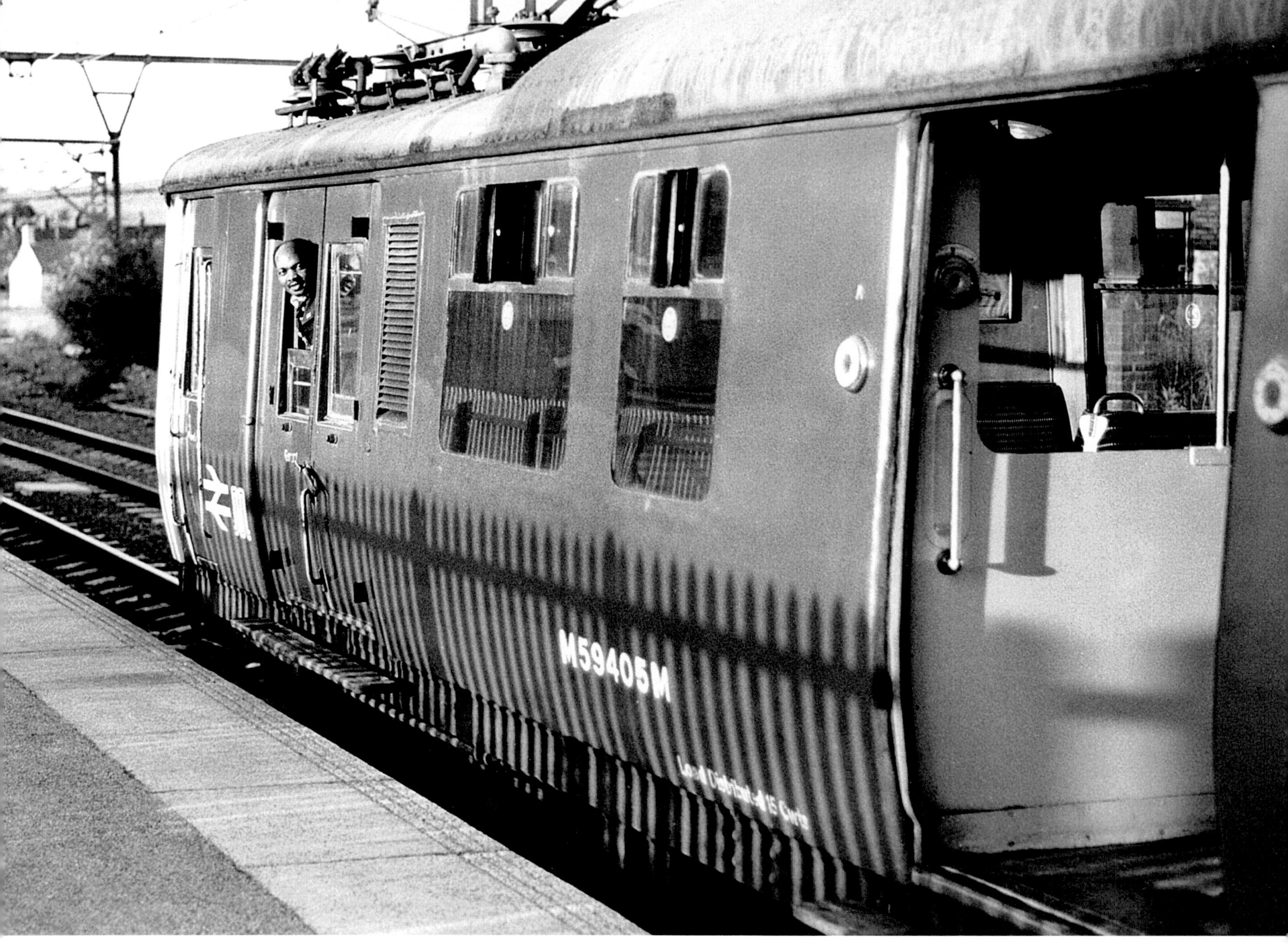

Mind the Doors, Hadfield, August 1980.
I can remember this guard asking me if I wanted to join the train. I said, 'No, I want to take your photograph. Give me a smile.' He duly obliged. Soon afterwards he gave the driver the signal to get the train under way. Its twin doors effortlessly closed and the train departed from Hadfield for Manchester Piccadilly, via Glossop. This electric multiple unit (EMU) is one of the LNER-designed Class 506s, which were based at Reddish Depot until it closed. Longsight continued to service them until they were eventually withdrawn.

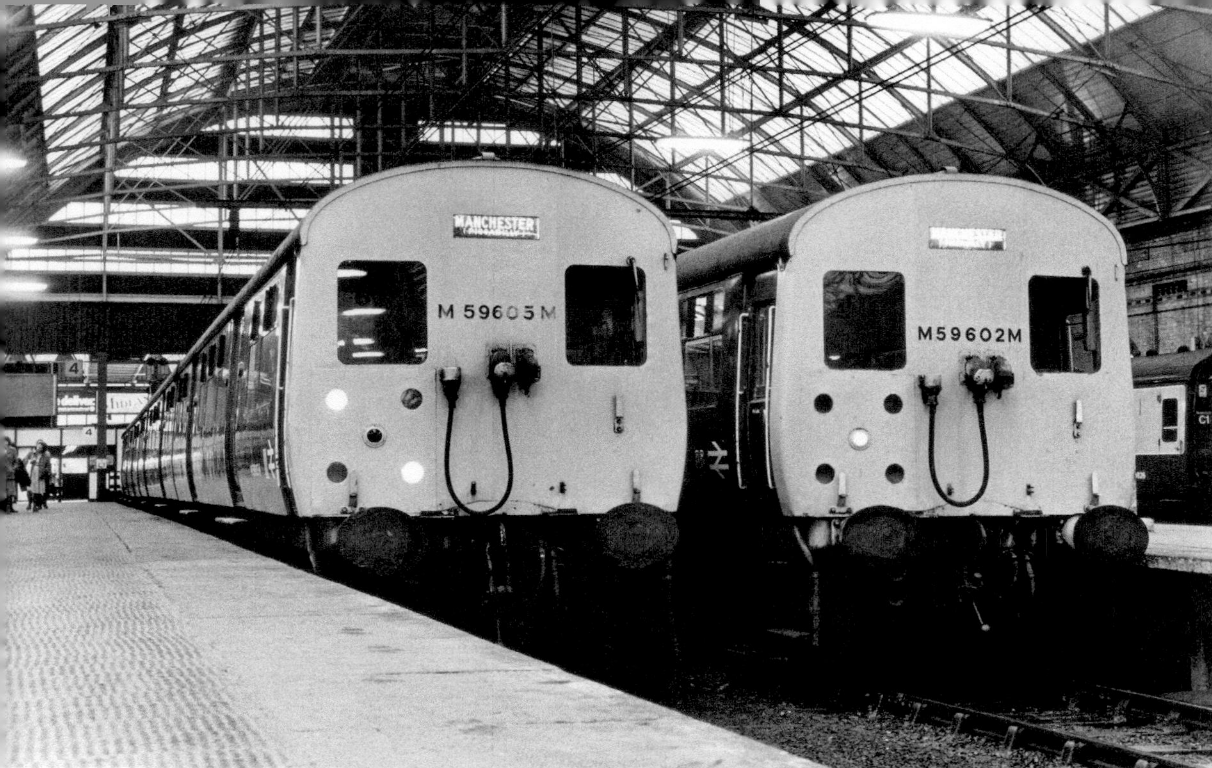

Waiting to Take People Home, Manchester Piccadilly, spring 1978.
Despite having Manchester Piccadilly on the destination blind, the Class 506 on the left is waiting to depart from the aforementioned station. The one on the right has just arrived. The imminent departure is bound for east Manchester suburbs and then on to the Derbyshire towns of Glossop and Hadfield. The doors have already closed and its vintage-style interior will be filled with homeward-bound commuters and shoppers.

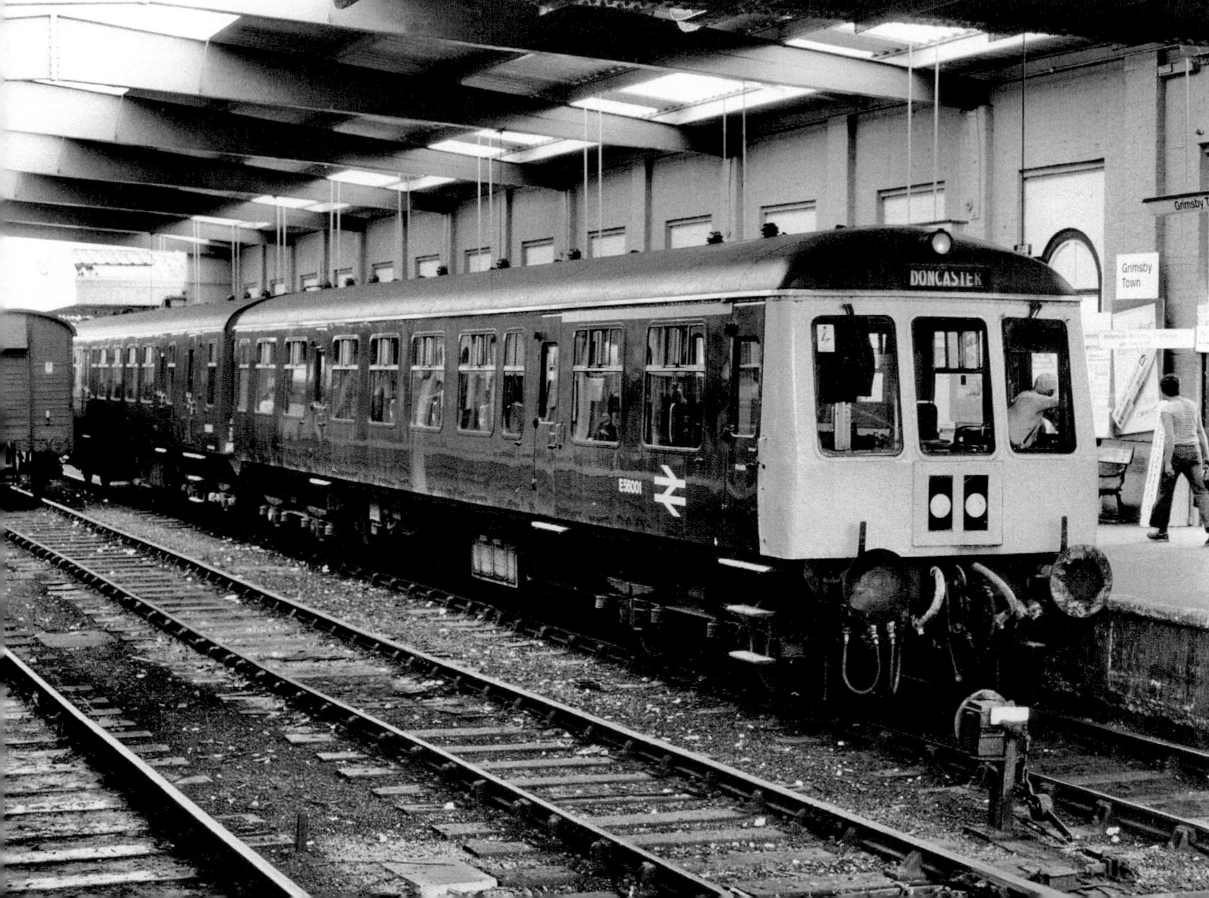

In Shirtsleeves, Grimsby Town, summer 1981.
It is a hot summer's day, so the driver of this Cleethorpes–Doncaster service is in his shirtsleeves. I can't help but wonder why he is leaning out of his droplight at Grimsby Town station. He might be taking in the famous fishing port's sea air. Maybe there is some delay receiving the buzzer from the guard and he is wondering what's causing it? Perhaps the buzzer isn't working and he is looking for the guard's green flag? He may be simply watching the platform activity. Who knows, but it is all part of the watching of a train about to depart that makes it so fascinating. This Class 114 two-car DMU is the first off the Derby production line E56001/E50001, dating from 1956. These sturdy and reliable DMUs were, for a long time, allocated to Lincoln Depot. They had quite a long life, some lasting in passenger service until 1992. A handful had a life extension after being converted for Royal Mail use. Two of these sets subsequently made it into preservation.

Female Driver, Doncaster, summer 1980.
The female driver of pristine 37064 looks down the platform prior to getting the 1D16, 17.09 Doncaster–Hull service under way on 23 August 1980. (Another photograph of this train appears on p.141 of my *British Rail Northern Scenes Coast to Coast* book, but is miscaptioned – my apologies.) Even if I do say so myself, this is a great photograph of a super-looking loco. Quite a few Class 37s continue in revenue-earning service on today's modern railway network. This is quite something for a loco type that is over 50 years old. Harry Needle had this example in his fleet fairly recently, based at Barrow Hill. It saw service on the mainline and visited preserved railway diesel galas. This suggested that after lasting so long it would eventually make it into preservation. Unfortunately this was not to be the case; sadly, it was scrapped at Stockton yard on 23 July 2010.

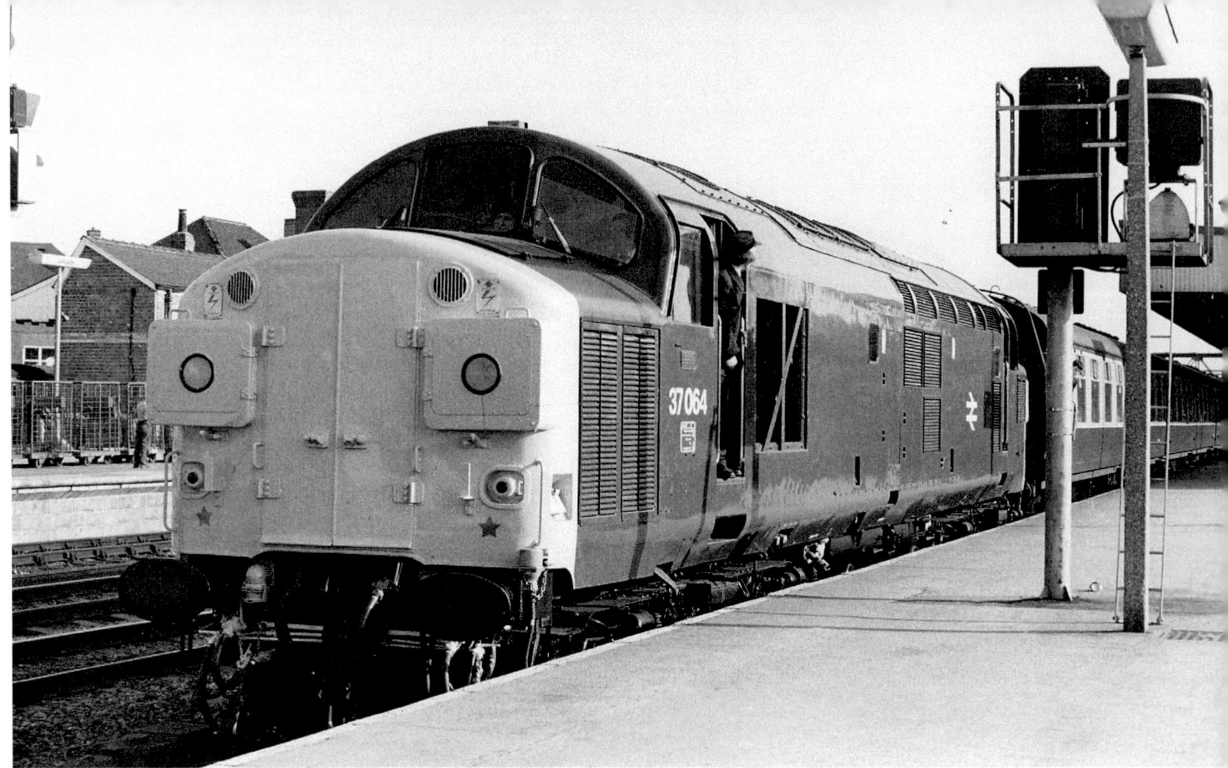

'Skeggy' Here We Come, Heckington, August 1980.
My title is a bit more exciting than the departure scene at sleepy Heckington station on the line to Skegness. The Class 114 DMU, bound for Boston and Skegness, is ready to depart after a few people have alighted. I can't remember anyone boarding the train. Heckington is a generally overlooked railway location on the Lincolnshire plains, in the shadow of the village's fantastic windmill. It proved to be an ideal place to photograph the streams of trains that made their way to and from the nearby popular holiday destination.

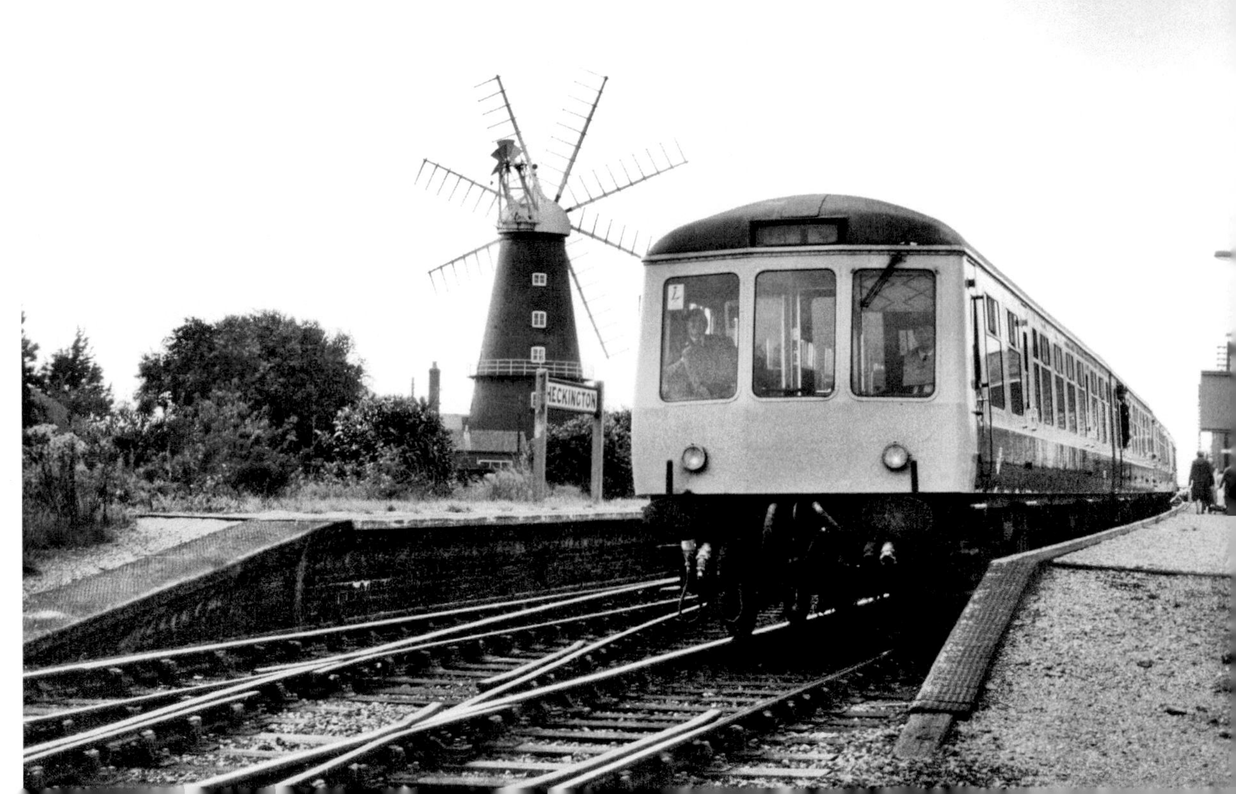

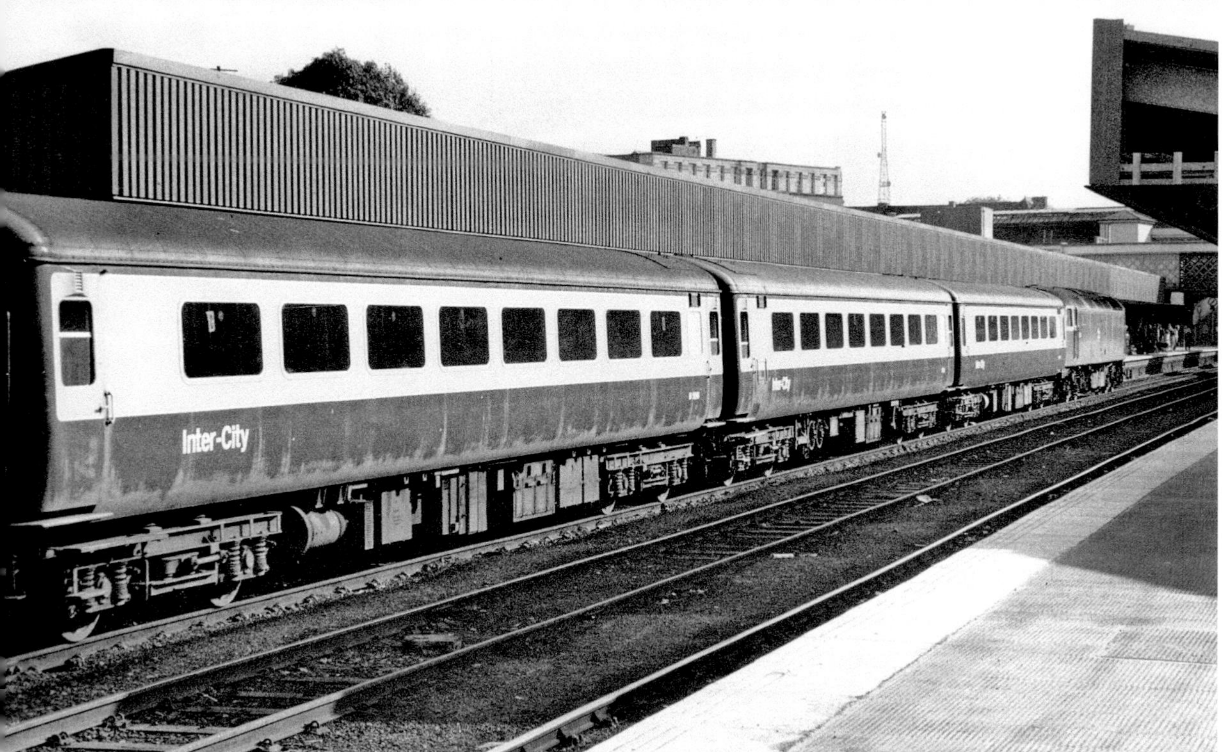

Inter-City Departure, Leicester, August 1980.

I have always liked BR Mark 2 air-conditioned coaching stock, in original blue-and-grey livery. I can remember it being introduced on West Coast Mainline services around 1973. Surely, I am not that old – well, I don't feel it. This train is made up of a complete set of Mark 2 stock, although there is probably a Mark 1 buffet car midway down the train – I have often wondered why they didn't build any Mark 2 versions. This Class 47-hauled train is bound for Sheffield and ready to depart on this gloriously sunny day. The 47 makes a change from the usual Class 45s that hauled these Midland Mainline Inter-City trains to and from London St Pancras.

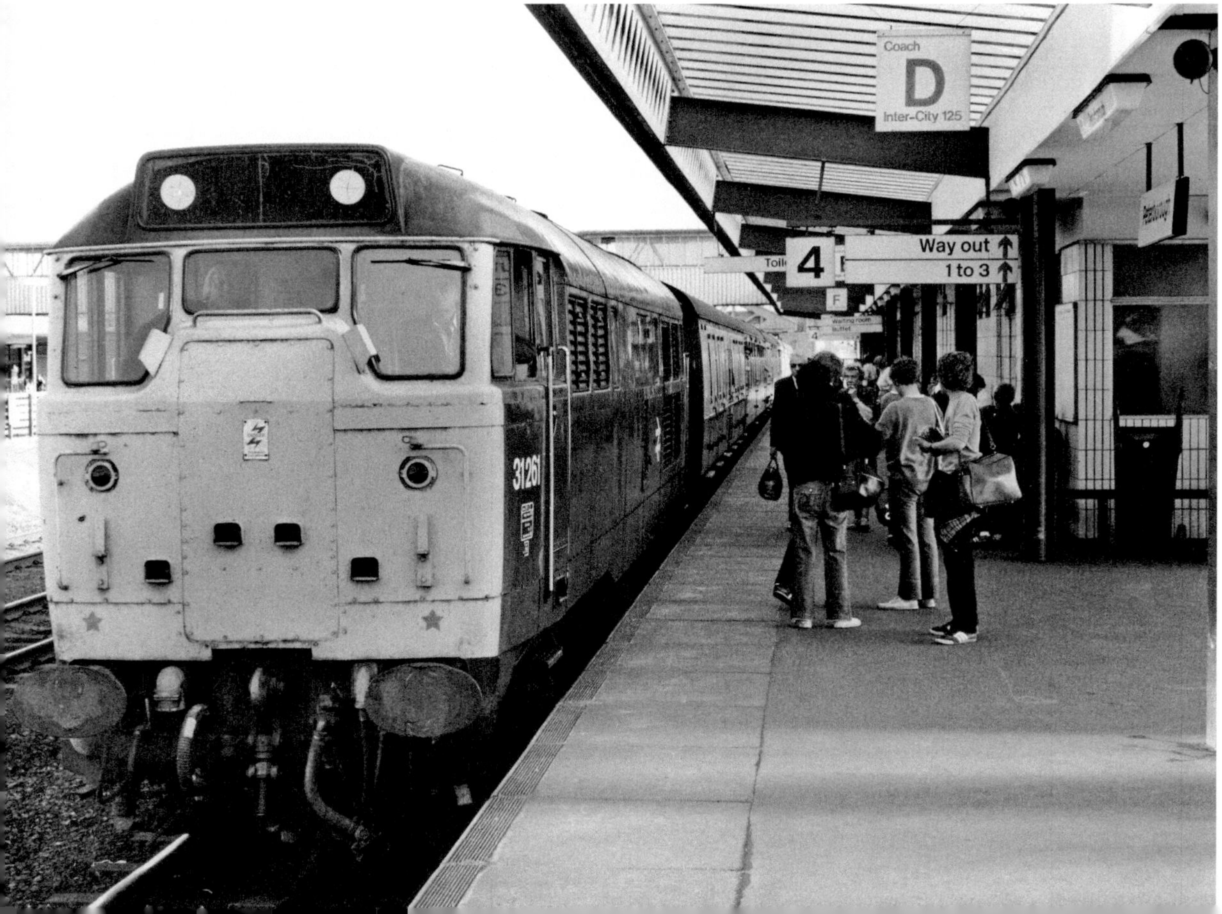

Change Here for the East Coast Mainline, Peterborough, August 1979.

Being from the North West of England, Class 31-hauled passenger trains were quite a novelty to me during the 1970s. However, they would soon become commonplace on the Hope Valley route. The Norwich–Birmingham New Street service was usually assigned to this class. When on my travels in the East Midlands, I would try to sample the delights of Class 31 haulage, bagging a short journey on one of these trains. In this shot, all the Mark 1 coaching stock slam doors are closed and the driver of 31261 is ready to get his westbound train under way from Peterborough's Platform 4. The group of holiday travellers walking down the platform arrived on the train from East Anglia. The odds are that they will next take an East Coast Mainline train to their final destination.

Just Time to Finish Reading My Magazine, Watford Junction, June 1978.

Watford Junction was terminus to the Class 501 suburban service from London Euston and Broad Street. There was usually time for the driver to catch up on their reading and have some refreshments prior to returning the train to the capital. This driver, comfortably ensconced in driving motor open brake second (DMBS) M61154, appears quite relaxed reading his periodical. I wonder which one it is? This train will soon depart for Euston. I grabbed this shot from the droplight of a Manchester Piccadilly–Euston Inter-City service, which back then generally called at the junction. The Class 501s were finally withdrawn from service during May 1985. However, ten DMBS cars were converted to Class 97/7 battery locomotives. Three complete sets became Class 936 Sandite units. Plus, rather curiously, two cars went to work at MOD Marchwood for a few years. The extended life of these few meant that a Class 501 was eventually saved for preservation.

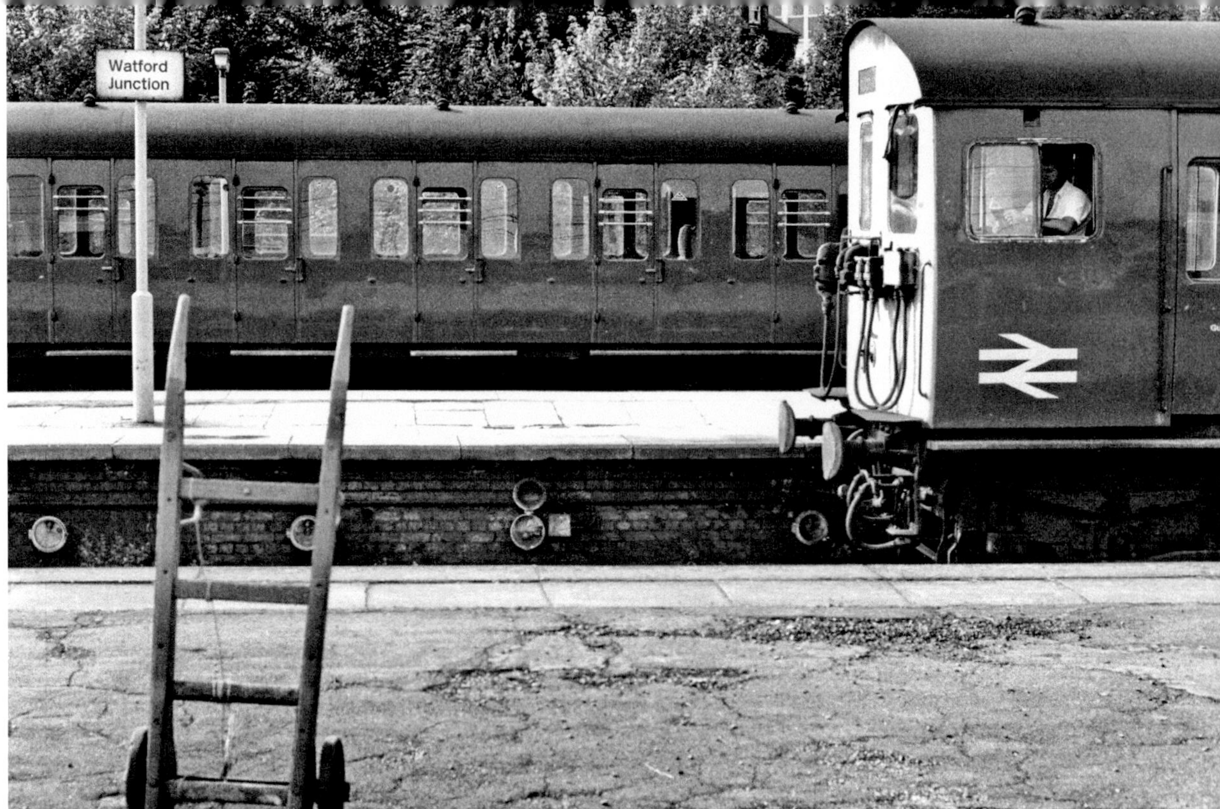

Inter-City 125, London Paddington, May 1979.

Just before departure time a passenger opens a big Mark 3 coach door to board high-speed train (HST) 253 006 at London Paddington. Bearing testament to their superb design, these trains, now over 40 years old, are still used on mainline passenger service. Nevertheless, the original Western Region Class 253 numbered formations and Eastern Region Class 254 numbered set formations have long gone. Probably because of my age, I like the original Inter-City 125 livery best. No doubt other enthusiasts will prefer one of the amazing varieties that followed.

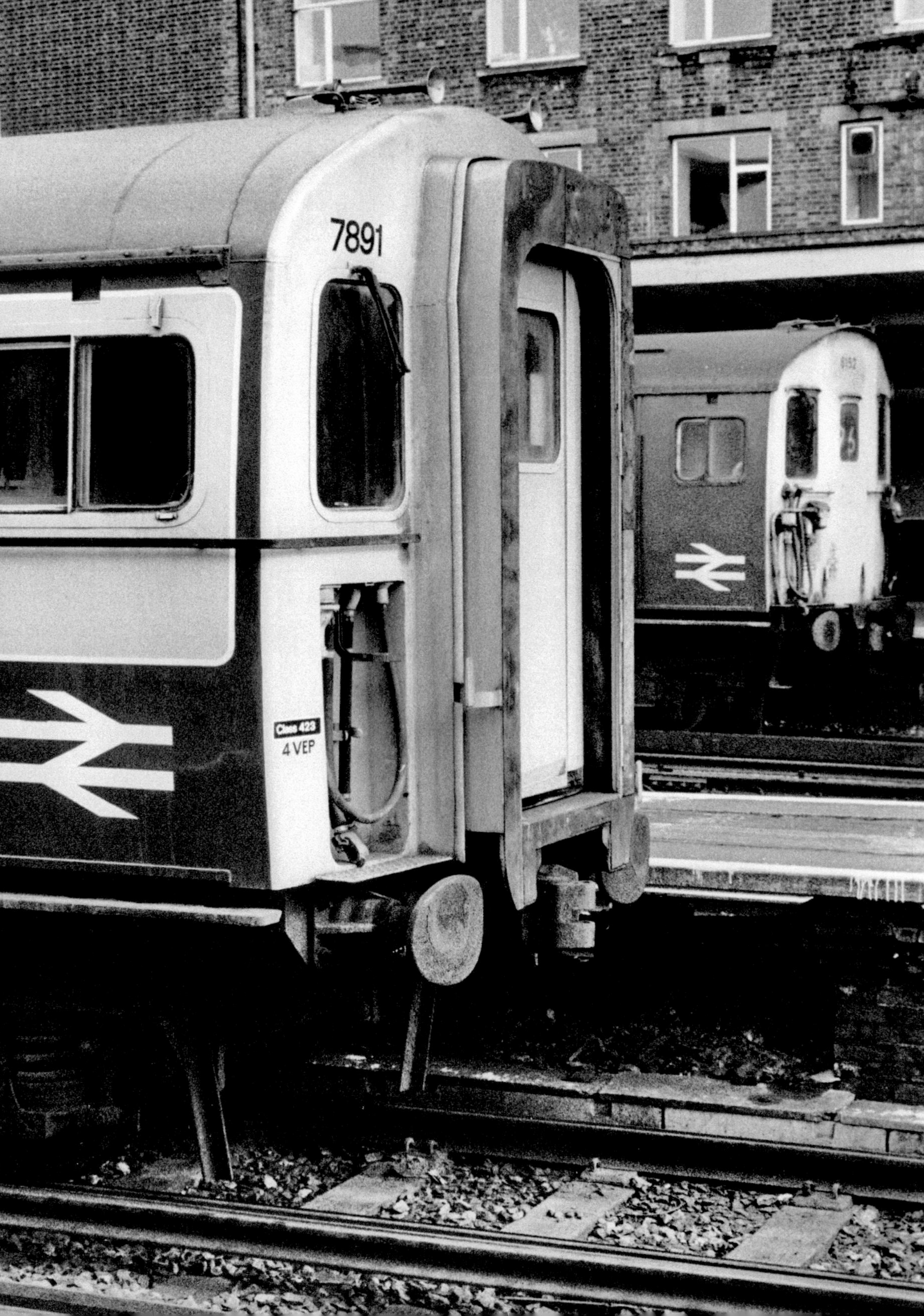

Southern Exotica, London Victoria, July 1979.

You might be wondering 'why the title?' and saying surely there is nothing exotic about this photograph. For me, a lad from Manchester, anything British Rail Southern was exotic. From an early age it conjured up thoughts of the mystique of the capital and its busy, seemingly cosmopolitan mainline stations. The thought of fast three-rail EMUs, boat trains and sunny south coast destinations added to my awe. In this pre-Jaffa Cake and Network South East livery period shot, I have captured on Ilford FP4 film a Class 423 (4 VEP), 7891, and Class 414 (2 HAP), 6152, ready to depart from London Victoria; the 423 is on one of the fast services I used to muse about during the early 1970s. This was while looking at the unobtainable in my Ian Allan *Combined Volume*, quite often on Manchester Victoria's Platform 11. I like to think it is bound for Dover Western Docks; unfortunately, I didn't make a record. The 414 is on one of the Southern's many much slower suburban services. In later years, I travelled on lots of the region's trains, mainly on business, and still found something exotic about them. Quite odd, you might think. This photograph is from one of the rolls of film that lay unprocessed for over twenty-five years.

ACE, London Waterloo, summer 1981.
The 'Atlantic Coast Express' (ACE) is arguably one of the best-named trains ever. Sadly, by the time I took this shot, the route of the train was a shadow of its former self and its name had disappeared from BR timetables. During the 1980s, the Class 50-hauled trains on the London Waterloo–Salisbury–Exeter Central/St Davids were the nearest thing to what had gone before. In this photograph 50046 *Ajax*, a member of a rather ace locomotive class, is ready to depart from Waterloo, bound for Exeter. After the end of Southern Region steam on the route, Western Region's Class 42 'Warships' took over haulage. When they were withdrawn, Southern Region Class 33 were utilised. By the 1980s, the 50s had started to make their mark by improving the service. The use of Inter-City 125s on many West of England services enabled this. Usurped Western Region-allocated Class 50s and displaced Mark 2 coaching stock were seconded to the old ACE route. These trains would soon become popular and legendary with '50 Bashers'.

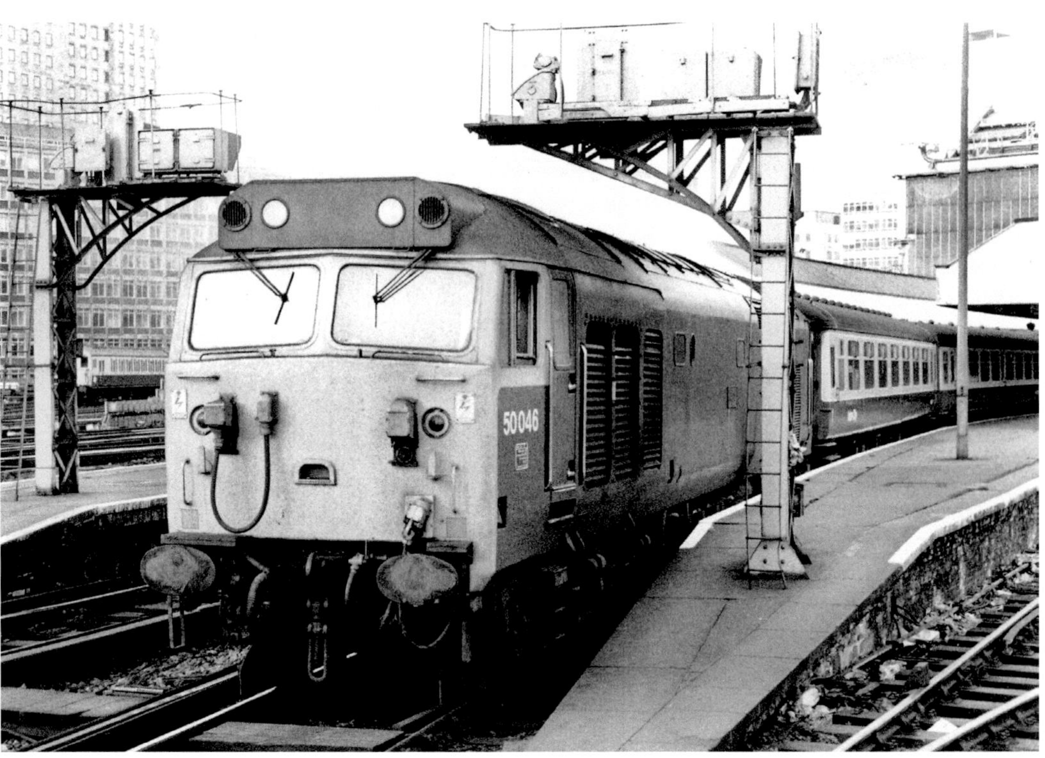

Slim Line and Full Bodied, Hastings, 25 May 1975.
Like many towns and cities on the rail network, Manchester was served by British Rail's weekly cut-price excursions. They were often known as Merrymakers. Early on the morning of 25 May 1975, my mates and I left Reddish North station aboard a BR Mystery Trip. It was a circuitous route via the Midland Mainline to Brent Junction, hauled by a Class 47. Then we headed south via Kensington Olympia with a pair of 33s at the head of the train. We were guessing the destination virtually all the way; surprisingly it turned out to be Hastings. During the day I saw lots of new railway-related things, one of which was the Hastings slim-line DEMU, Class 201. I thought they were most unusual. Soon after our empty coaching stock had drawn out of the station, I managed to bag this photograph. What makes this shot special to me is that it was the first time I had seen a Hastings DEMU standing alongside a normal-sized train. The Class 421 (4 CIG) 7369 is ready to depart with a London-bound train. Class 201 1017 is awaiting its next passenger duty.

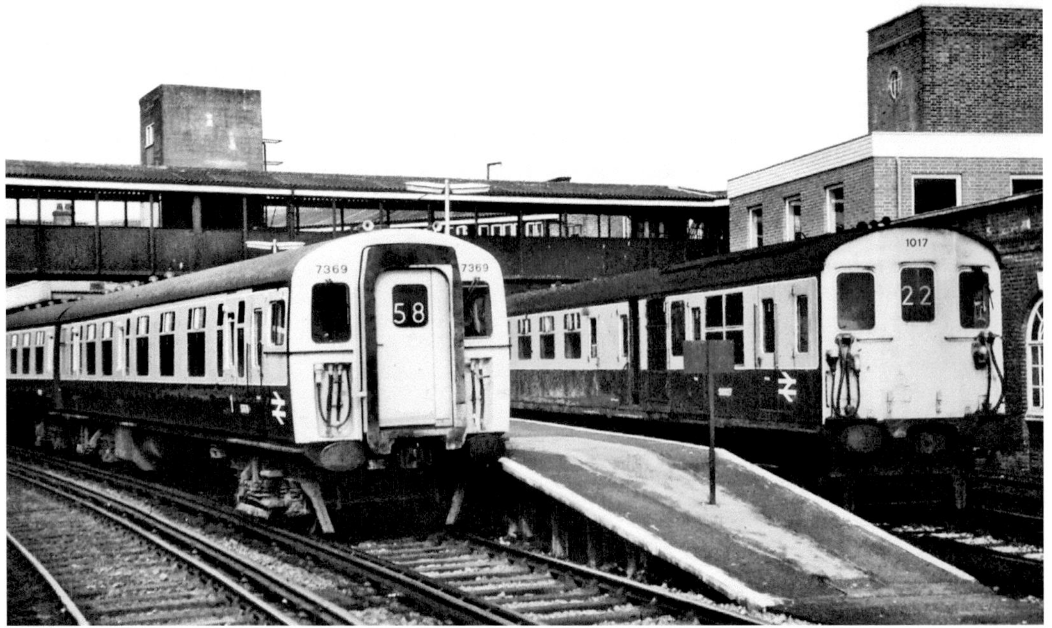

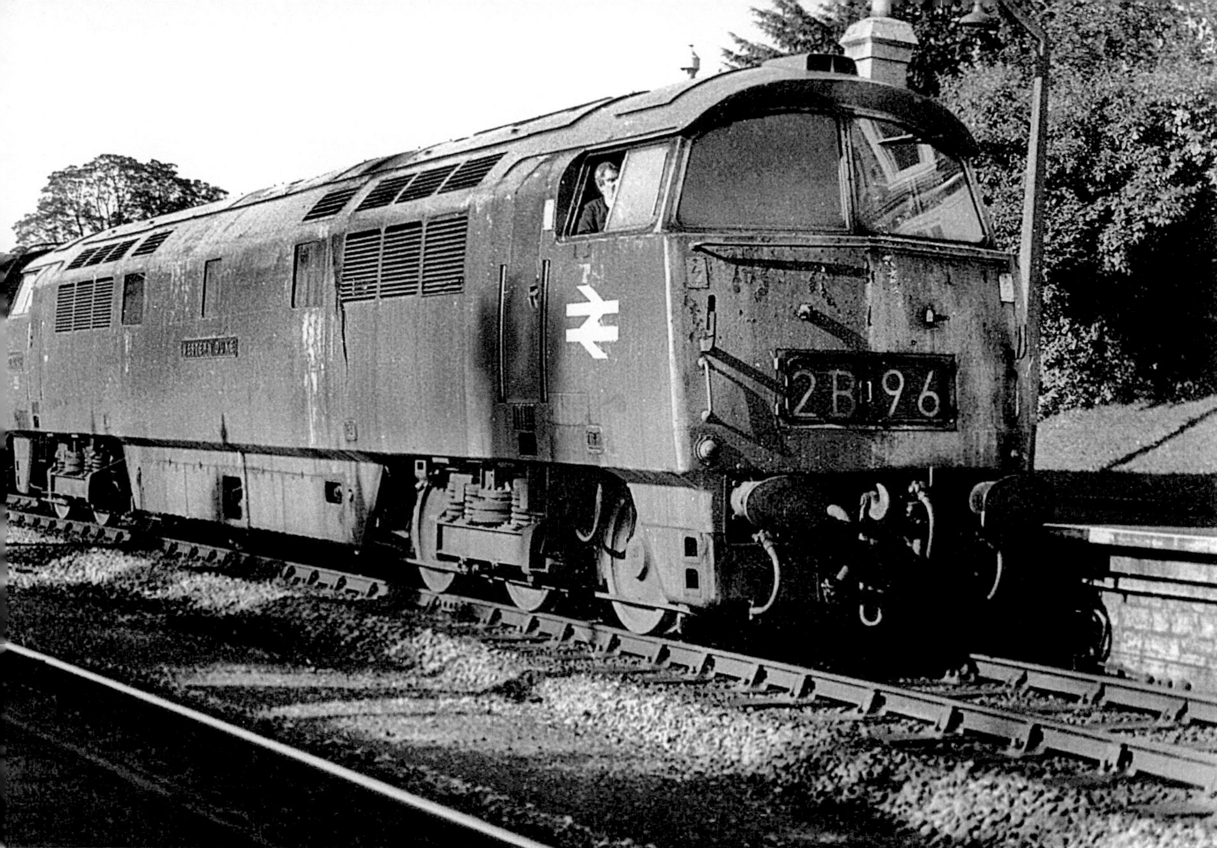

***Western Duke*, Torquay, July 1973.**
Get ready for 1043 *Western Duke*'s engine roar and accompanying plume of black clag as the driver brings on the power. It will happen any minute now. The loco's second man is looking straight ahead as he and the driver wait for the Torquay station's lower-quadrant signal to drop. This is the afternoon return working of the summer-timetabled service to Plymouth from Paignton. This service was intended to take day-tripping holidaymakers to Plymouth after breakfast and then bring them back in time for tea. It proved rather popular and was a great opportunity to have a low-cost run behind a 'Western'. This of course included the challenging Devon Banks – unmissable! Upon arrival at Newton Abbot the train would be pointing in the wrong direction. This meant the loco had to run round and couple up to the other end of the train, allowing passengers time to stretch their legs on the station. I travelled on it several times and did take the opportunity to get off, although I ran round rather than strolled: there was so much to see, but little time to do so. Early 1970s Newton Abbot was a fantastic place for the rail enthusiast, especially the depot area – 'Westerns' a plenty!

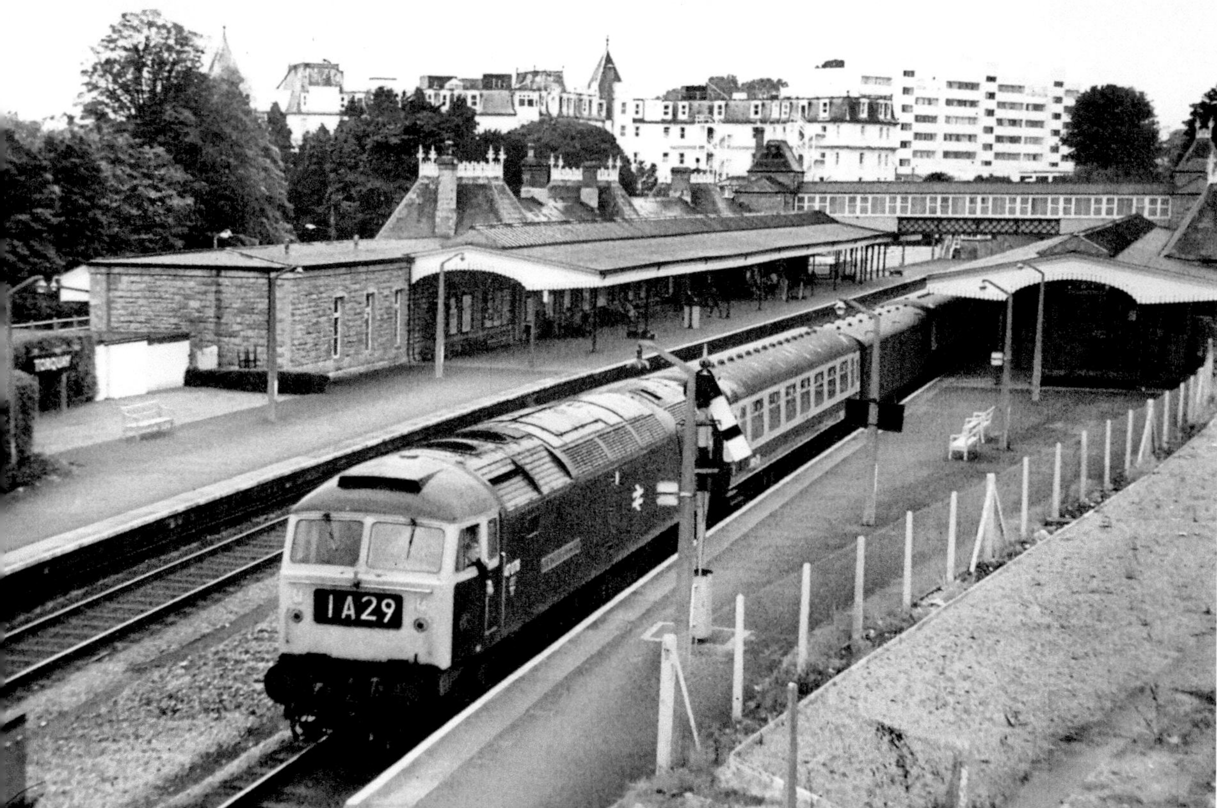

***Sir Daniel Gooch*, Torquay, July 1974.**
Torquay's up line lower-quadrant signal has dropped. The driver is waiting for the guard's green flag to be waved and whistle to be blown. It looks like the driver is taking in the Torquay sea air while he waits. The loco is 47074 *Sir Daniel Gooch* and the train is bound for London Paddington on this rather uncharacter-istically overcast day. Curiously the first Mark 2 coach is separated from the rest of the passenger-carrying coaches by an ex-GWR non-gangwayed full brake. Was the first coach locked out or had it been separated from the rest of the train because a dignitary would be travelling in it?

Dusk at York, May 1981.

For me, dusk and night-time long-distance train departures have always held that extra bit of excitement. In this photograph it will soon be dark as this evening Class 47-hauled train to Liverpool Lime Street waits to depart from York. Disappointingly this service was not hauled by a Class 40, which invariably did the honours. Along with North Wales Coast trains, this service was a favourite of the steadily increasing numbers of 'Class 40 Bashers'.

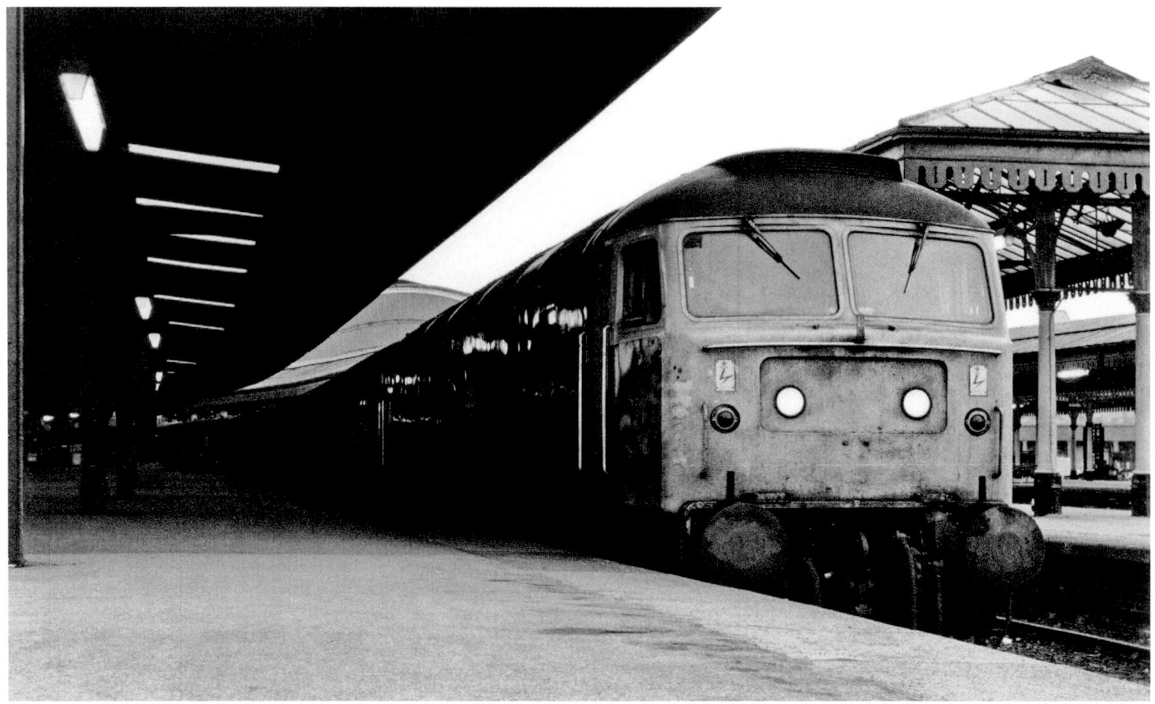

Settle & Carlisle Express, Carlisle, May 1974.

To maximise my train-travel mileage I made full use of BR's many special offers. This enabled my Saturday job money to literally go further. I used to work on the *Manchester Evening News*' 'Football Pink' picture desk – fantastic and very hectic. On the occasion of this photograph I had got myself to Carlisle using a Round-Robin ticket. This allowed me to head north via the West Coast Mainline and return via the Settle & Carlisle route. This photograph shows an unidentified Class 45 waiting to depart from Carlisle, bound for Glasgow Central via Dumfries. Rather than heading back south I would have much preferred to go north on this train. How many of us have watched a train, ready to depart, wishing we could go on it? My homeward run on the Settle & Carlisle Line was my first and rather wet. No complaints about the poor weather – full marks for the added atmosphere that came with it.

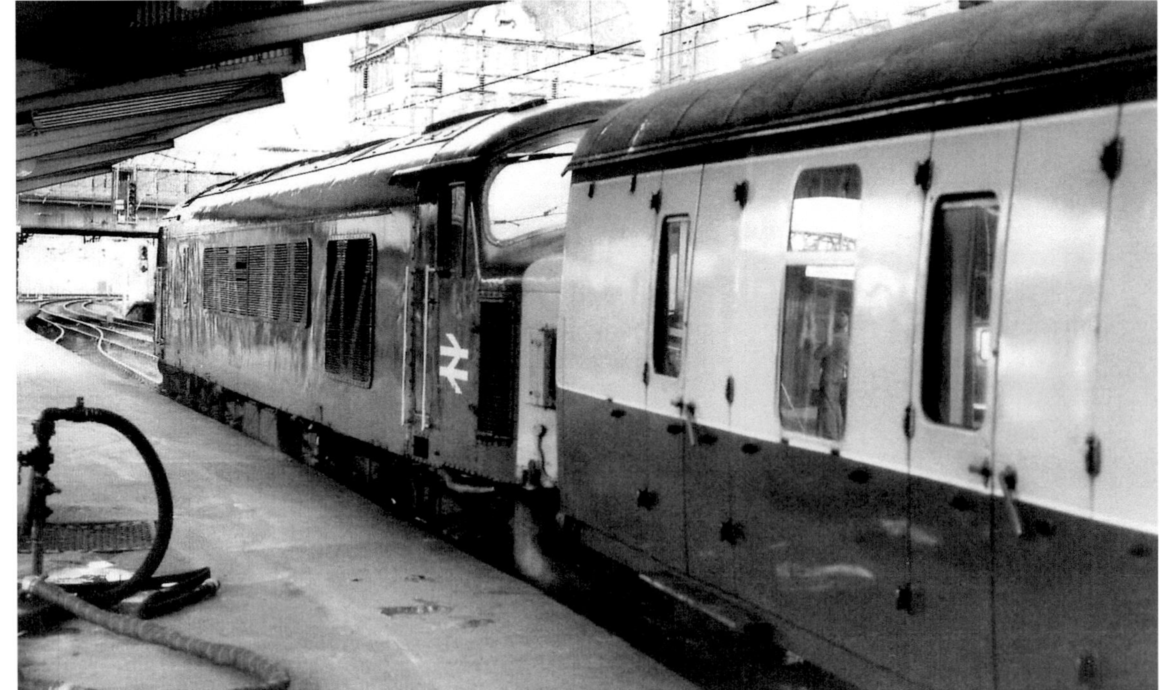

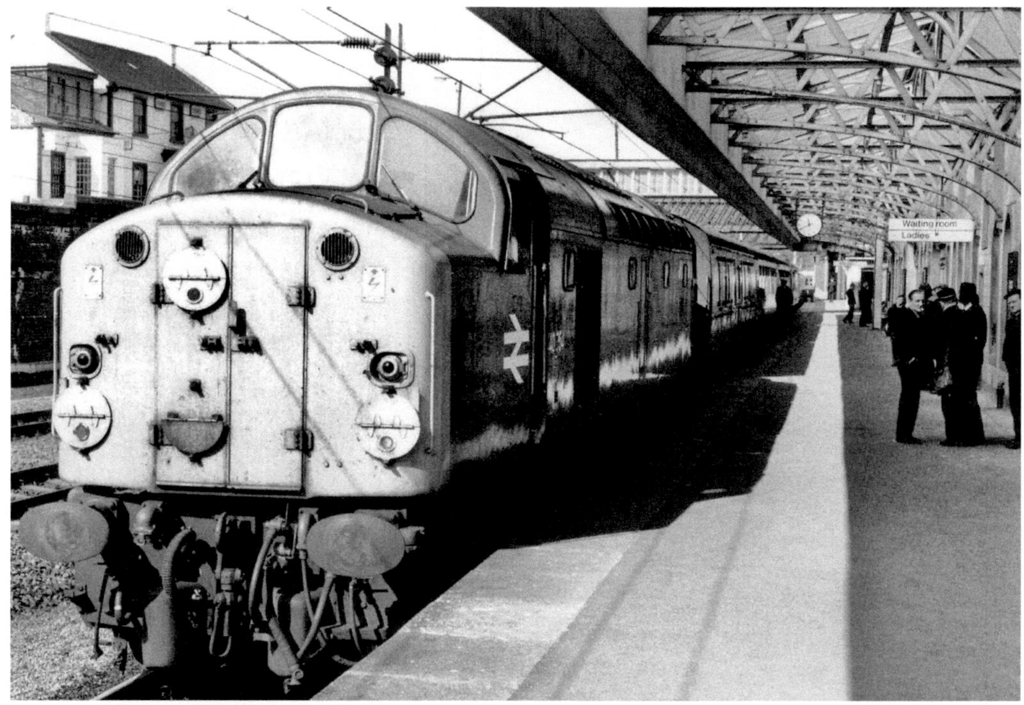

The Edinburgh Portion, Carstairs, 9 April 1977.
It's 11.40 a.m. on the station clock and 40054 is waiting to depart from Carstairs with the Edinburgh portion of the early morning train from Manchester Victoria. The train was in two parts: one for Glasgow Central, the other for Edinburgh. Nowadays there is a chord south of the station that leads off the West Coast Mainline. This obviates the need for trains from the south having to be reversed at Carstairs station, which had previously been the case. The reversing practice was necessary to enable them to use the chord from the northerly direction, also south of the station. When trains split at Carstairs the Glasgow portion was quickly uncoupled. The electric loco that brought the train from the south continued north with its truncated consist. The portion left behind had a diesel loco coupled to the south-facing end and then departed for Edinburgh. This is exactly what happened in the case of the train shown in this photograph. Carstairs was a large, fully equipped station back then; sadly, now it is a shadow of its former self.

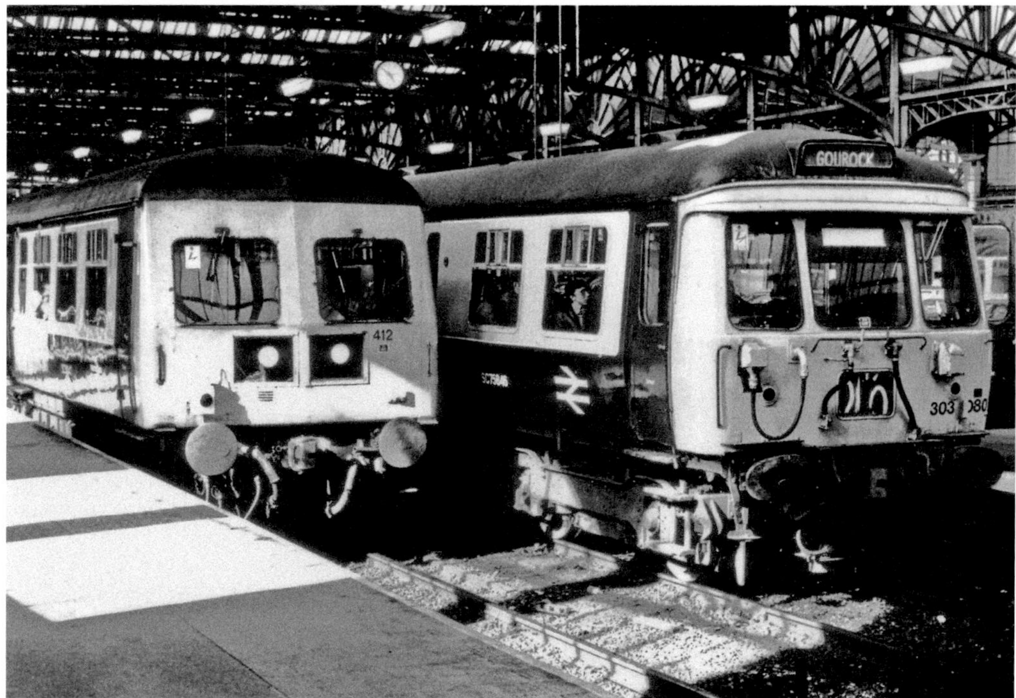

Blue Train, Glasgow Central, summer 1979.
During the 1960s I saw lots of books and posters with images depicting the Glasgow area's rather stylish 'Blue Train' EMUs – Class 303 and 311. Like Southern EMUs, I found them rather exotic and for a long time alluringly inaccessible. Little did I know that during the 1980s Class 303s would be drafted into the Manchester area, primarily to replace withdrawn Hadfield/Glossop Class 506 EMUs, and became commonplace. During this visit to Glasgow I didn't have enough time to sample either of the tempting delights depicted in this photograph. Both trains were ready to depart and I was soon to return home on the afternoon service to Manchester Victoria. Class 87-hauled to Preston, then a 47 on the final leg. The train to the left is one of the Class 126 Swindon-built DMU oddballs. It uniquely had the standard Swindon front at one end and a flat front, similar to a Southern EMU, at the other end. I guess the idea was to be able to couple two flat-front ends, together creating a gangwayed double full-length train. Good in theory, not in practice, if the train ends were the wrong way round. The train on the right is 303 080; it is ready to depart for Gourock – a rather pleasant destination.

Right: Inter-City sleeper, Glasgow Queen Street, August 1981.

The attraction of a sleeping-car train is shared by many. In recent years the now universally known Venice Simplon-Orient-Express has added style, romance and mystique to the concept. This Inter-City Sleeper, hauled by 27022, isn't bound for anywhere romantic, though. It is about to depart for the carriage sidings. This overnight train from Inverness left the Highland capital at 11.50 p.m., with the Edinburgh portion. Berths were ready for passengers at 10.15 p.m. The two portions split at Perth – the operation tended to wake me up when I travelled on it. Bleary eyed, I would peer through the corridor window to catch some of the activity. Arrival at Glasgow was at 5.46 a.m. Passengers were allowed until 7.30 a.m. (8 a.m. on Sundays) to vacate. In theory, this time frame allowed plenty of time for a good night's sleep, but I wonder how many people did get one while travelling aboard the vintage Mark 1 sleeping cars? I enjoyed every minute and wish I could repeat the journey now. In this shot the last passenger is in the process of vacating the train: the trolley already has a suitcase on it. They have nipped back to their berth for the rest of the luggage. Soon the driver will fire up the 27 and the train will be eased out of the station. During the day, it will be cleaned and serviced ready for the 11.30 p.m. departure from Queen Street, bound for Inverness.

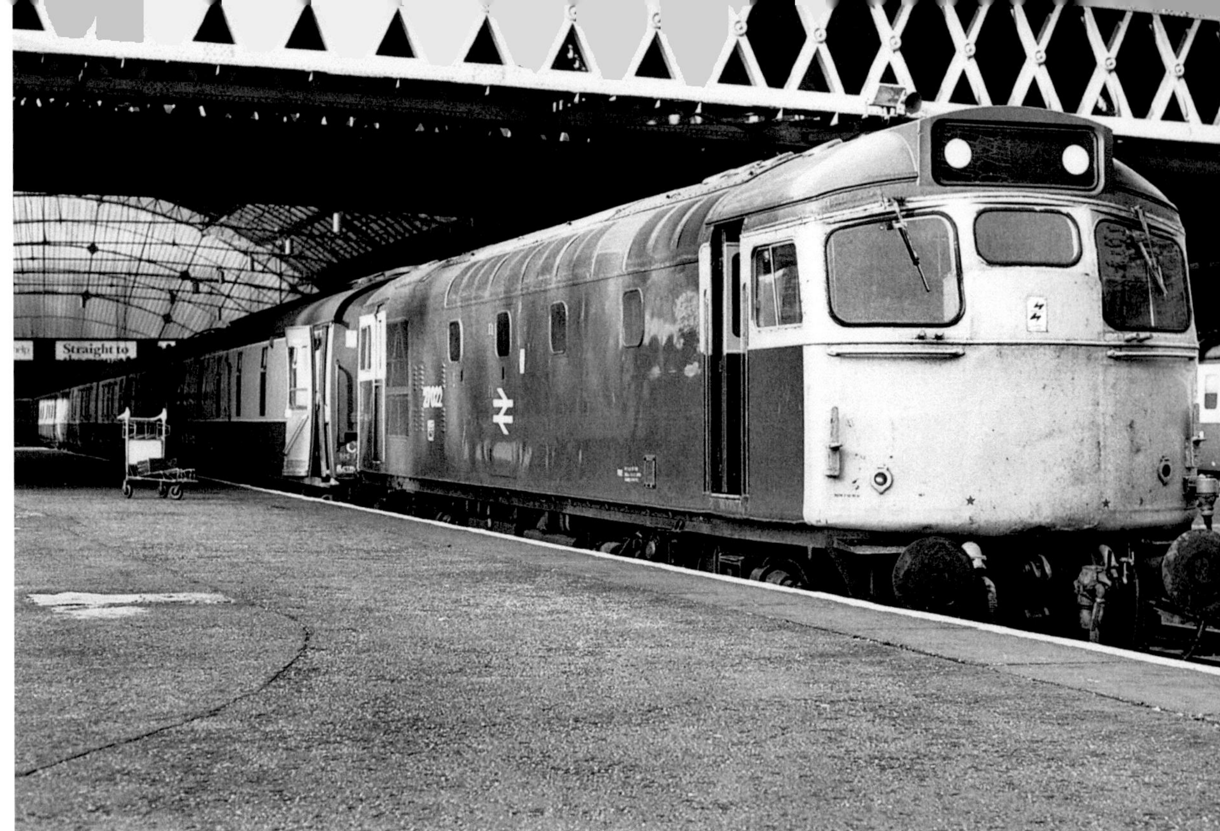

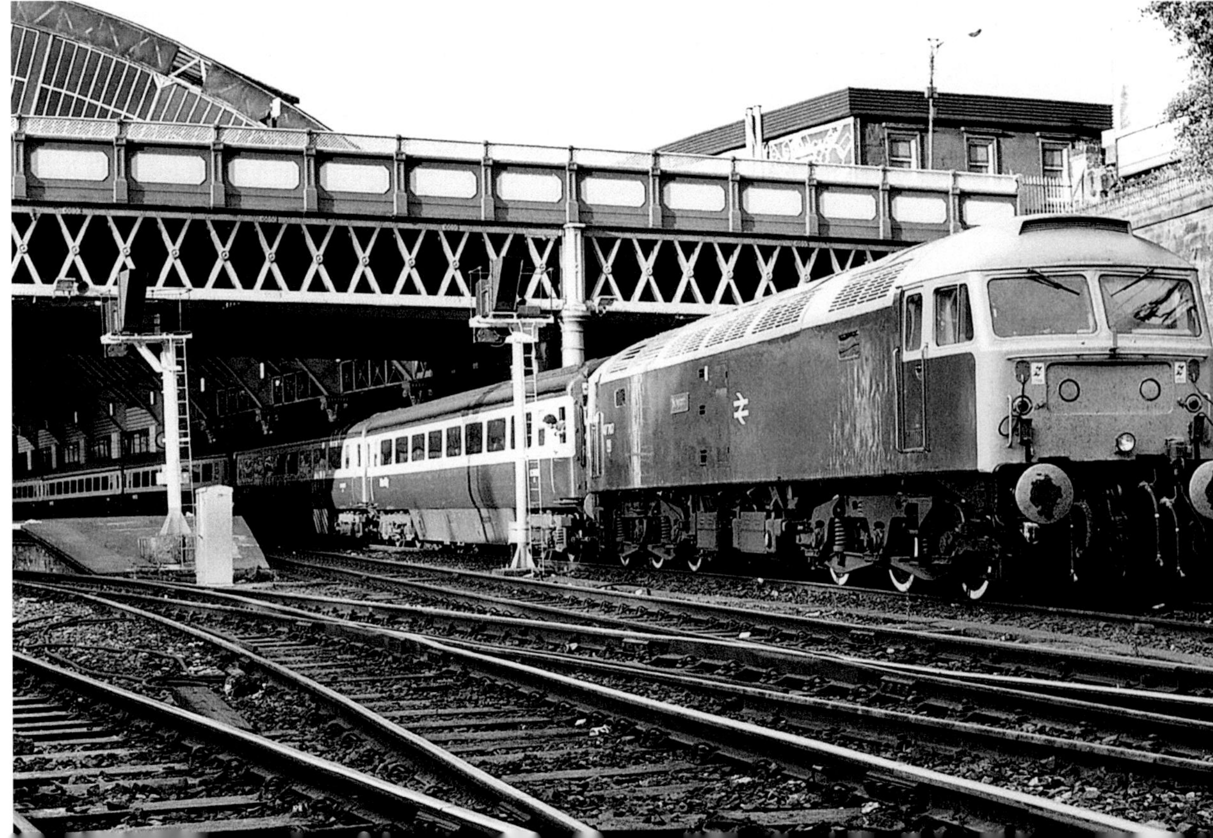

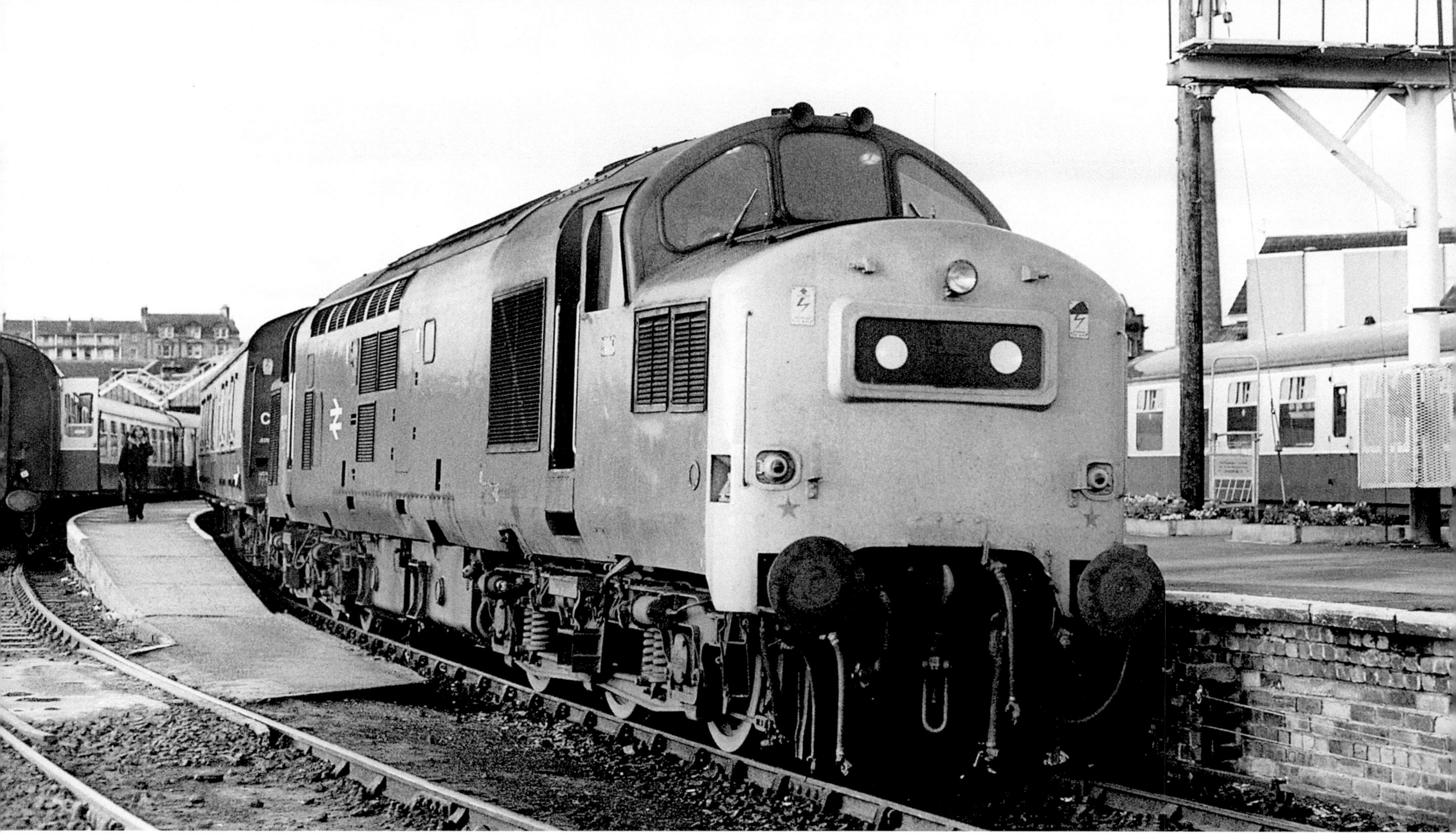

Left: Holyrood, Glasgow Queen Street, August 1981.
This is an early morning push-pull service to Edinburgh, hauled by 47707 *Holyrood*, waiting to depart from Glasgow Queen Street. The enthusiast leaning out of the first carriage door droplight appears keen for the train to get under way. No doubt he will partake in a little bit of 'window hanging' as this fast service makes its way to Waverley station. The novel Edinburgh–Glasgow push-pull formation replaced the equally novel top-and-tail trains (a Class 27 at either end of a rake of Mark 2 coaches). The new trains comprised a fleet of specially converted Class 47s along with rakes of Mark 3 coaches coupled to a Mark 2 driving van trailer (DVT). The push-pulls were a vast improvement on what had gone before. Based on their success the loco and rolling stock fleet was augmented to enable these trains to also serve Aberdeen. Tragically, during July 1984, *Holyrood* pushed the 5.30 p.m. Edinburgh–Glasgow into a cow at high speed. The impact, compounded by the effect of a heavyweight loco pushing a relatively lightweight set of coaches, caused the train to derail badly. Thirteen passengers lost their lives and seventeen were seriously injured.

Above: Ready to Depart for the Far North, Inverness, August 1982.
By the time this photograph was taken, ex-Eastern Region Class 37s were infiltrating the Highlands. The long reign of the Class 26 was beginning to come to an end. This crack-of-dawn service to Wick and Thurso, hauled by a fine-looking 37, is waiting to depart from Inverness. Having arrived on the sleeper from Glasgow, I quickly bagged this shot and then ran round the platforms to board it. I took it all the way to Thurso from where I was bound for the Orkneys using the P&O ferry from Scrabster.

2 THE ENTHUSIAST

INTRODUCTION

Rail enthusiasts were very much part of the 1970s and '80s British Rail scene. I for one loved every minute of my time spent riding trains and amongst BR's environs. For sure I was not alone even though a lot of my travels were solo.

During the early part of the 1970s rail enthusiasm was still recovering from the blow of BR steam traction coming to an end on 11 August 1968. (My dad took me to see the 15-guinea special at Manchester Victoria, and got a driver to autograph my *Railway Magazine*.) The effect was compounded by the fact that BR banned any steam on their network, apart from specials hauled by the *Flying Scotsman*. This concession was a little academic because the locomotive was languishing in America. This sad state of affairs meant that many of the people who had spent their time chasing steam turned their backs on the 'Big Railway' and focused their attention on locomotive and railway preservation. Thank goodness they did – what a fantastic legacy we now have. Fortunately, by 1972 steam was allowed to return to the BR network. After the ban was lifted, steam railtours began to flourish and still run today.

Coming up behind the BR steam era was a new generation fascinated by the often-derided 'tin boxes' (locomotives and multiple units), which had so quickly usurped the long reign of steam during the 1950s and '60s. No doubt the newbies caught the bug on train rides to the seaside, walks by the railway and visits to fledgling preservation centres and railways. Plus, of course, there were the loco-spotting expeditions that were often prompted by their elders and peers.

I caught my lifelong bug thanks to my mum and dad, as they could tell I liked trains a lot. I can vividly remember being taken to see what I liked best while still in my pram. They had to run with me if we could hear a train coming as I didn't want to miss it. From being very little, Reddish North station and yard, and Reddish Motive Power Depot were among my favourite haunts. The depot serviced the Woodhead electric locos (Class 76 and 77) and the 'Midland Pullman', which I saw several times. Best of all were annual holiday journeys and days out by train. Whilst steam was still prevalent, I was captivated by the electric blue- and Brunswick green-liveried new order. Class 40s, 76s and the vintage Manchester–Altrincham electric units were my favourites. The latter had compartments with leather straps to adjust the window droplights. Coupled to my passion for trains, I was captivated by the general atmosphere, buzz and excitement of it all. I guess so many enthusiasts will have similar stories to tell, no matter how old they are. This new generation and those that followed meant that the train enthusiast would once again be very much part of the British Rail scene from the early 1970s.

To be a rail enthusiast was easy. In general there was freedom to roam depots and sidings because there were often no rigid health-and-safety or security constraints. This made it simple to 'cop' locos and photograph them. Open days made this aspect legitimate. Cheap travel using BR special offers, 'Runabout' tickets and their unbelievably cheap Merrymaker day excursions (for example, £2 for Manchester to Torquay and back) were irresistible. Regular society railtours added to the opportunity to clock up intergalactic annual mileages by train. If you worked on the railway, rail travel was generally free. If you had little money, long days on stations could cost nothing or just the few pence needed to buy a platform ticket.

Planning outings could be a fascinating challenge, maximising how much you could cram in. The regional and later all-line timetables were invaluable. Geography became second nature, along with time management. Knowledge of the multifaceted railway world was avidly soaked up – regularly studying magazines and books made this inevitable. Ian Allan's *Combined Volumes* ensured we knew all about the different types of locomotives and multiple units, along with their numbers. Their Locoshed books told us which depots they were allocated to. Updates in the *Railway Magazine* and *Railway World* told us about changes and withdrawals – far slower than Internet updates, but effective.

We learnt such a lot about all sorts of things, and still do, while pursuing our hobby – endlessly riveting and fascinating.

The early demise of the less fortunate post-1955 Modernisation Plan designs, such as the 'Metro-Vic' and 'Baby Deltic', went largely unnoticed. However, the withdrawal of the Western Region 'Warship' class spawned a new phenomenon in rail enthusiasm. It later became known as 'Bashing': chasing certain classes of locomotive, particularly those with just a few years left to run on BR metals. Thousands of miles would be clocked up riding behind certain locos and travelling to see them. The first type to really energise people was the Class 52 'Western': everything about them ensured they had a big following. Their distinctive look, size, superb 'Western' nameplates, power (fast Inter-City trains were their forte) and of course noise were a heady mix. I can well remember 'Platform Enders' at Newton Abbot shouting 'Western!!!' as one appeared, especially during the scorching hot summer of 1976. This was their final full year in service. Even lesser locomotives such as the Class 24 began to attract a strong following. The big locomotives really caught people's attention, though; in particular the Class 40, 44/45/46 'Peak', the once ubiquitous 47, 50 and the mighty 55 'Deltic'. In time, every loco, and even the lesser thought of multiple units, had 'Bashers'. This has translated into many examples being preserved and some even hauling well-filled charter trains on the modern railway network. A credit to all concerned.

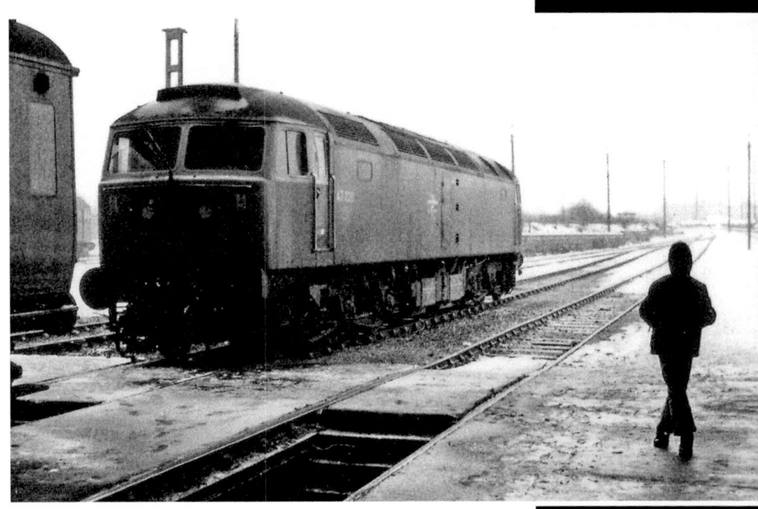

Above: It's cold out there, Birkenhead Motive Power Depot (MPD), January 1978. During the 1970s and '80s, access to all areas was possible at most depots, except for notables such as Old Oak Common and Gateshead. In this shot a sensibly clad young enthusiast stares out from the shelter of Birkenhead Depot's servicing shed at 47226, which was standing in the freezing cold yard. The rather dilapidated ex-steam shed and its yard were full of locos – Class 08s, 25s, 40s and 47s – most of which were outside. Despite the weather it was a brilliant visit – very atmospheric!

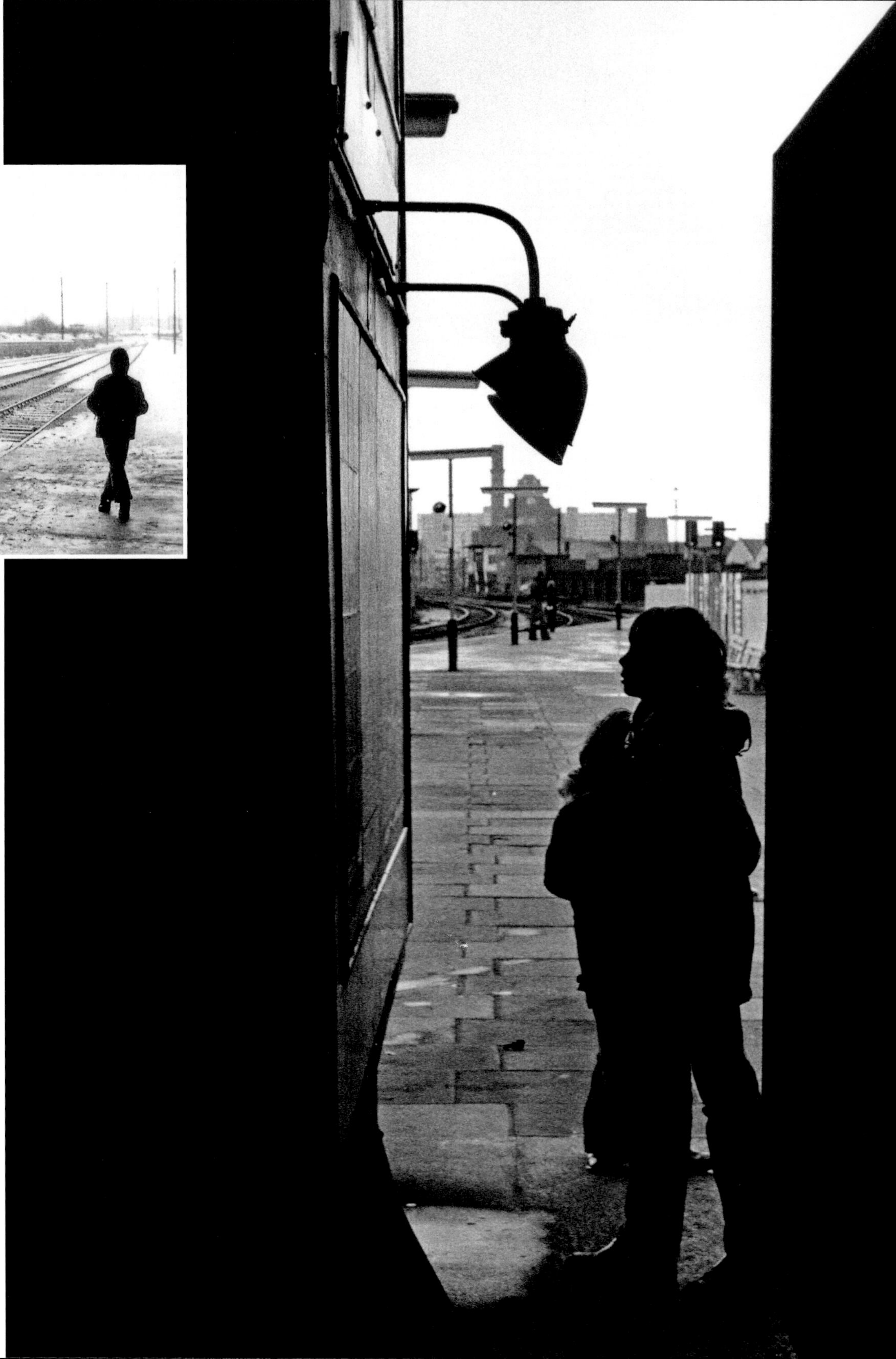

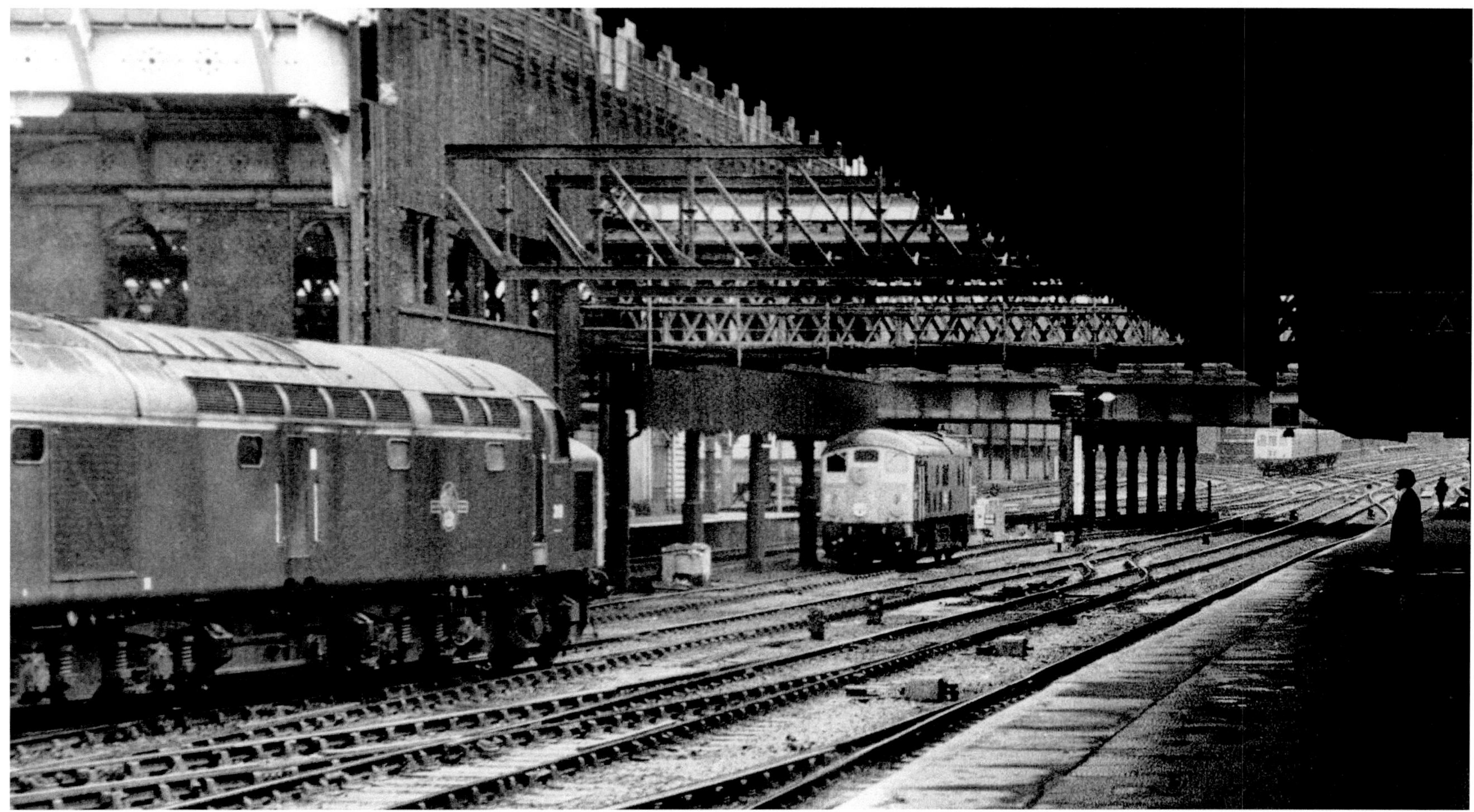

Left: **What's Next? Manchester Victoria, winter 1978.**
The weather is cold and grim, but clearly of no consequence to these keen loco spotters. The hyper-atmospheric surroundings of this sprawling station are legendary. Those were the days! Trains were plentiful and there were lots of vantage points. The timetable board on Platform 12/13 was ideal for finding out what was coming next. Of course arrival knowledge relied on the Tannoy operator being clearly heard; no dot matrix information boxes back then. The regular freights and light engine movements were surprise bonuses. Countless train enthusiasts, over many generations, have spent a huge amount of totally engrossing hours within the station's confines. My good friend and former vice chairman of the East Lancashire Railway Preservation Society, David Flood, has often spoken to me about the terrific times he spent there – in particular, as a young lad during the late 1950s and early '60s. He has a photograph of himself trainspotting on Platform 12, taken by master railway photographer Jim Carter.

Above: **What a Vista! Manchester Victoria, winter 1973.**
For generations of rail enthusiasts Platform 11 was best of all for watching trains at Manchester Victoria. The platform continued into and through the by then closed Manchester Exchange, making it the longest platform in the world! It was in the *Guinness Book of Records*. During the early 1970s it was still possible to walk its full length, providing another brilliant vantage point to watch trains. In this shot pre-TOPS-numbered Class 40, 318, passes through with an eastbound freight. Adjacent to Platform 12, an unidentified 'Skin Head 24' on station pilot duties waits for its next assignment. Meanwhile, a Metro-Camm Class 101 two-car DMU drifts down Miles Platting Bank towards Platform 14.

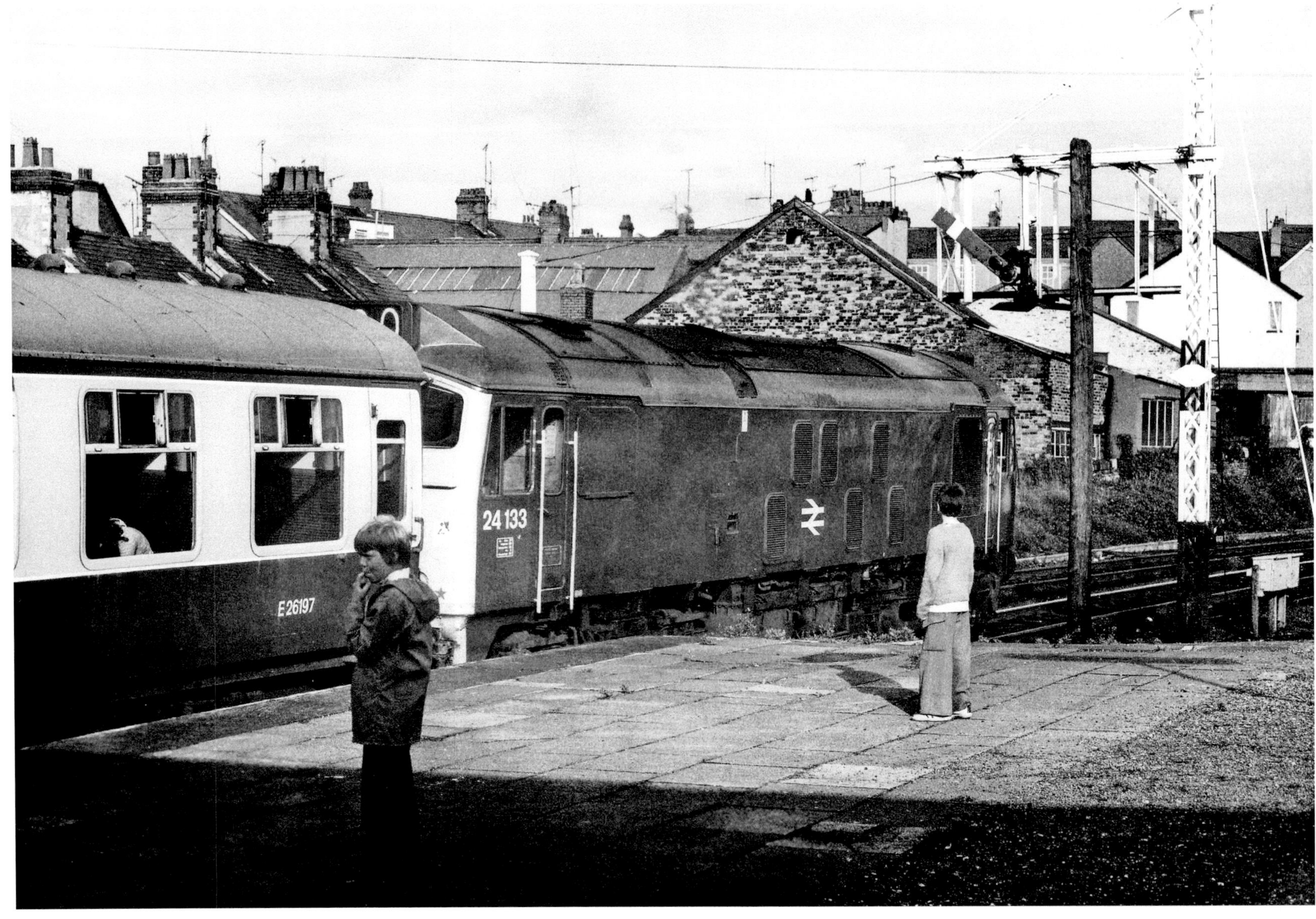

Take your Finger Out of your Mouth, Llandudno Junction, summer 1977.
The Junction was a great place to escape to, especially while on family holidays at nearby seaside resorts, such as Llandudno, Colwyn Bay and Abergele. Its adjacent loco shed provided added interest to the regular stream of trains calling and passing through the station. During the summer months, loco-hauled passenger trains made regular appearances. This train was bound for Crewe, hauled by one of the by then rare Class 24 survivors. This later variation headcode box-fitted example was unique, having a standard version at one end and a Class 27-style one at the other. Sadly it didn't make it into preservation, but fortunately four earlier 'Skin Head' (no headcode box) versions did. By 1980, Llandudno Junction and the North Wales Coast Line had become a Mecca for 'Class 40 Bashers'. The route had become the domain of this threatened and ever popular class of locomotive.

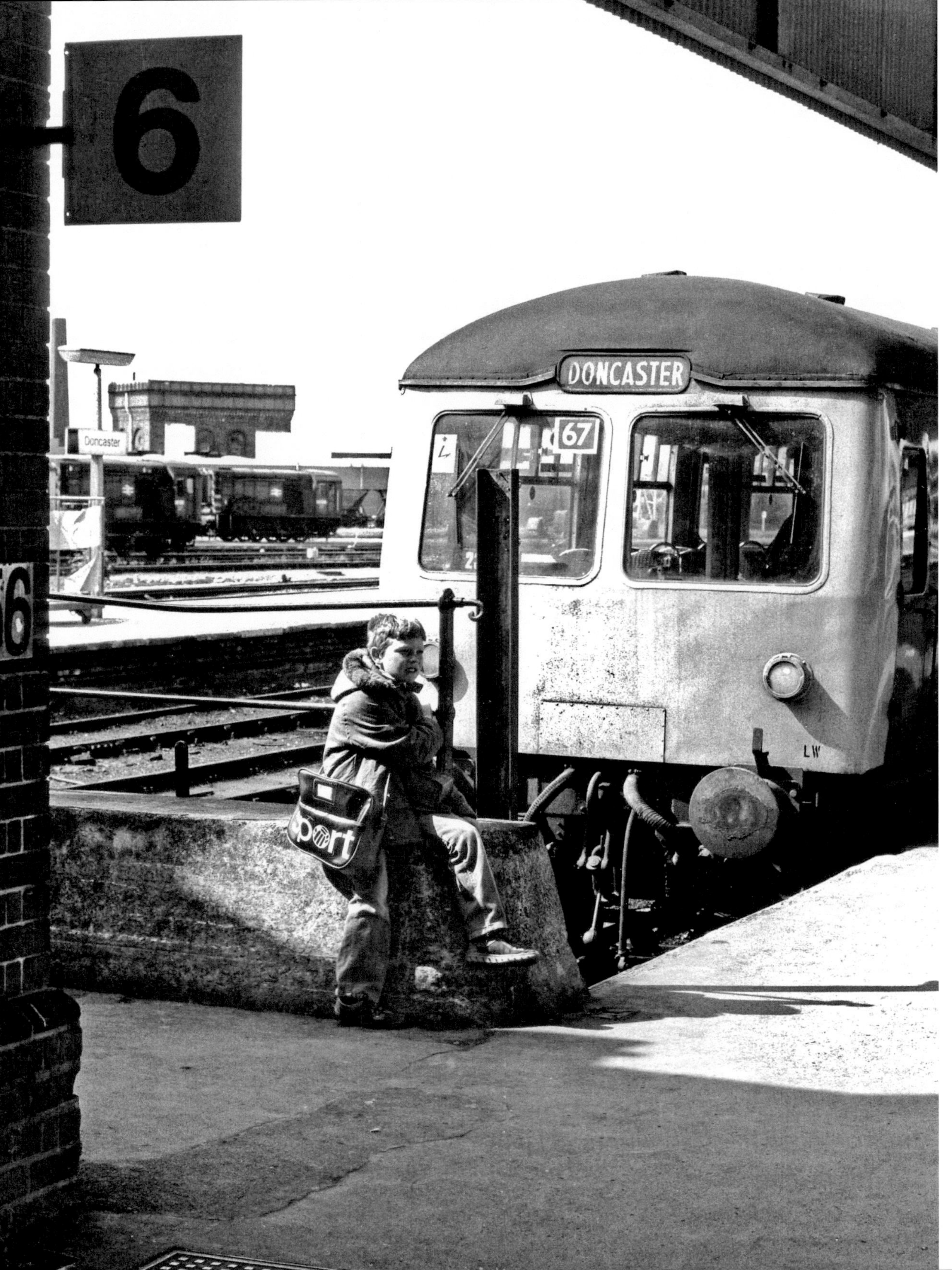

Phew, it's Hot! Doncaster, summer 1979. Despite it being quite hot, this enthusiast is steadfastly wearing his all-weather outfit, complete with regulation sports bag. The bag will be filled with all sorts of essential items such as butties, pop, magazines, timetables, a *Combined Volume*, *Locoshed* book, camera, pens and paper. No wonder he is feeling the effects of the weather.

Pen and Paper in Hand, Guide Bridge, winter 1973.

I met this fellow loco spotter at Manchester Victoria station, where he asked me how best to see some Class 76 electrics. I suggested he took a train from Manchester Piccadilly to Guide Bridge. I decided to tag along, hoping for something interesting to photograph. Unfortunately, when we got there the only loco activity was a few Class 40 moves. However, he wasn't disappointed with the nearby Stabling Point, which was filled with Class 76s. In this photograph, Class 40 306 rumbles through shortly before taking the Denton spur. It was later to become a celebrity loco and was subsequently preserved in good operational condition. This photograph is especially for the irrepressible John Stephens, chairman of the Class 40 Preservation Society and lifetime train enthusiast. During late 2015, out of the blue, he managed to arrange the purchase of this loco. John never ceases to amaze me. It is now part of the society's fine stud of three operational Class 40s, 40106, 40135 and mainline-certified 40145.

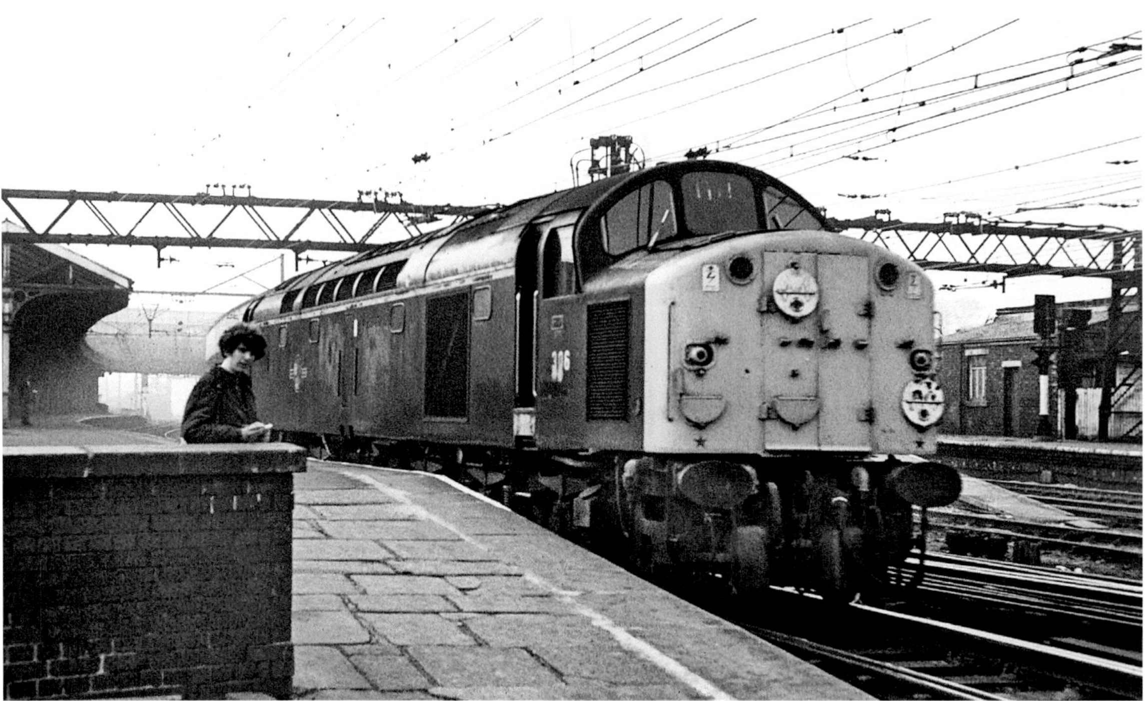

Dull Day at Basingstoke, summer 1975.

In this shot it is perhaps clear why many enthusiasts walked away from the 'Big Railway' when steam came to an end on British Rail. Many preferred to spend their time on preserved railways, the fairly local Bluebell Railway being a prime example. It is not surprising, when you think that just ten years previously this part of the Southern Region could boast awesome 'Merchant Navy' and 'West Country' steam locos hauling fast trains. This enthusiast only has 33115 to captivate him. In fairness to Basingstoke, it did still have plenty of railway activity to keep him occupied.

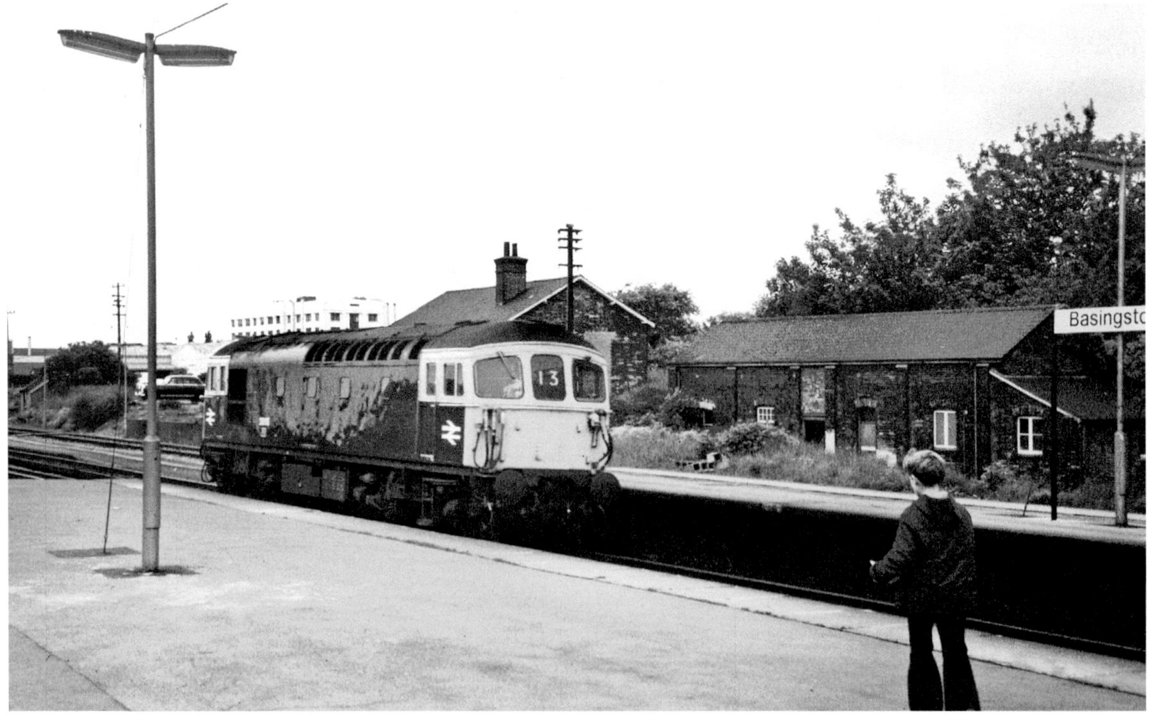

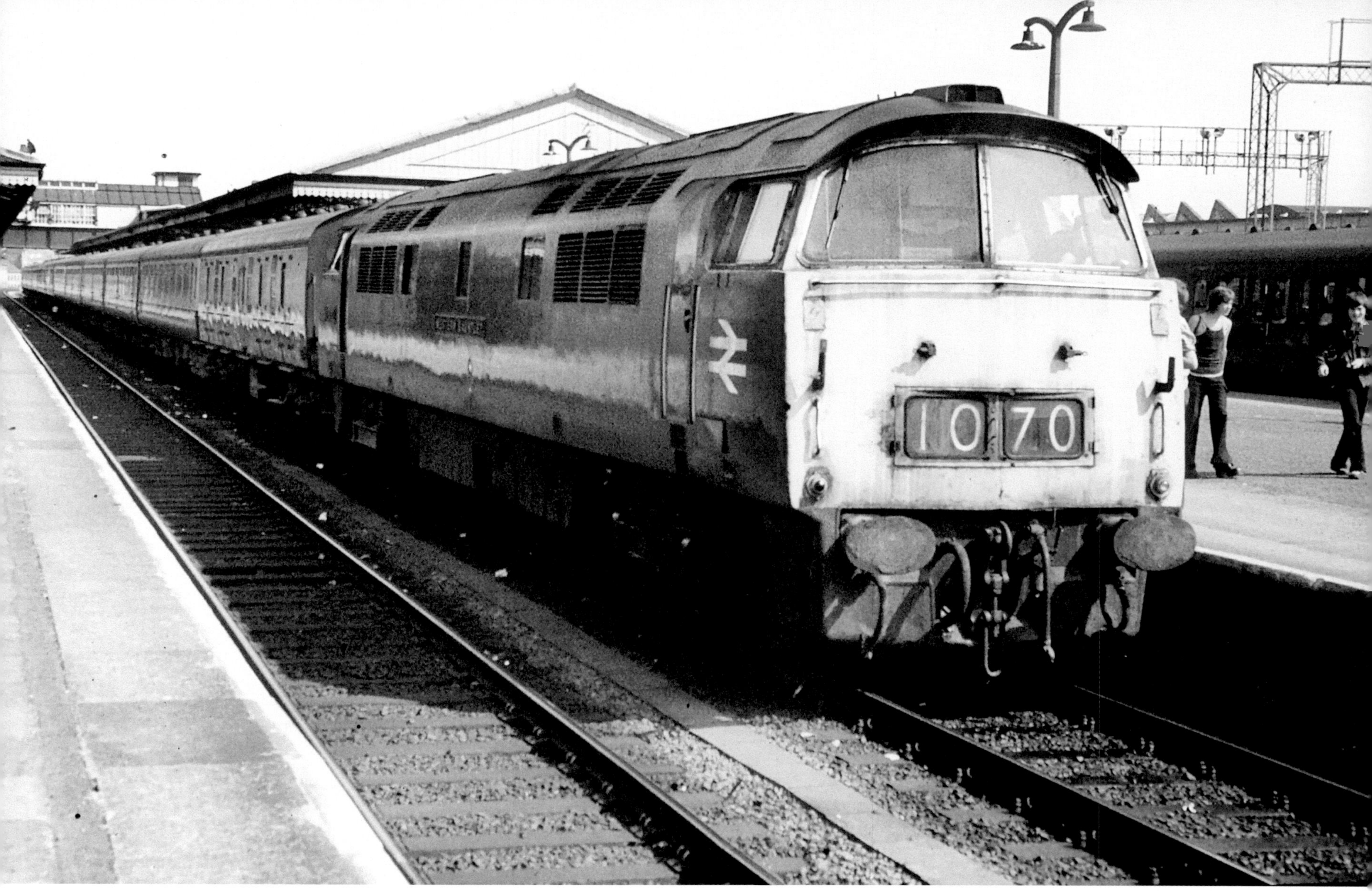

Chasing 'Westerns', Newton Abbot, summer 1976.

The long hot summer of 1976 was the last full year of Class 52 'Western' service on British Rail, chasing 'Westerns' was a must-do activity. Sadly, by the end of the following February they had all been withdrawn. This really was the Indian summer for the class. Fortunately the remaining examples were still being used extensively on the West of England Mainline serving Torbay, Plymouth and Penzance. If you had the money, bargain-priced 'Runabout' tickets were ideal for clocking up the miles hauled by this iconic class of loco. If funds were low and you were lucky enough to take your family holiday on the 'English Riviera', this main hub of activity was a great place to while away the days. If you lived locally, even better – it must have been too good to miss. Like Llandudno Junction, Newton Abbot had the added bonus of an adjacent depot – perfect! The young chaps walking past the loco are clearly enjoying every minute. Note one of them is sporting one of the then fashionable tank tops. *Western Gauntlet* (great use of the then redundant headcode box), 1070, waits to depart with an Inter-City service from London Paddington to Plymouth.

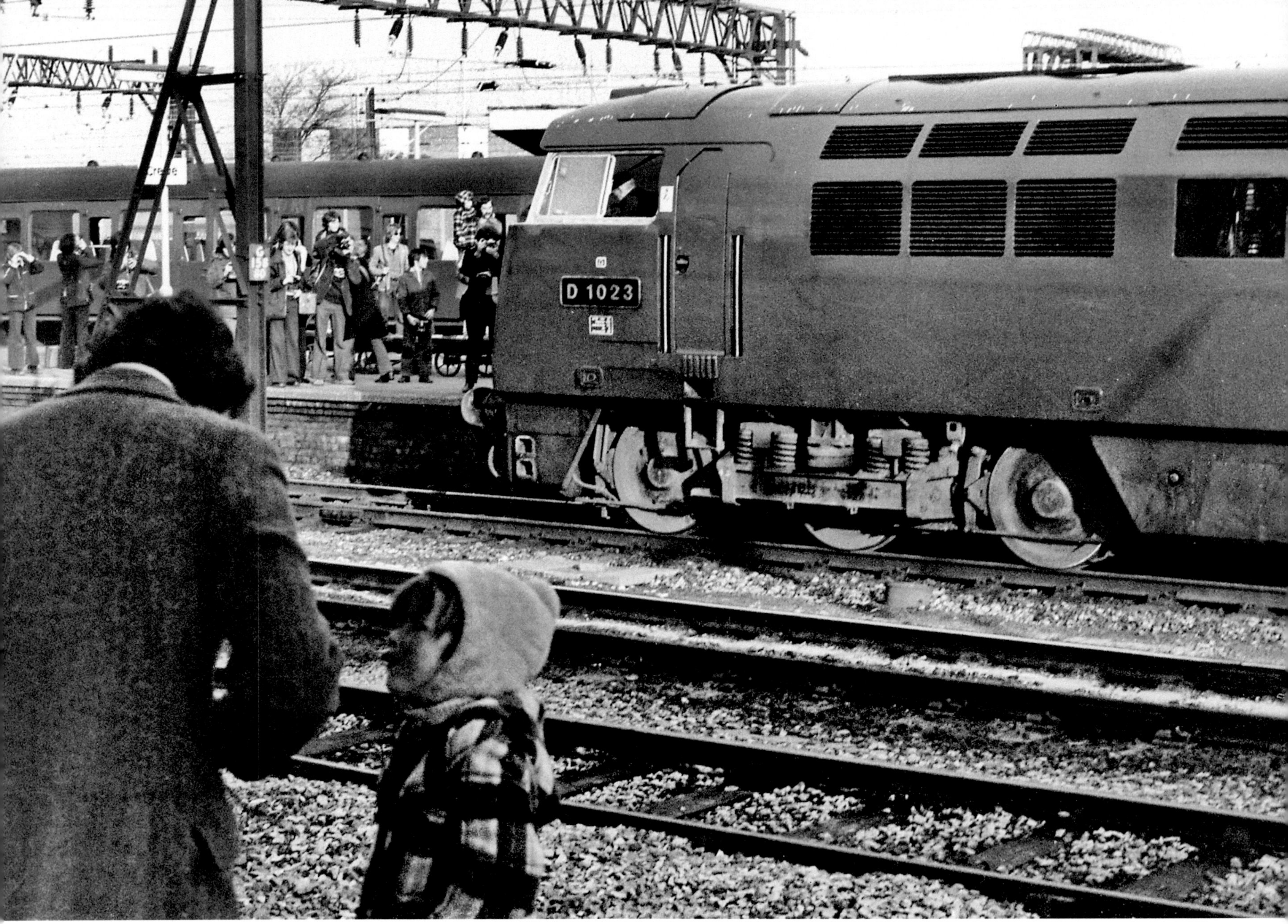

Can We Go Home Now? Crewe, 29 January 1977.
This was an unmissable event, 'Western' Class 52 1023 *Western Fusilier* hauled the Railway Pictorial Publications Railtours' 'Western Memorial' railtour from London Paddington, via Bristol Parkway, Severn Tunnel Junction, Hereford, Shrewsbury and Crewe (returning via Wrexham instead of Crewe). The train was packed and followers of the class watched the train along its circuitous route. This shot was taken just as the loco had pulled the railtour into the station. The platforms were crowded with fans of the soon-to-be withdrawn 'Westerns'.

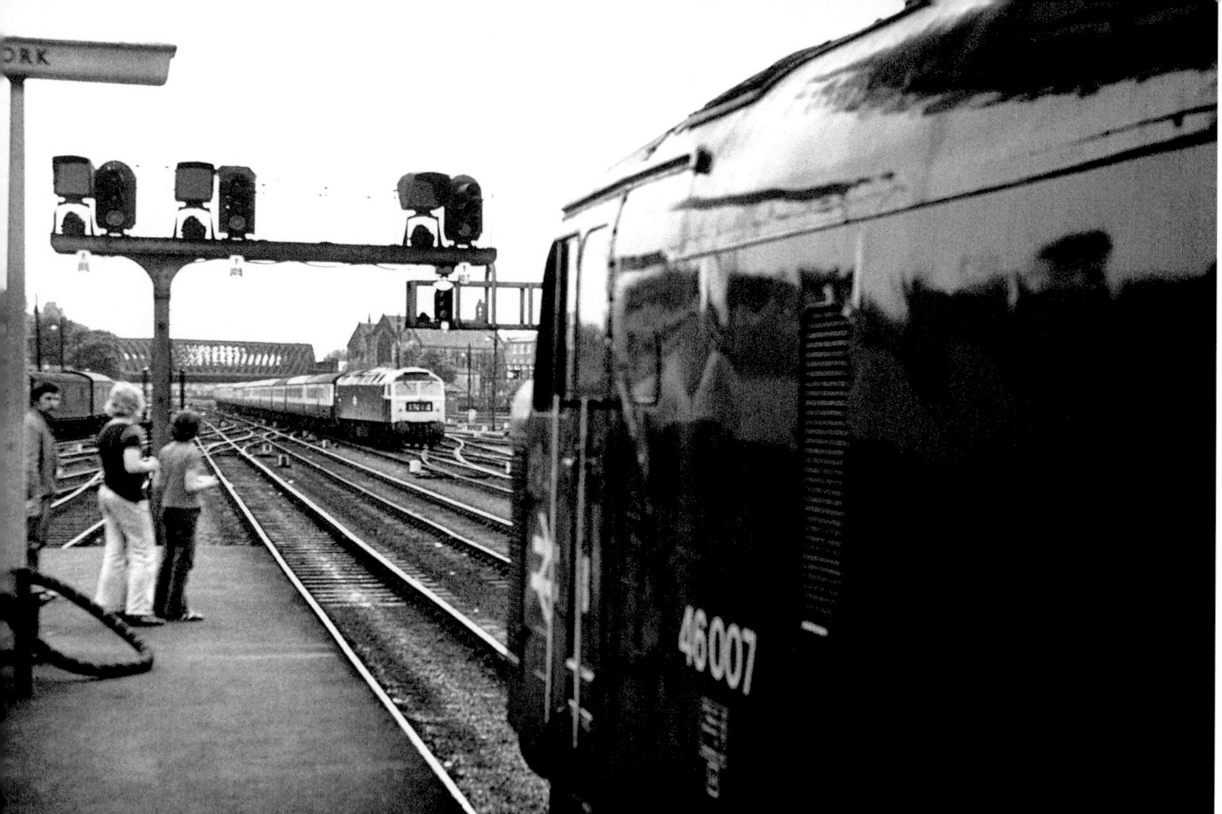

This is York, August 1975.
A great way to spend an afternoon: 46007 waits to depart with a Bristol-bound train, while an unidentified Class 47 approaches with an Anglo-Scottish train. Superb entertainment, there was something to enthral every few minutes. A few years later York would become a Mecca for enthusiasts wishing to view the numerous comings and goings of the awesome Class 55 'Deltics'. I bet there are plenty of people reading this book, like me, who spent many a fantastic day at York railway station. I still find it pretty good, but nowhere near as good as during the 1970s. Older enthusiasts will no doubt remember the station filled with LNER steam locos, with bucketfuls of nostalgia.

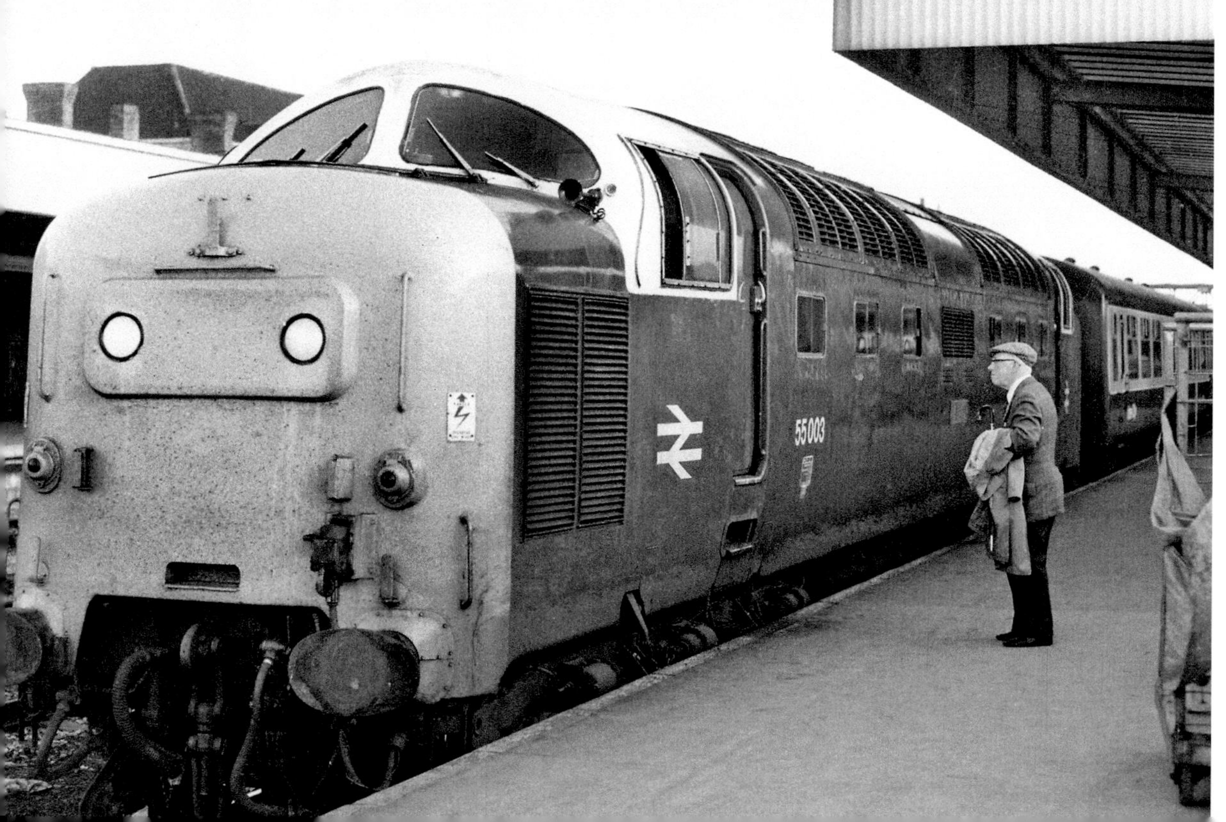

Not as Good as an A4, Doncaster, 14 August 1980.
Finsbury Park-allocated 'Deltic' racehorse 55003 *Meld* pauses at Doncaster station, while hauling 1L42, the 12.20 p.m. King's Cross–York. No doubt this older gentleman was a dyed-in-the-wool LNER/BR steam man. Nevertheless, he appears captivated by the mighty 'Deltic'. Twenty years earlier the 'A' Class ex-LNER 'Pacific' steam locos still reigned supreme on the East Coast Mainline – he would have remembered them vividly, and I guess he would also have remembered their 1930s heyday. I should have spent a few minutes talking to him. My loss.

Brass Rubbing, Doncaster, 15 September 1979.

Probably the fastest brass rubbers in the land. A well-planned operation is under way to get a tracing of the builder's plate and nameplate of 55012 *Crepello* on Doncaster's Platform 1. It won't be long before the 7 a.m. Hull–London King's Cross departs, so they had to be quick. Far cheaper than buying the actual plates, a roll end of wallpaper was often used – mum and dad's permission being advisable. I wonder if the intrepid enthusiasts' efforts have stood the test of time? The first time I saw this being undertaken was on a Class 52 'Western'. The length of their nameplates would need a pretty long roll of paper.

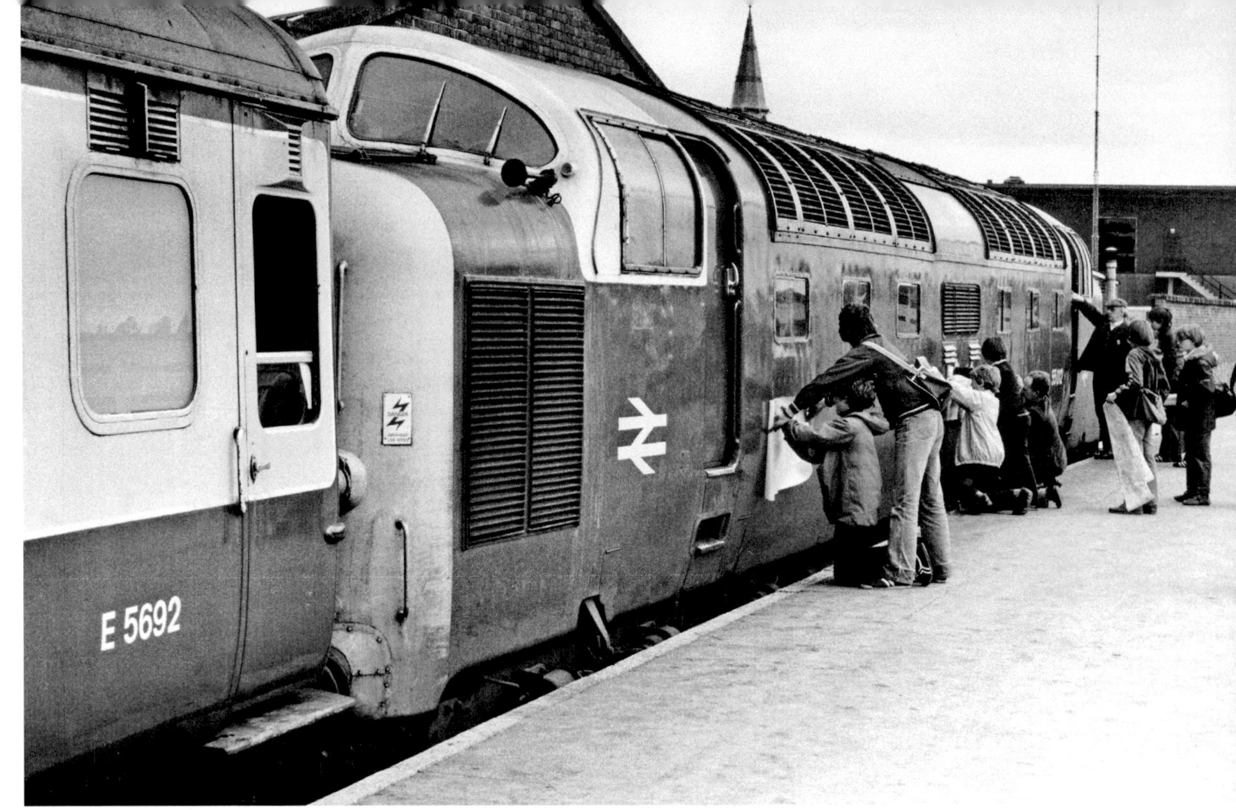

Not the Best Place to Sit? York, 8 April 1978.

A few years ago, 'Deltic' man Martin Walker told me that he thought he was the young enthusiast featured in this photograph. Wouldn't that be great? Whoever it is, 55011 *The Royal Northumberland Fusiliers* has really captivated his attention. I guess nowadays sitting there wouldn't be allowed.

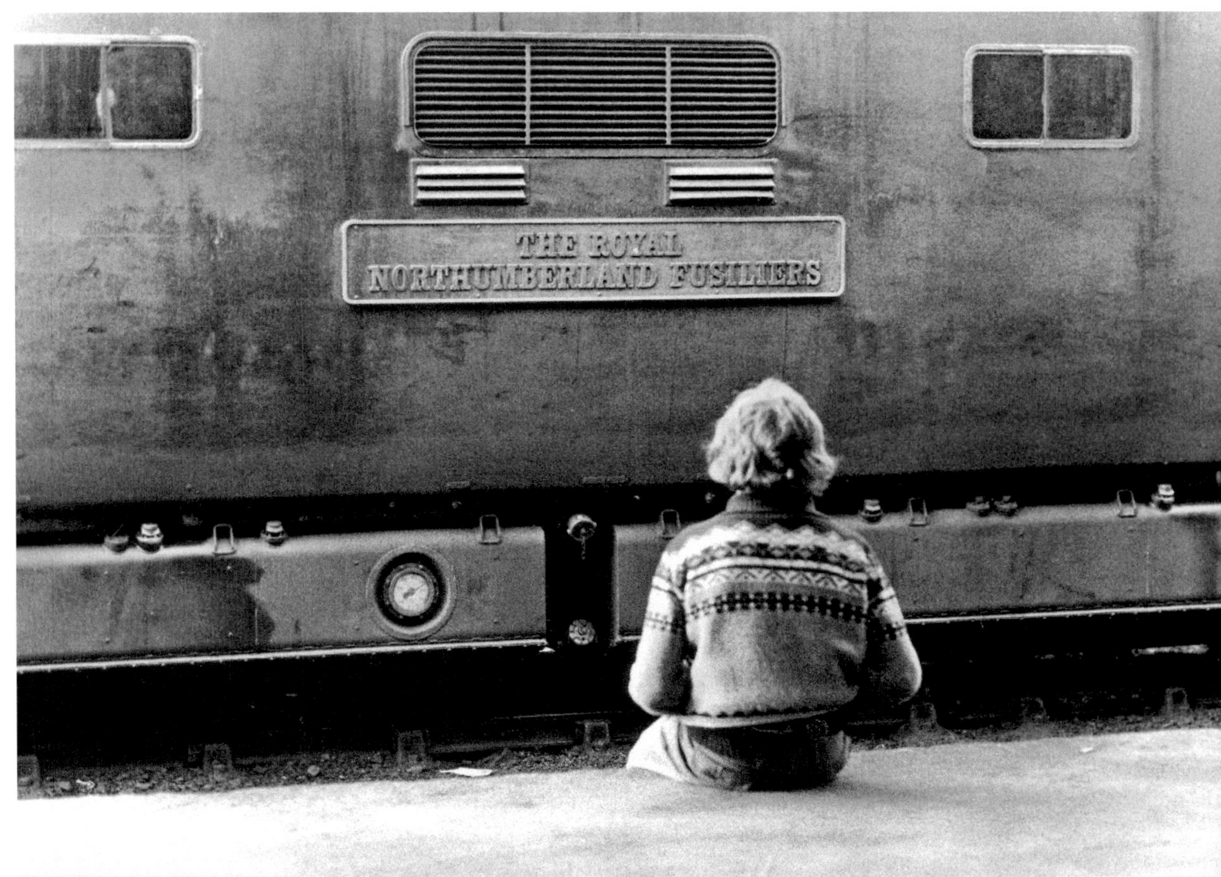

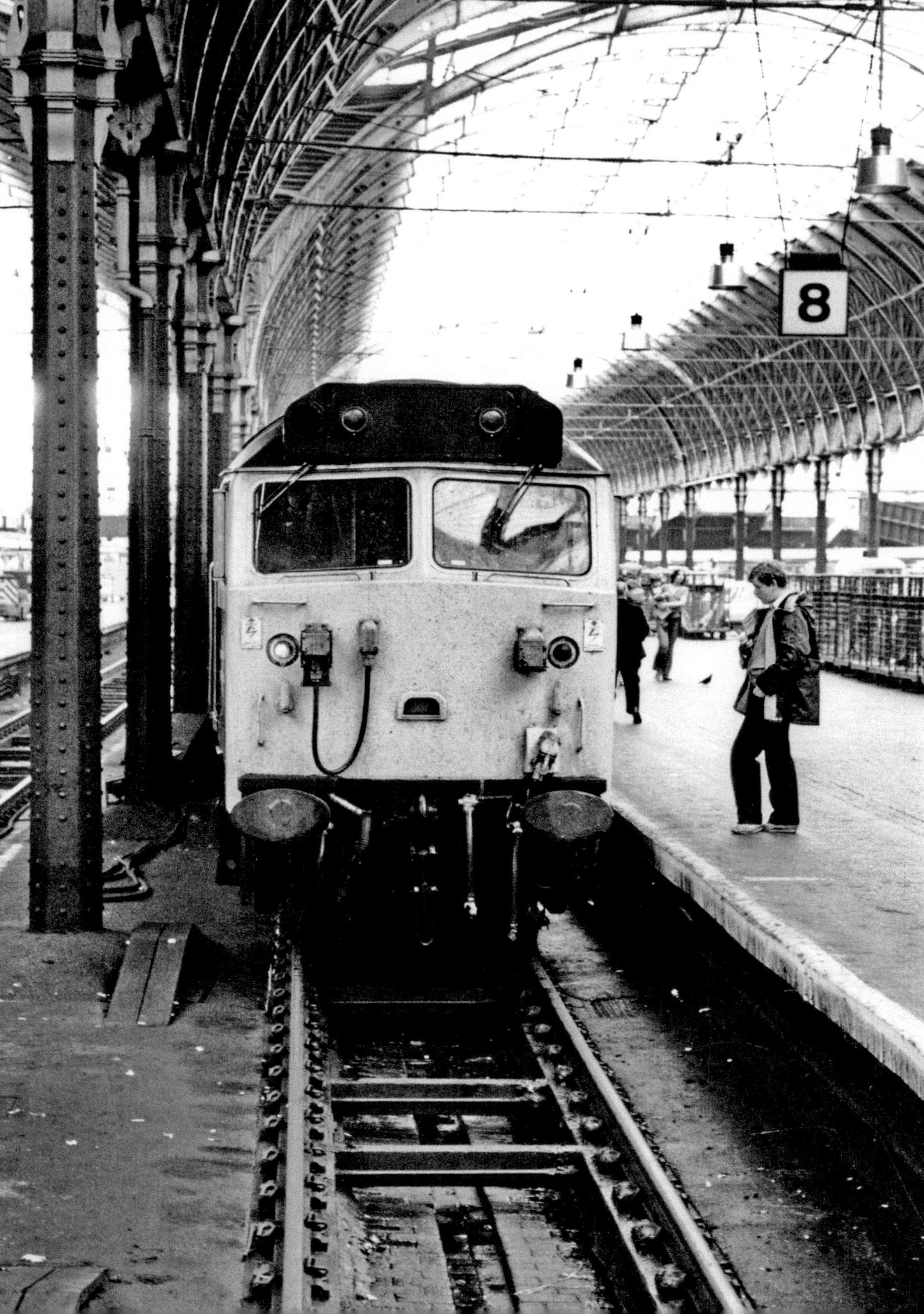

In Deep Concentration, London Paddington, summer 1981.
By the time this photograph was taken, a passion for Class 50 'Hoovers' was beginning to take hold. After the demise of the Class 40 and 55 during the first half of the 1980s, 'Class 50 bashing' became the preferred activity by many enthusiasts. Previously derided by some because they usurped the Class 52 'Western', the Class 50 were undeniably fine machines. This enthusiast is clearly deep in concentration examining the finer points of 50035 *Ark Royal*.

I would rather be at Crewe, Stoke-on-Trent, November 1979.
Not all mainline city stations were full of activity. Stoke-on-Trent could have seemingly long dreary periods, unlike relatively nearby Crewe. These enthusiasts look like they are suffering the effects of such a period. They only have the pair of Class 25s to interest them. The station would come alive for a little while when an electric-hauled Manchester Piccadilly–London Euston, Birmingham/Cardiff Inter-City service called. There was also Class 304 and 310 EMU services, plus Class 120 DMU Crewe–Lincoln trains to break up the prevailing quiet spells. Sporadic freights also helped. Clay for the Potteries from Cornwall, coal and steel to and from British Steel Corporation (BSC) Shelton, and sand for glass from Oakamoor were the main source of freight-train action. The pair of 25s may well have been waiting to work a freight train out of the station's sidings.

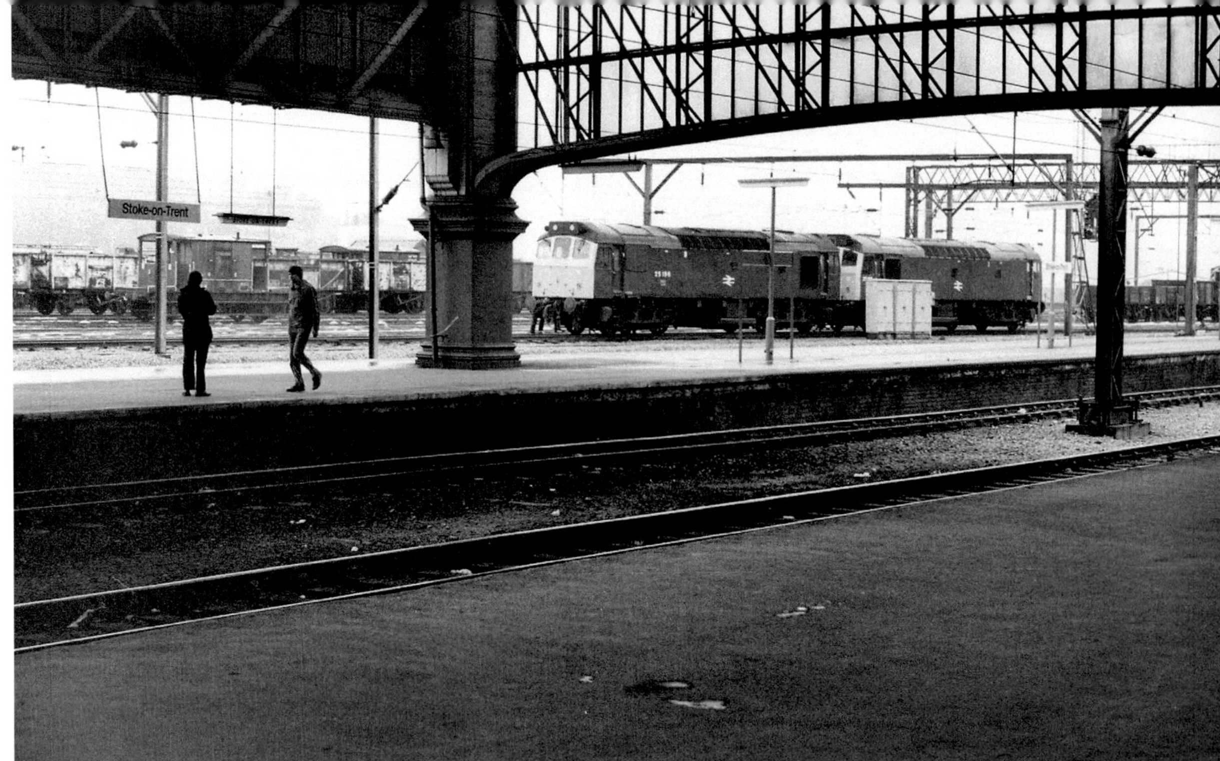

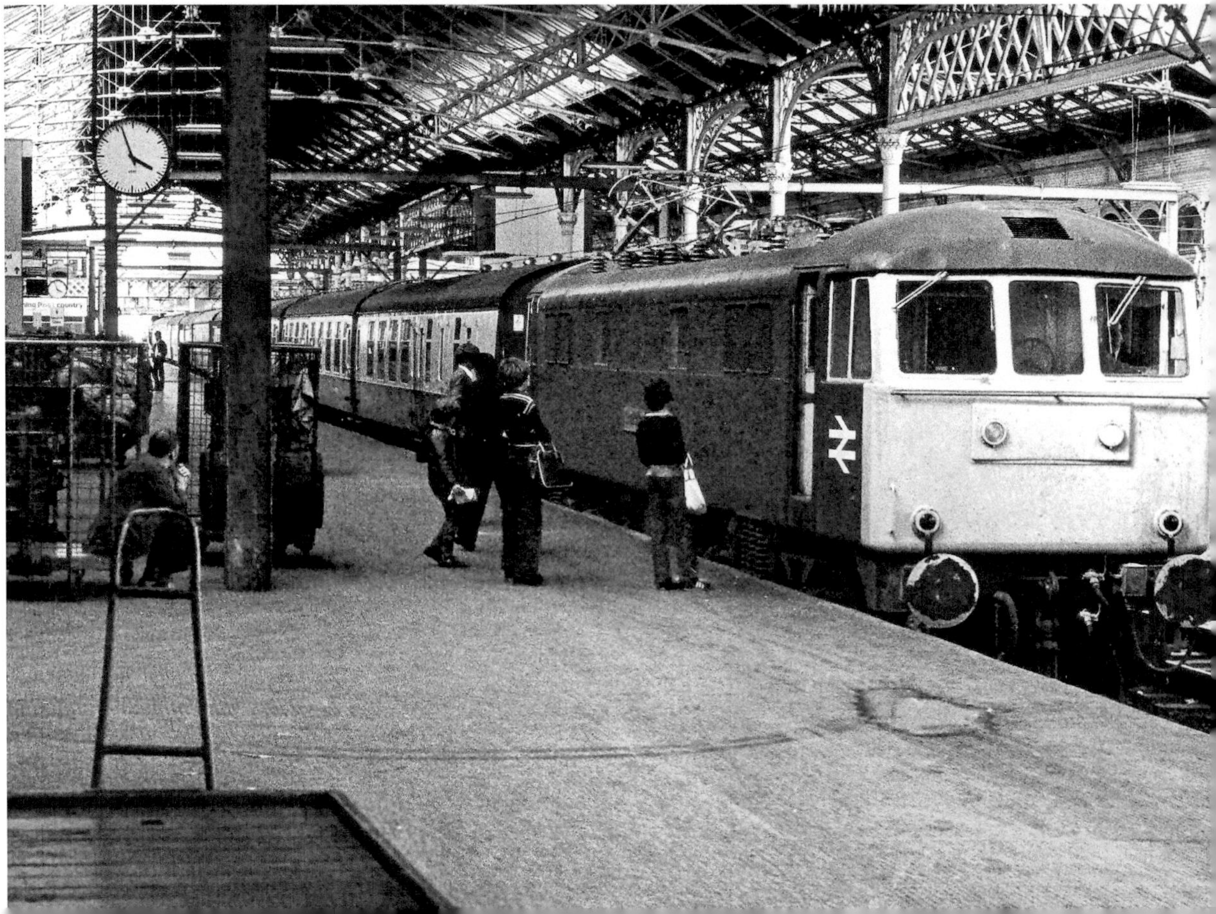

'I wonder if we can cab it? Preston, Easter 1980.
Sometimes a kindly driver would allow an enthusiast to cab a loco. Even better, a short cab ride if the loco was being detached from the train. I remember being offered a run in the cab of a Class 86 from Longsight Depot to Manchester Piccadilly. No doubt these lads would have loved the opportunity to pile into the cab, but on this occasion they were out of luck. They must have said to each other, 'I wonder if we can cab it?' This unidentified 86/2 loco has just arrived with the 12.55 p.m. Edinburgh–Liverpool Lime Street.

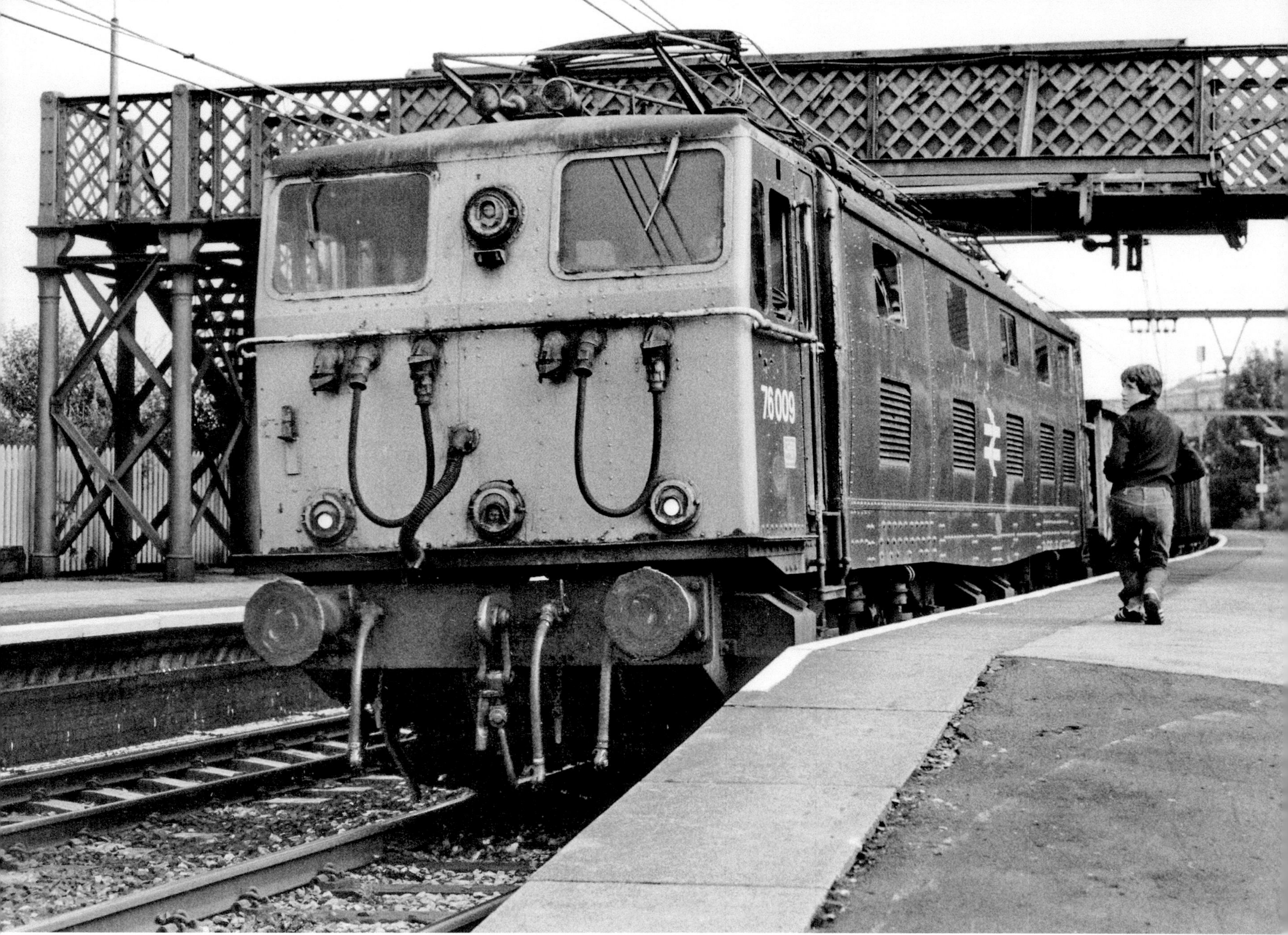

In Search of the Master Shot, Dinting, August 1980.
Photography is very much part of railway enthusiasm. This fellow photographer, no doubt on a quest for the ultimate Class 76 master shot, has just bagged a photograph of 76009 passing through Dinting station with an eastbound mixed freight. I wonder if he fulfilled his quest? He most likely got a good shot because of his low-level photograph-taking position. The approaching loco probably looked quite impressive when his film was developed, especially if he left pressing the shutter until just the right moment: not too close, not too far away.

'Farewell 24s', Crewe, 24 April 1976.
It wasn't just the big locos, such as soon-to-be withdrawn Class 40s, 52s and 55s, that mustered up enough interest to fill 'Farewell to …' railtours. This is the 24 April 1976 'Farewell 24s' railtour hauled by 24133 and 24085. It is departing from Crewe bound for Holyhead and Blaenau Ffestiniog. At the time, I and many other enthusiasts thought the Class 24s' days were numbered, hence the railtour. Whilst 24085 was put into store the following month, 24133 remained in service until 1978; 133 worked several more railtours in the meantime. The last Class 24 in BR service is now preserved 24081. It was withdrawn during October 1980 – over four years after 24133 and 24085 hauled 'Farewell 24s'.

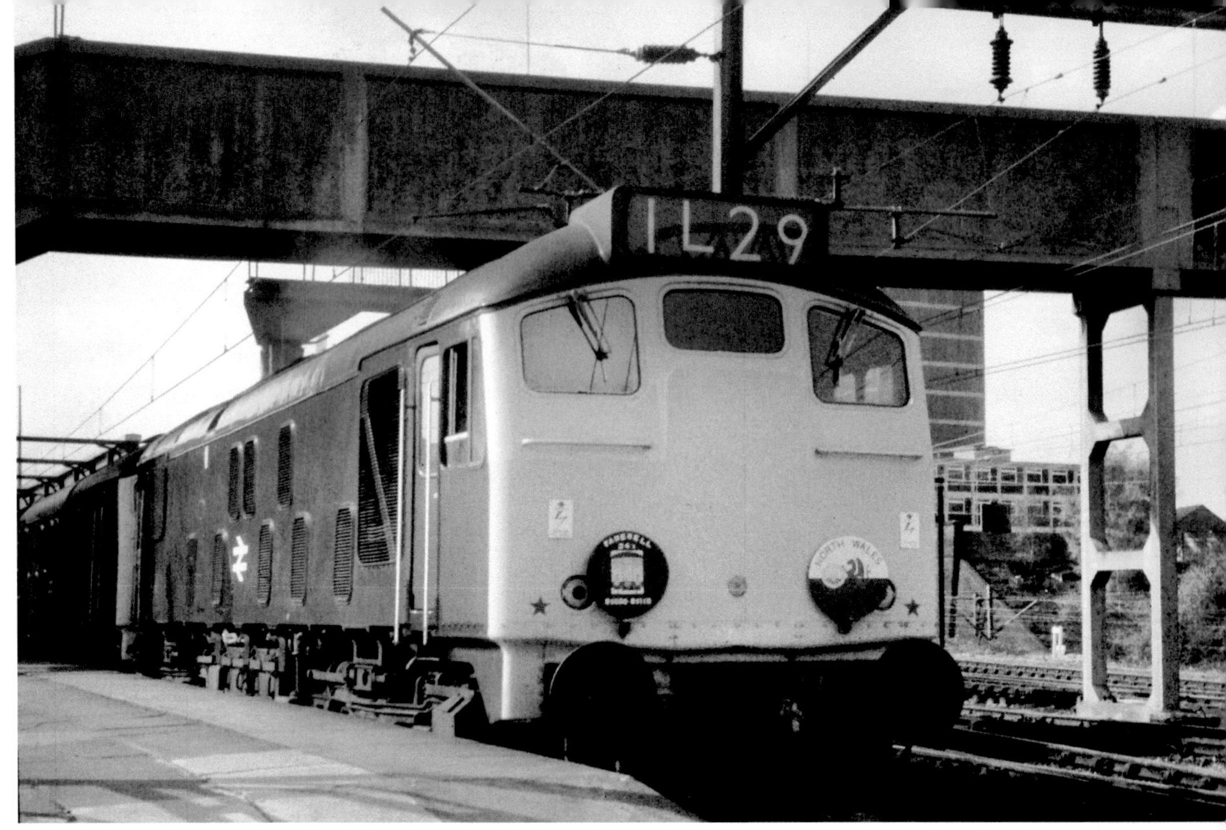

'The York Ranger', Doncaster, summer 1980.
In a bid to cater for both steam and modern traction rail fans, a number of longer established railway societies ran railtours to suit all. They often utilised a variety of steam, diesel and electric traction in their tour itinerary. However, in the case of the Midland & Great Northern (M&GN) Joint Railway Society's 'The York Ranger', I am not sure if this was the case. One thing is for sure: the modern enthusiast fraternity would have been satisfied with the choice of large logo-liveried 47170 *County of Norfolk* to haul the train. I photographed the train as it paused at Doncaster while heading south. The bicycling enthusiast will have been pleased he turned up just as it drew into the station.

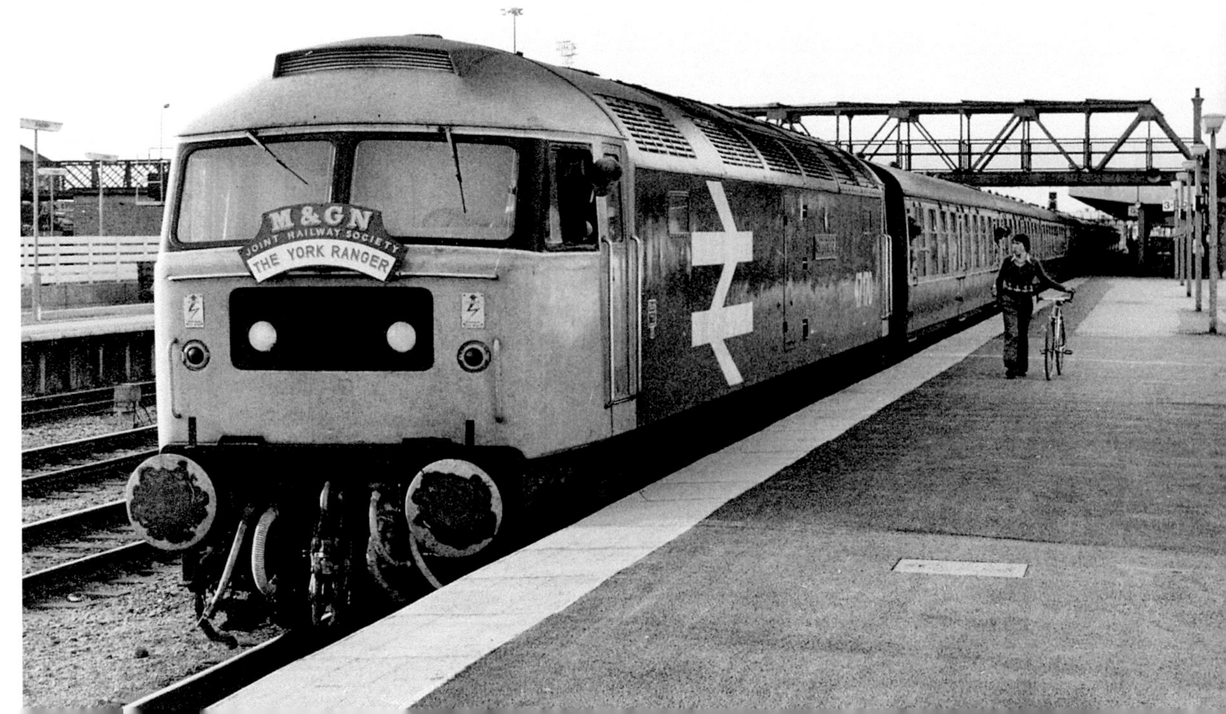

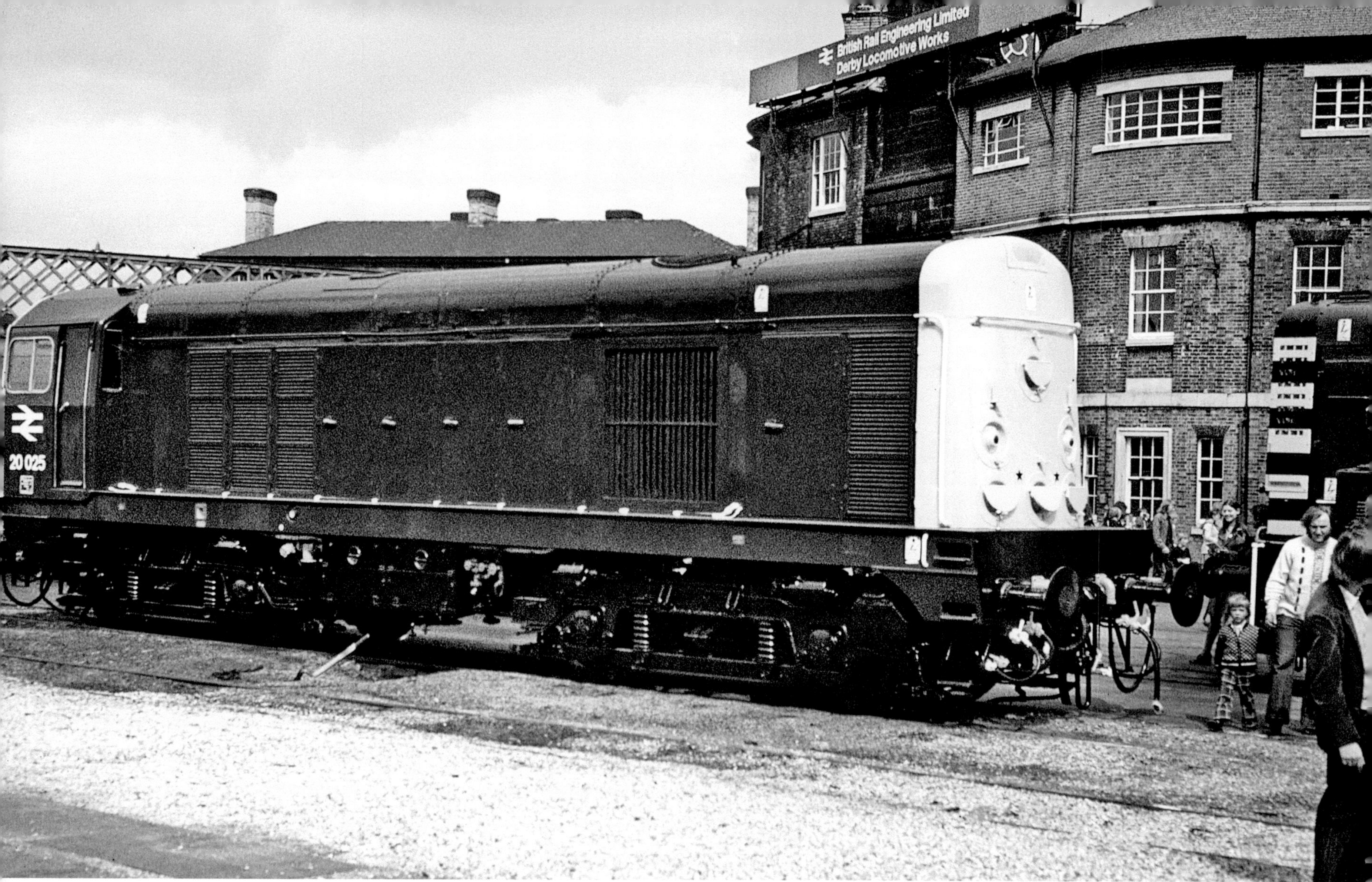

Open Day, Derby, 4 September 1976.
Throughout the BR network, open days were held at depots and loco works. They were a great way for enthusiasts, families of rail workers and local people to explore and get to know these fantastic places. Quite often locos and rolling stock would be drafted in to augment the exhibits. There were stalls manned by fledgling preservation societies and, my all-time favourite, BR's Collectors' Corner. The latter had a great place near to Euston station where you could buy BR's cast offs, including posters, signs, nameplates, labels, buttons, chairs, crockery and cutlery. Having a stall at open days allowed enthusiasts the opportunity to buy something off them, without having to trek down to London. A commonplace feature was the prominent placement of an ex-works-condition loco. In this case, at BREL Derby works 1976 open day, freshly outshopped 20025 looks splendid, although it doesn't seem to have caught the eye of visitors. I understand a month before this shot was taken the loco was fully stripped down in the main erecting shop. Impressive!

I Like Diesels Best, Leeds station, summer 1976.

Steam specials were plentiful by the time this photograph was taken. BR's late 1960s embargo on running them had been lifted and quite a few beautifully restored steam locos were regularly hauling trains on allotted routes. Runs between York or Leeds and Carnforth or the Cumbrian coast were popular. Carnforth's Steamtown provided home and servicing facilities to several mainline operational steamers. In this shot LNER-liveried 1306 *Mayflower* is rather tellingly being totally ignored by this young rail enthusiast. No doubt he preferred Leeds regular Class 40, 45/46 and 55 loco-hauled activity. Check out the kindly police sergeant talking to an enthusiast.

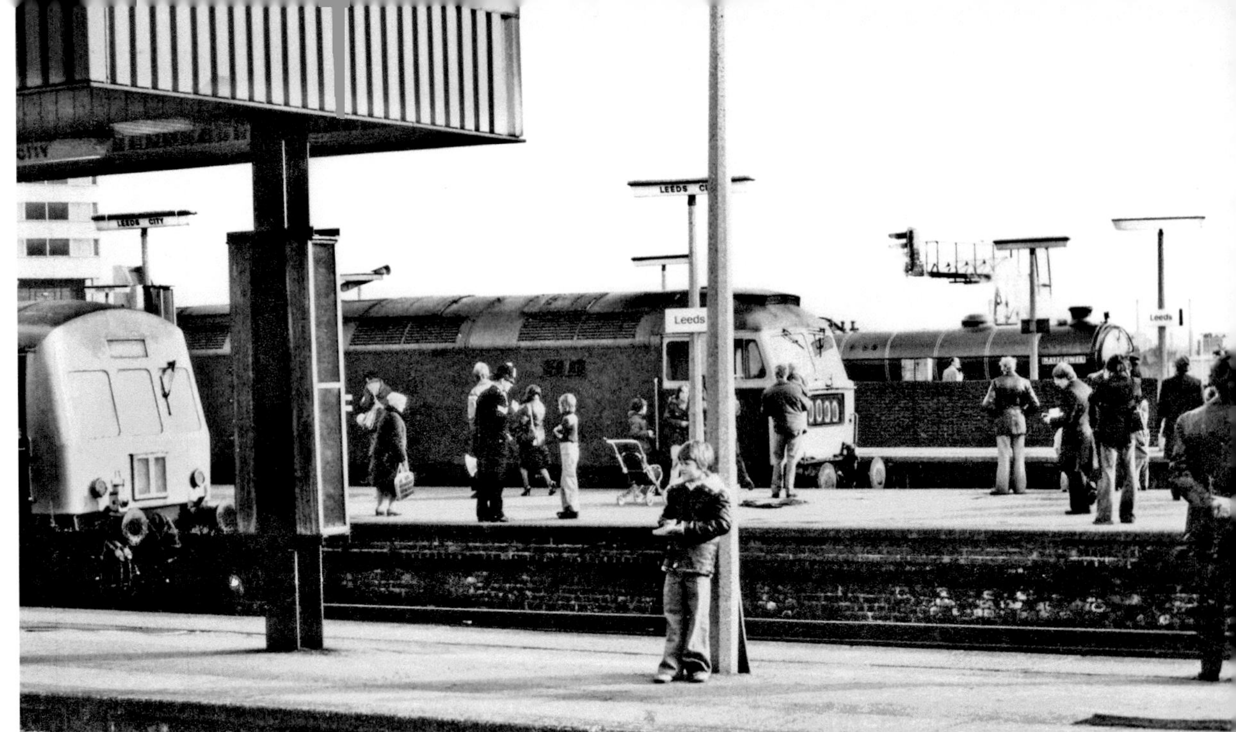

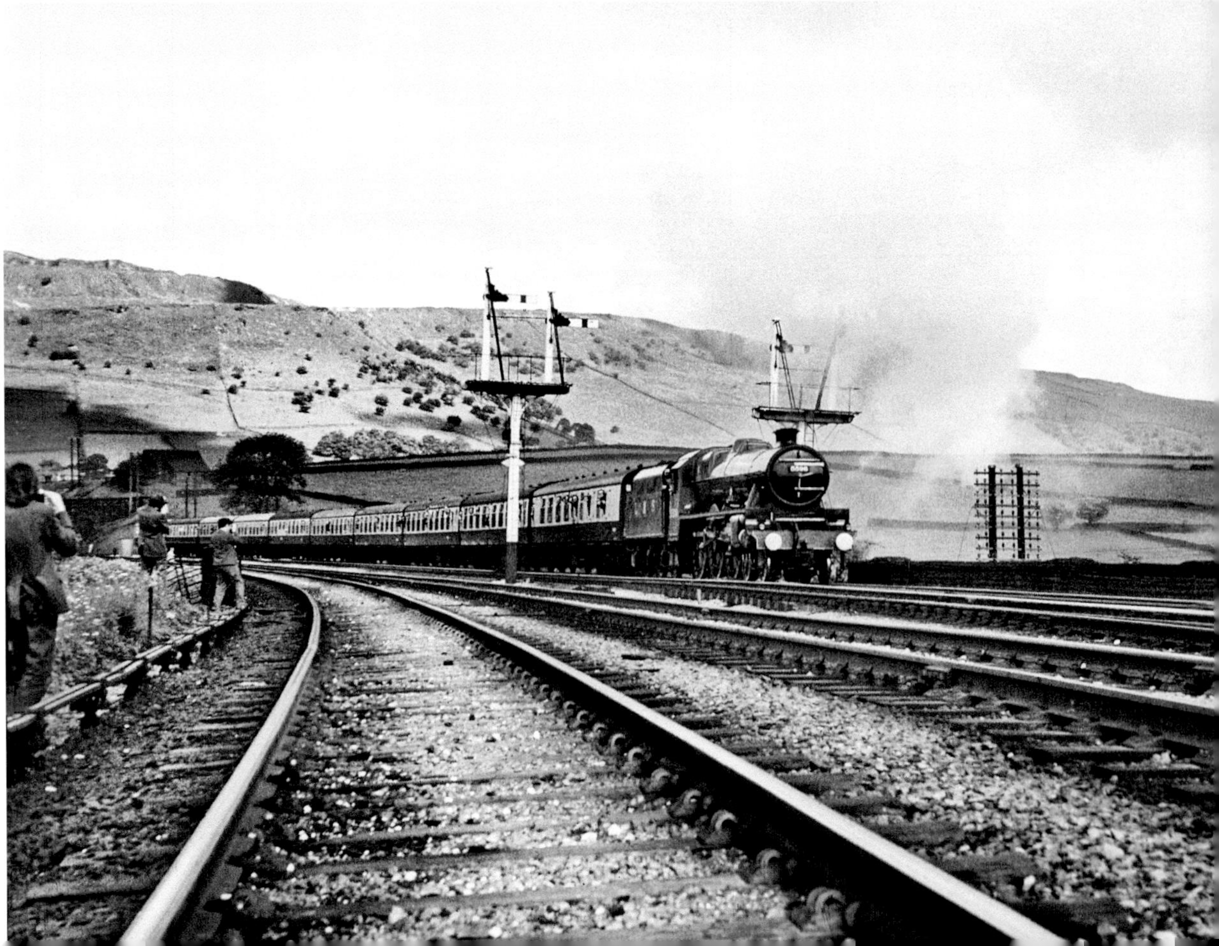

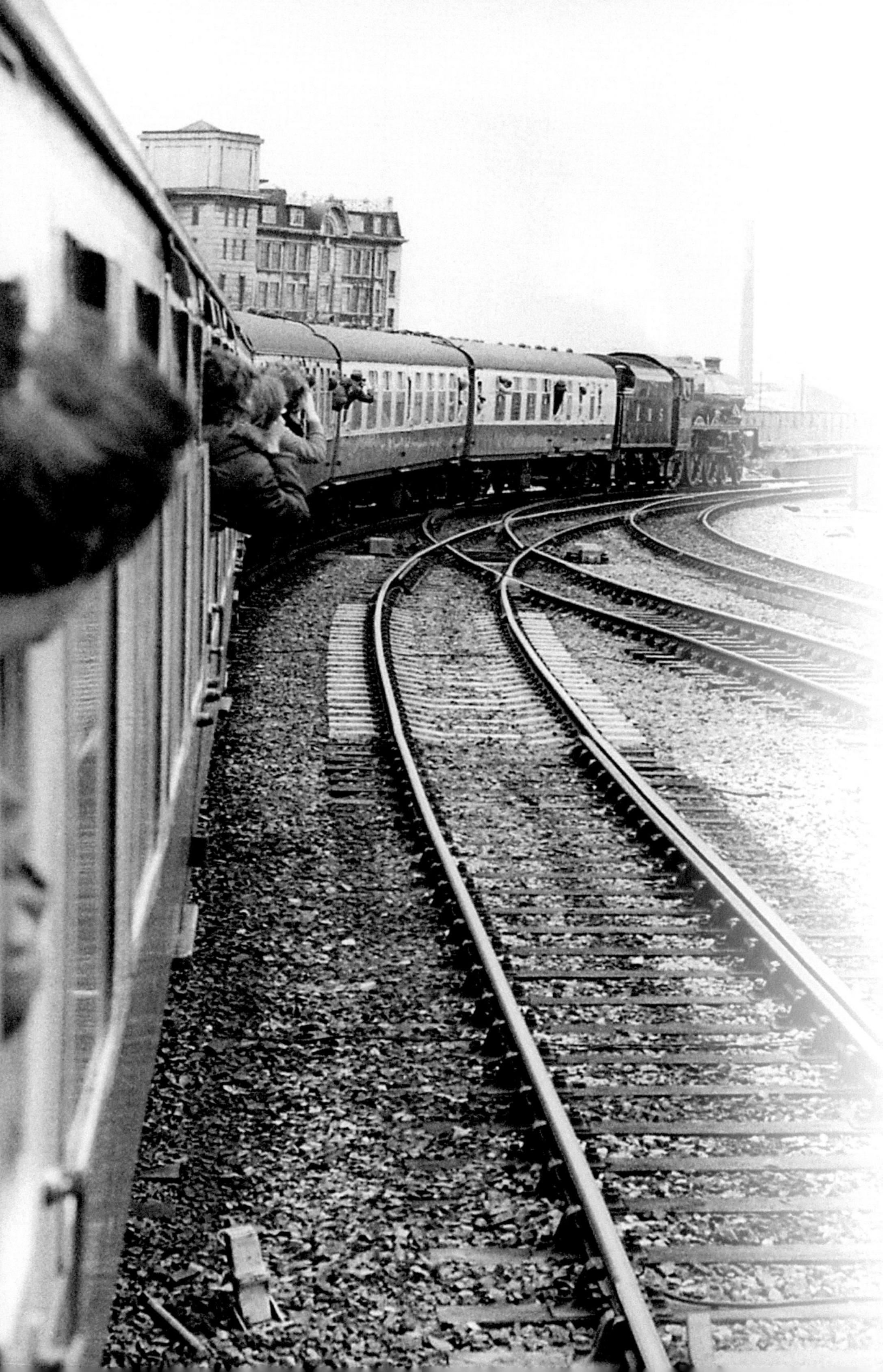

Left: Mind Your Head, Ordsall, 27 July 1980.
During the 150-year anniversary Rainhill celebration period, there were a lot of steam-hauled special trains. During the summer of 1980, British Rail ran a series between Manchester Victoria, Edge Hill and Liverpool Lime Street. Despite primarily being a diesel and electric fan, I couldn't resist buying a ticket to ride the first train. The 5690 *Leander*-hauled special was packed with enthusiasts, many of whom 'window hung' throughout the journey. Not the safest of practices, but a great way to soak up the nostalgic experience and something that was equally prevalent on modern traction railtours.

Opposite bottom: Bahamas, Chinley, 17 June 1973.
When I was 12, I became a member of the Bahamas Locomotive Society based at Dinting. One of my mates and I used to travel on the 125 bus there from Denton. For a little while we were working members – I still have my membership card somewhere. I can remember the telephone number of the society was Glossop 5596, the same number as their ex-LMS loco. The loco was still in great condition, having been overhauled at Hunslet works soon after withdrawal from Stockport MPD during 1966. The lifting of the steam ban on BR meant it could return to the network hauling railtours. I think this is its first outing after the ban. Having a little bit of a connection to the loco, I felt the need to capture its return on film. Over the preceding years I had looked at lots of steam train photographs taken at this classic location, Chinley North Junction so I decided to have a go at emulating them. I reckon I didn't do too badly. My photo position was protected by the signalman in the box behind me, so I was safe. This railtour started and finished at Manchester Piccadilly. The section between there and Guide Bridge was hauled by a Class 76. 5596 wasn't allowed in the confines of Piccadilly. I wish I had gone to a station between Manchester and Guide Bridge to take a shot of the 76 hauling the train. Nearby Ashburys, Gorton or Fairfield would have been ideal.

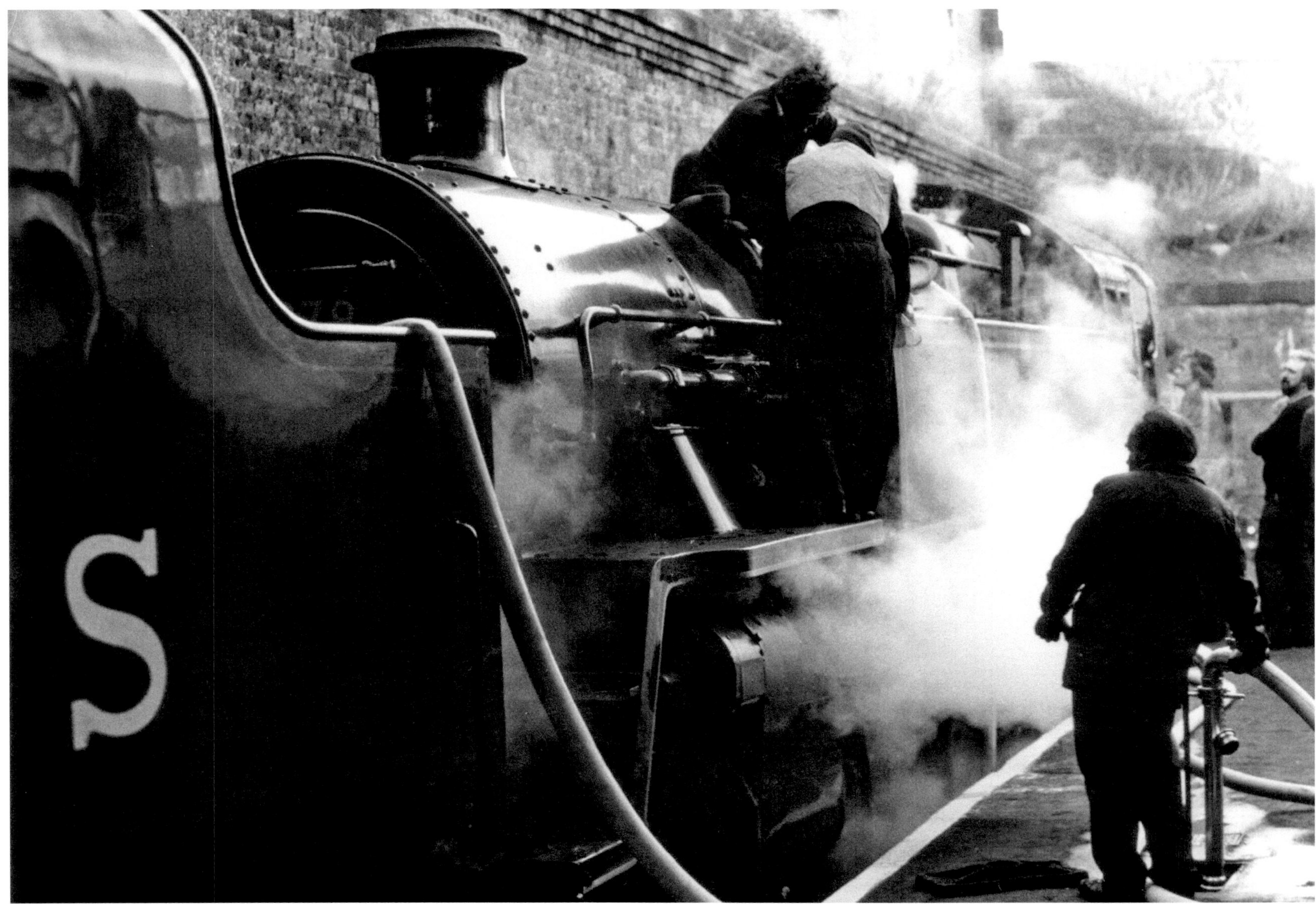

Snake Fighting, Manchester Victoria, 19 April 1980.
The flurry of steam-hauled trains during 1980 must have been a dream come true for steam enthusiasts. The year's Rainhill celebrations seemed to be a green light for the approval of all sorts of steam loco-hauled railtours. The routes taken and loco combinations were in some cases better than during pre-August 1968 BR steam days. This shot shows Standard Class tank loco 80079 being watered at the end of Manchester Victoria's Platform 16. Volunteers are doing the honours using the platform hydrant to water the locos. Sorting the tangle of pipes reminded me of snake fighting. The loco has recently arrived double heading with 'Black 5' 5000. It's 19 April 1980 Steam Locomotive Operators' Association (SLOA) charter 'The Black Countryman' steam-hauled from Hereford, via Chester, Skelton Junction and Guide Bridge, to Manchester Victoria. The train originated at Birmingham New Street; 47090 took it to Hereford. The steam locos were replaced by 40178 for part of the run back to New Street. At Stockport 85013 replaced the 'Whistler'.

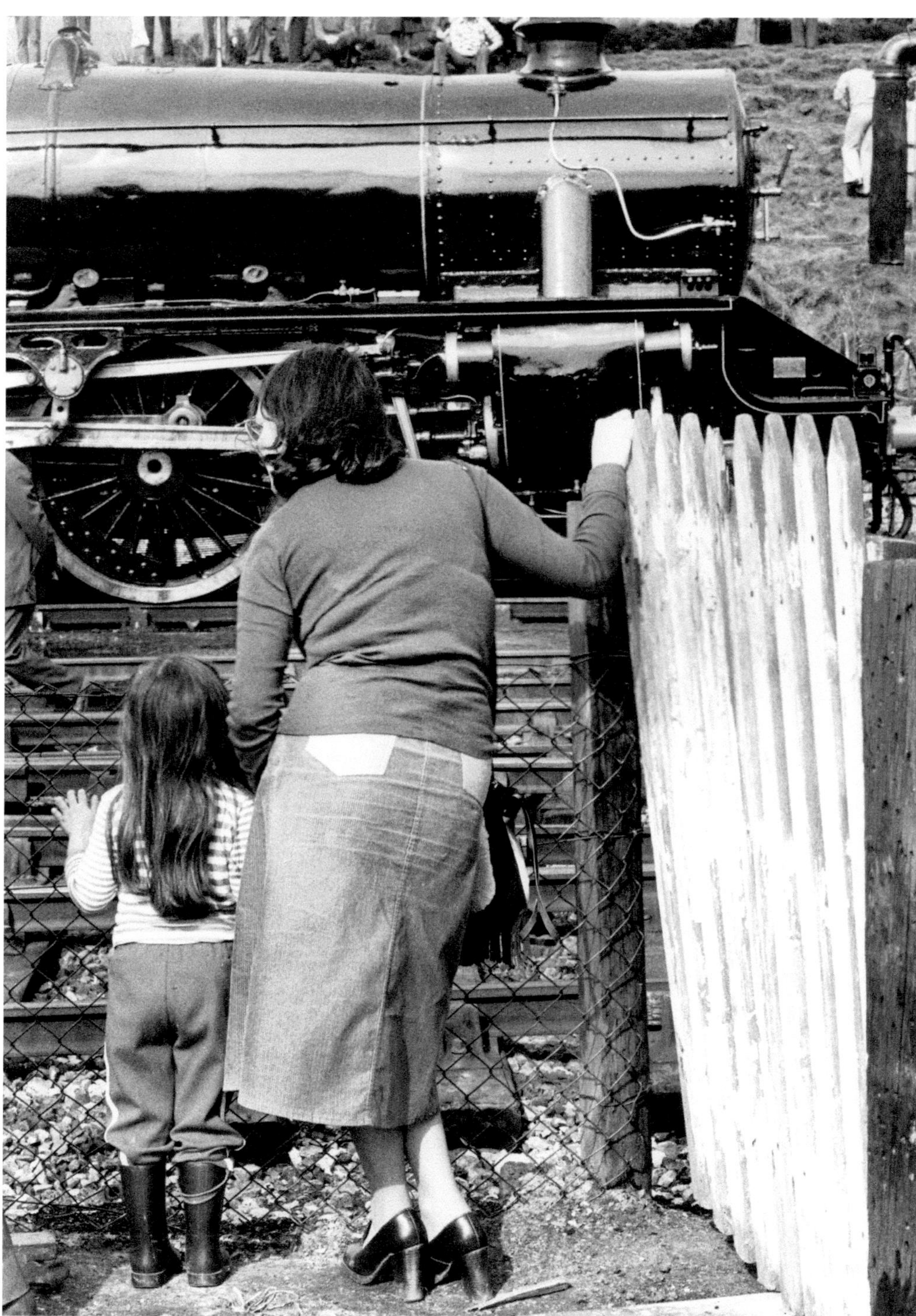

Not Just for Men and Boys, Dinting, 14 April 1979.
Railway centres sprang up around the end of
the steam era. They were usually redundant
depots, which provided restoration, storage and
servicing facilities. Those at Carnforth, Didcot,
Southall, Southport and Bulmers Cider at Hereford
immediately came to mind. They were open to the
public and proved to be very popular. Brake van and
cab rides were their forte. Sadly quite a few have
since closed, including my local centre at Dinting. In
this shot, taken at Dinting, a mother and daughter
are captivated by the sight of LMS-liveried 'Black 5'
5305 being serviced. The loco had hauled the
'Humberside Envoy' from Hull to Dinting.

3 SIGNS

INTRODUCTION

Signs are everywhere, although we might not notice them all. Those that we do see we quickly read and process, often subconsciously. We discard what isn't applicable or don't like. We take note and respond accordingly to what we do like or is applicable. During a car journey, whether driving or not, we do all this in quick succession. Our roads are packed with myriad signs for a vast array of reasons. For example, they can warn, help, manage and influence us. There are other occasions when we slowly read every sign and sometimes use them to distract us. I do that in unsettling places like doctors or dental surgeries, and hospital waiting rooms. I also do it in less scary places where you can end up hanging around for longer than you would like. Car tyre and exhaust replacement workshops immediately spring to mind.

Signs are very much part of our environment and our world would be a more naked and less interesting place without them. Some stay with us for a long time, while others are very transient: here today gone tomorrow. Progress and change often sweeps them away, turning them into part of our history. Sometimes they remain by default, having been forgotten about or retaining purpose. Those that have been with us for a long time are part of our, and quite often the previous generation's, history – that

history can be economic, technical and social. Signs can play on our emotions – fear, nostalgia, humour. All of which I find fascinating and thought provoking.

Wherever I go I love looking at signs, and have consciously paid them special attention from an early age. Railways are bursting with signs doing all the things I have mentioned, and plenty more besides. When out with my camera I like to include them in my photographs – sometimes as the main feature, or as part of the overall vista, adding depth and more interest. During the 1970s and '80s British Rail presented me with a treasure trove of signs to capture on film. Many of the pieces of hardware I pointed my camera at are now desirable must-haves for railwayana collectors. Their value is now at levels unimaginable all those years ago. Nostalgia and rarity make a difference. Enamel signs, especially totems, fall into this category. Items that have an association with a popular locomotive class, such as a nameplate, builder's plate or 'flamecut', tend to fetch the largest prices. I like the lesser-coveted signs best: the posters and handwritten notices. Having said that, some posters can be rather expensive. I hope you enjoy my varied selection of sign photographs and accompanying captions. They have jogged my memory and made me smile in the process of captioning and marshalling them together.

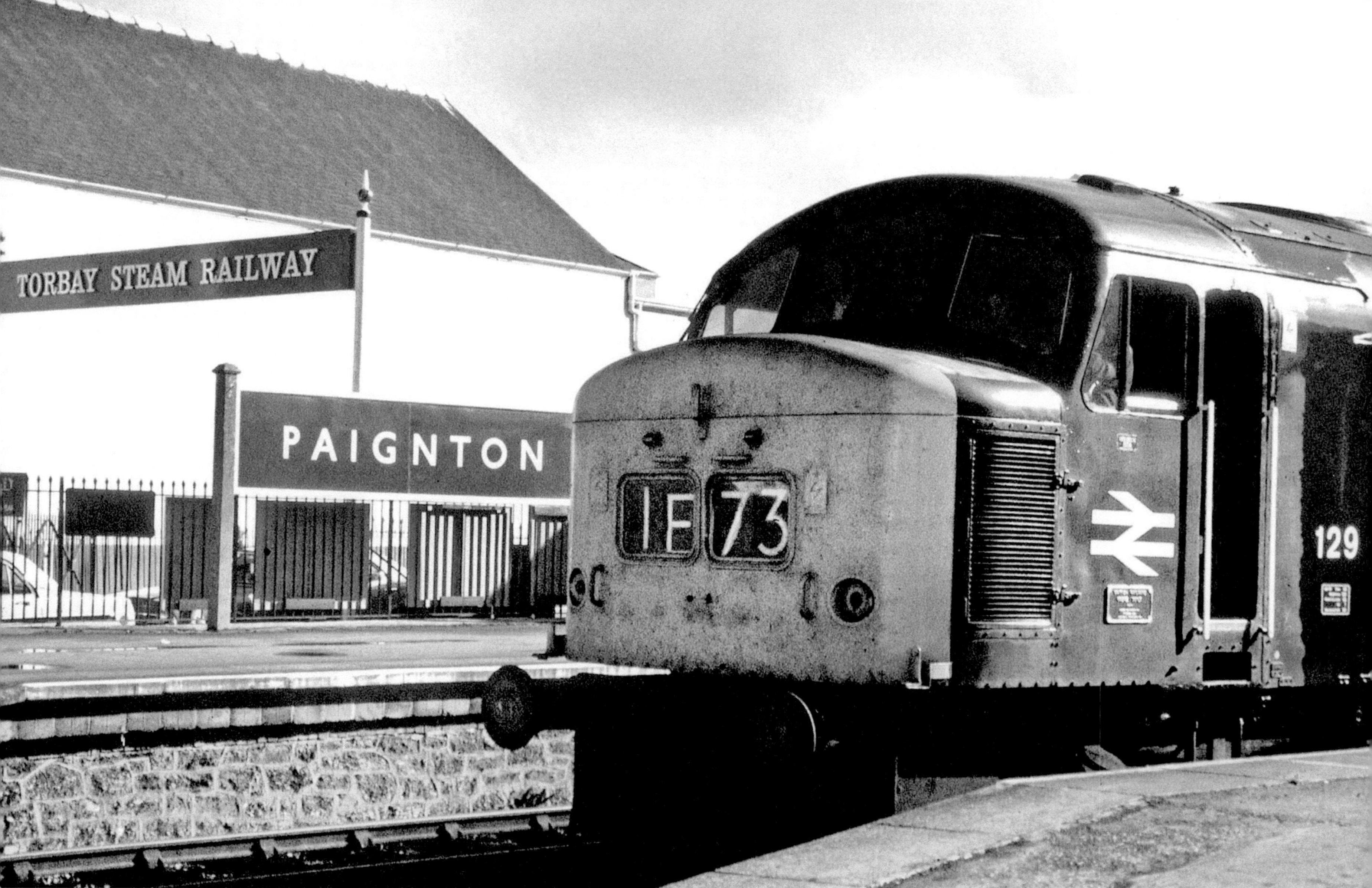

'The Devonian', Paignton, July 1973.

How many interesting signs can you see in this photograph, primarily of a Class 45 'Peak' loco? It is waiting to depart from Paignton with 'The Devonian', which was destined for Bradford. Nearest the camera is the soon-to-be-abandoned headcode blinds on the locomotive's nose end. In this case it reads 1E7 – the 1 indicating an express passenger train. The most noticeable sign is the large enamel Paignton running-in board. It is in a distinctive and definitely GWR-influenced British Railways Western Region white lettering on brown background. Did it survive and become a prized part of someone's railwayana collection? If so, how much would it be worth? Next is the large Southfork Ranch (Dallas)-style Torbay Steam Railway sign. It welcomed visitors to the newly opened steam railway linking Paignton with Kingswear. BR closed the line the previous year, on 30 December 1972. On the loco cab side, from top to bottom, is a sticker stating the depot it is allocated to, followed by the universally recognised BR double arrow logo. In addition, the cast builder's plate is firmly secured to the cab side. On the bodyside is the pre-TOPS number 129 (45073) and the loco data panel. This fine-looking loco was amongst the first of the class members to be withdrawn, lasting until October 1981. It was scrapped the following year at BREL Derby.

Western Totem, Newton Abbot, July 1973.
British Railways Western Region enamel signage abounds in this shot. The most eye-catching is the Newton Abbot totem sign – I wouldn't be surprised if someone would now pay £2,000 for it. By far the most expensive signs shown in this photograph are the Class 52 'Westerns' cast nameplate and number plate. They are D1061 *Western Envoy*; I guess their value is scarily high. The loco is waiting to depart for Paignton with a service from London Paddington. If only I could climb into a time machine and go back to Torbay during the summer of 1973. Back then 'Westerns' still reigned supreme. Ideally once or twice a week would suit me. I am sure there would be plenty of others who would want to join me.

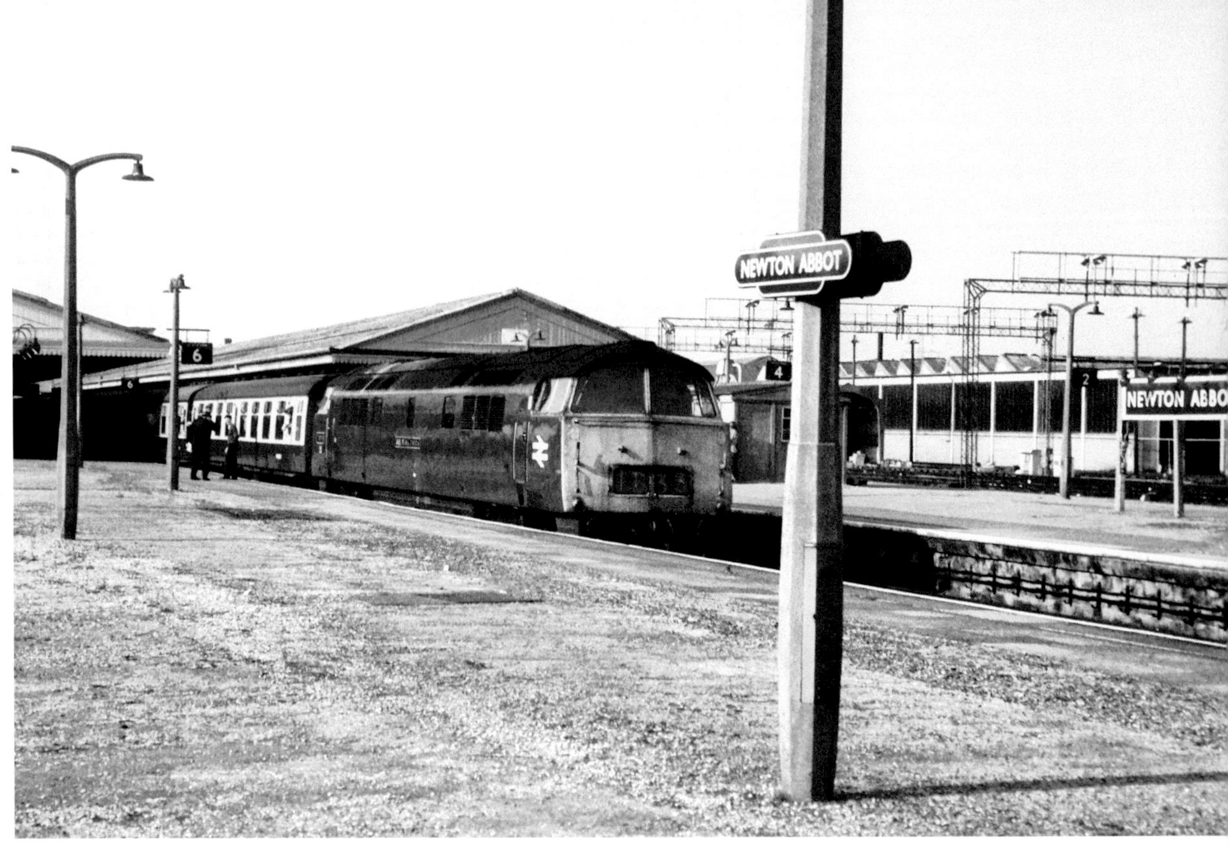

Waiting Patiently, Bristol Temple Meads, July 1973.
This group of passengers are waiting patiently for their connections in distinctly GWR surroundings. There is no doubt where the location is, thanks to the appropriately bold chocolate-on-cream ceramic-lettered sign 'Bristol'. I wonder if the couple to the right are discussing the British Rail posters? They are certainly eye-catching, proclaiming aspects of the modern rail system. However, they would pale in comparison to the pre-1965 era of British Railway posters, particularly those featuring artwork by famous artists such as Terence Cuneo.

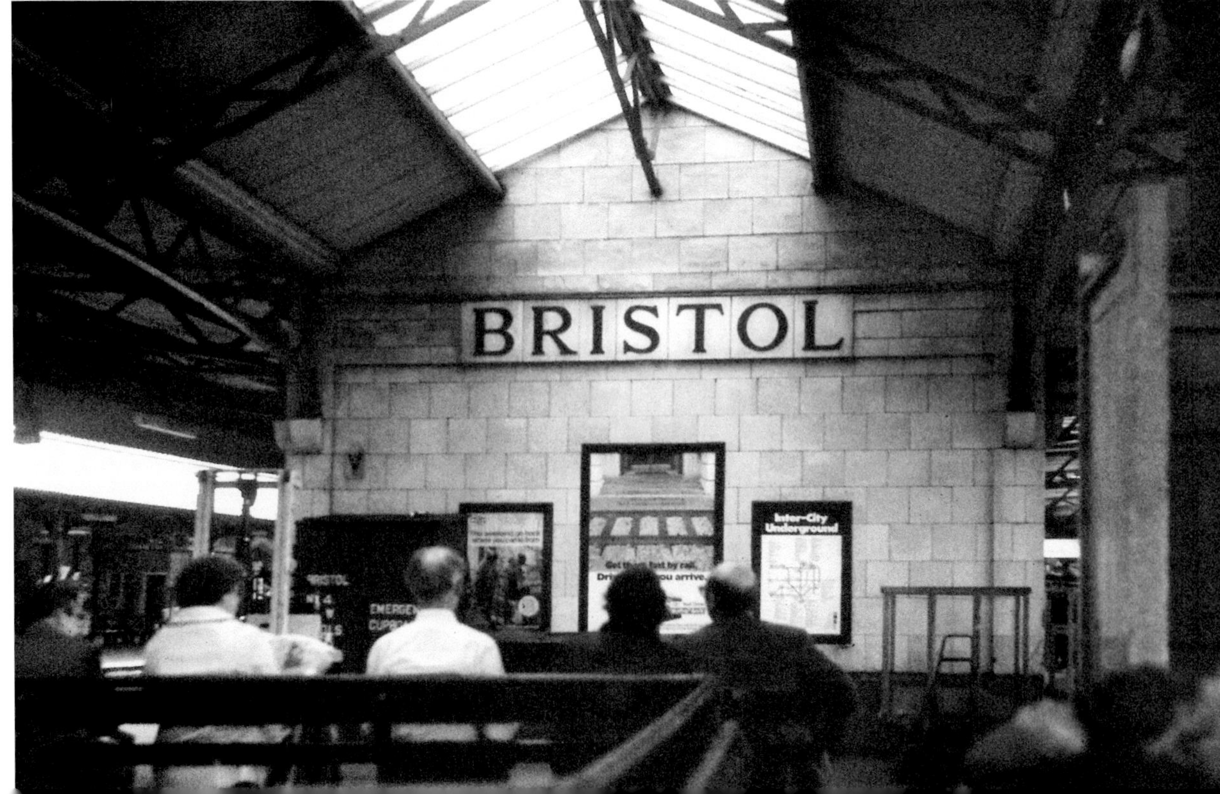

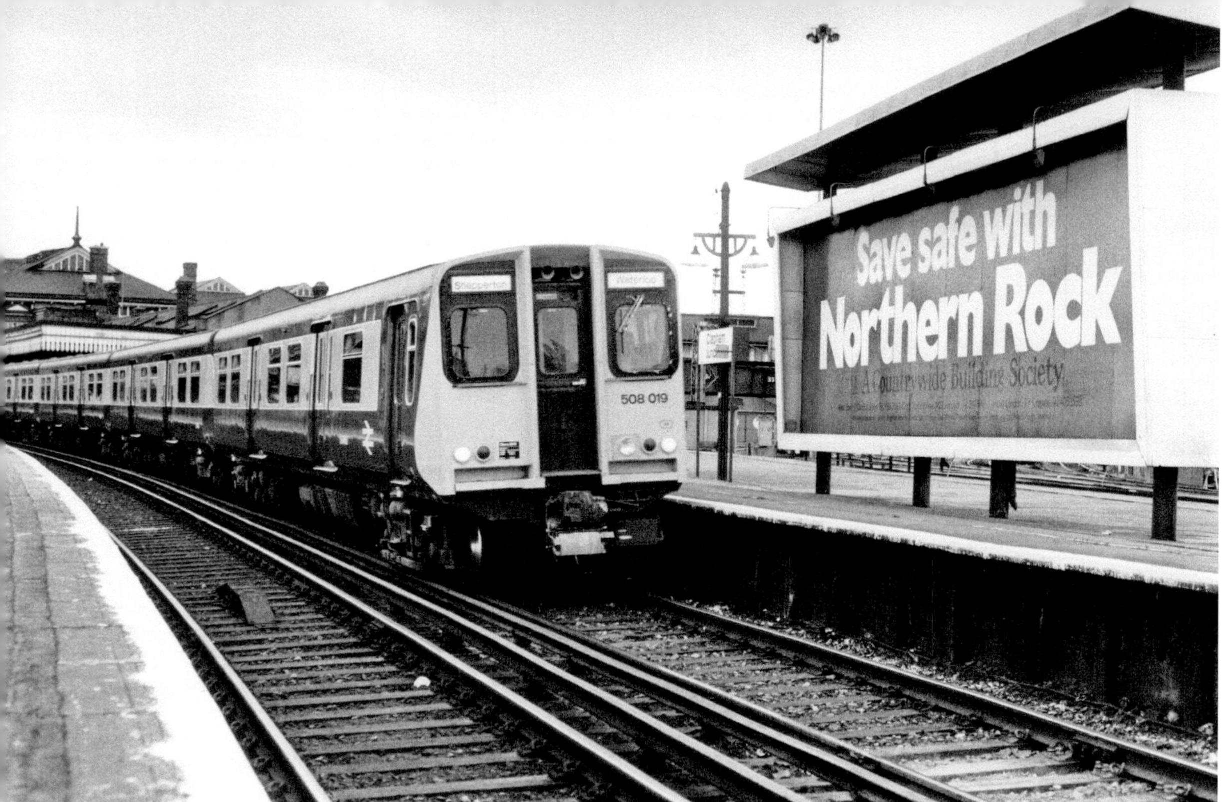

'Save safe with Northern Rock', Clapham Junction, July 1980.
Brand-new EMU 508019, on a Shepperton–London Waterloo service, glides past this wonderfully big and bold billboard poster. It clearly extols the virtues of saving with Northern Rock; it was inconceivable that the company would get into so much financial trouble a little over twenty-five years later. This modernist or Dan Dare space age-styled billboard was a throwback to the steam age - most of Clapham Junction was when I took this photograph. Over the years the posters pasted to it must have generated a lot of custom for the products and services being advertised. This must surely have been one of the best places on the BR network to advertise to a captive audience: the amount of trains, filled with passengers, passing through the station was colossal. I wonder how much BR charged to advertise on it? The Southern Region's fleet of 508 EMUs would soon be transferred to the Merseyrail system to replace the LMS-designed Class 502s and 503s.

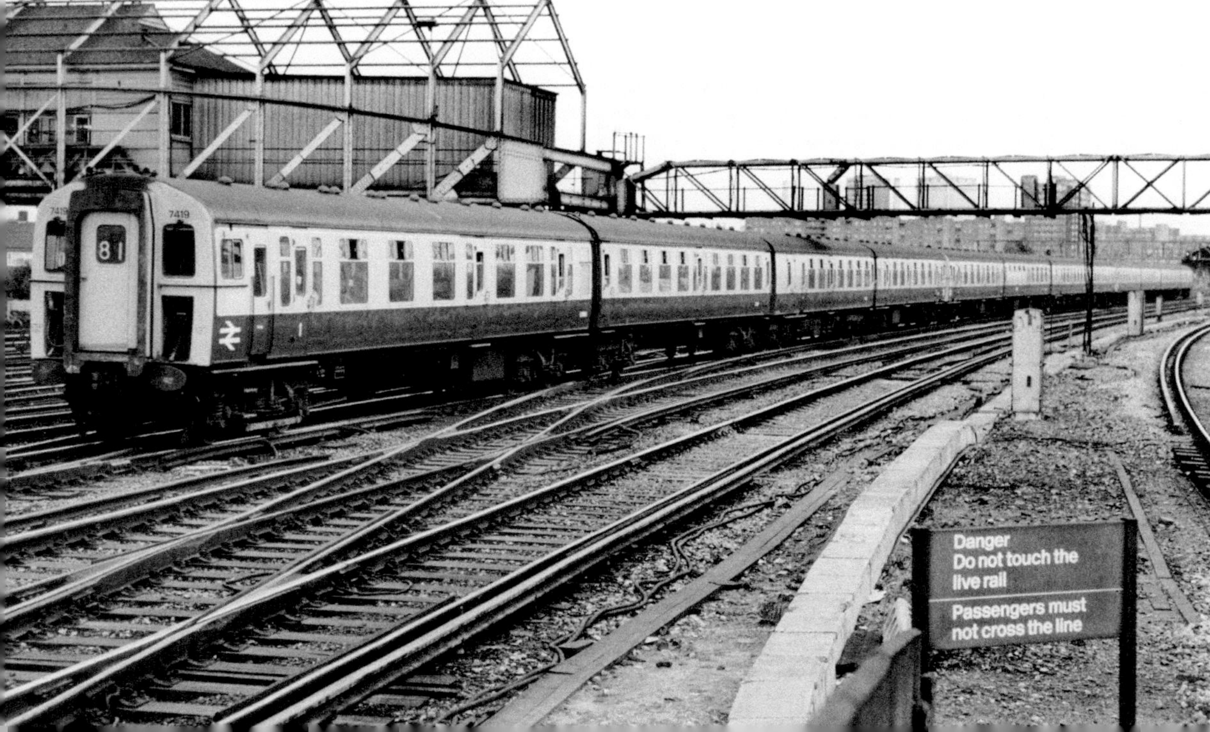

'Do not touch the live rail!, Clapham Junction, June 1980.
A 3 x 4 car set of Class 421 (4 CIG) EMUs, headed by 7419, sweep past the rather precarious bridge signal box at Clapham Junction. The train carries the headcode 81, which indicates it is a London Waterloo–Portsmouth Harbour service. The sign at the end of the platform warning people not to touch the live rail isn't easy to miss. A live third rail to power trains has been in common use for many decades. I wonder if the concept would be acceptable now if it had just been invented? Imagine the deep intake of breath from health-and-safety officials.

'Shunters Only', London Waterloo, May 1980.
This Mark 1 second-class brake coach provides a rest room for Waterloo's shunters. It comes complete with compartments, which they must have found very cosy. We know it is just for them because they have the words 'Shunters Only' clearly chalked on the blue section of the bodyside. Woe betide anyone else who set foot in the coach. I was tempted to peep in, but feared the consequences. Was it a permanent fixture or temporary accommodation?

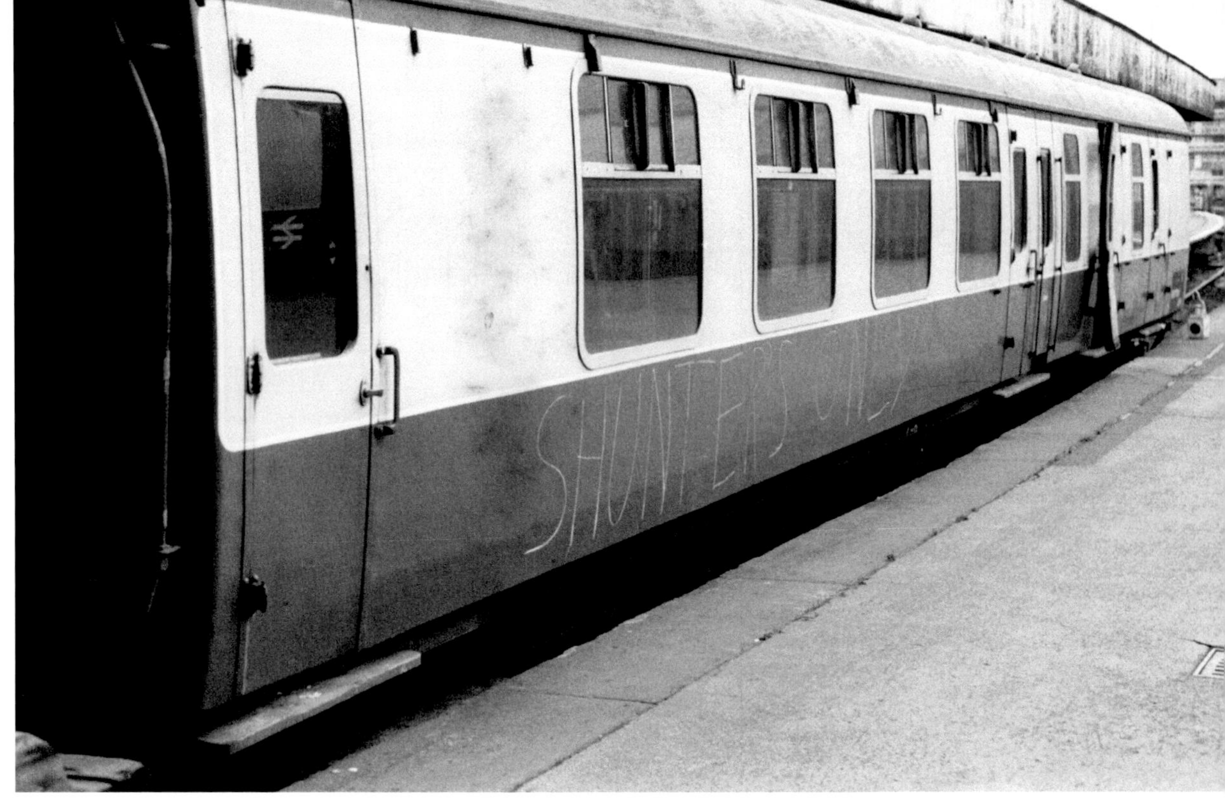

Overground and Underground Signs, London Paddington, May 1978.
London Underground Circle Line C69 Class EMU arrives at London Paddington. The mix of BR's rather bland corporate black-on-white signage literally pales in comparison with the Underground 'Target' sign on the station's Platforms 15 and 16. The 'blank canvas' plain grey bodysides of C69 stock were soon to become popular with graffiti artists, which some people would call art and others vandalism. Even though I have a passion for art, I would go with the latter because the stock's livery was so classy – a case of less is more.

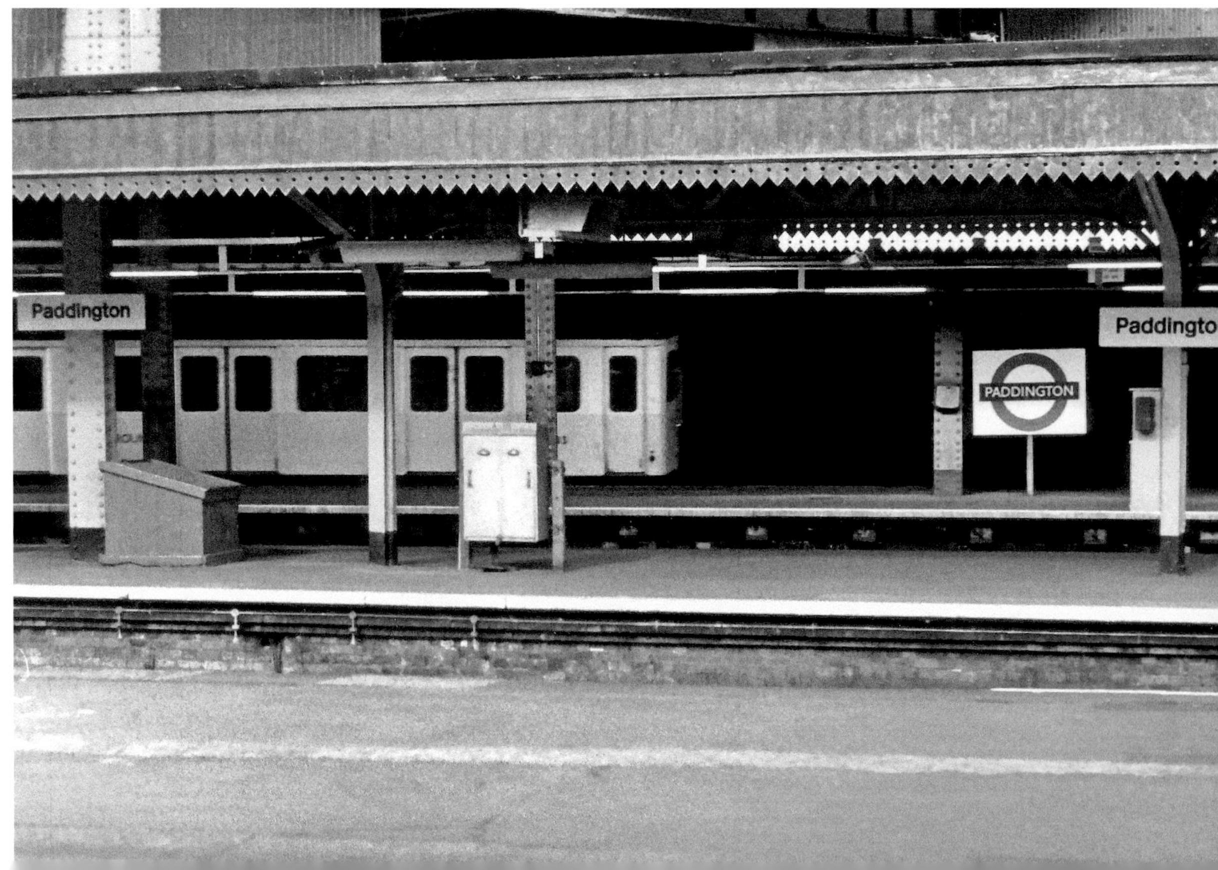

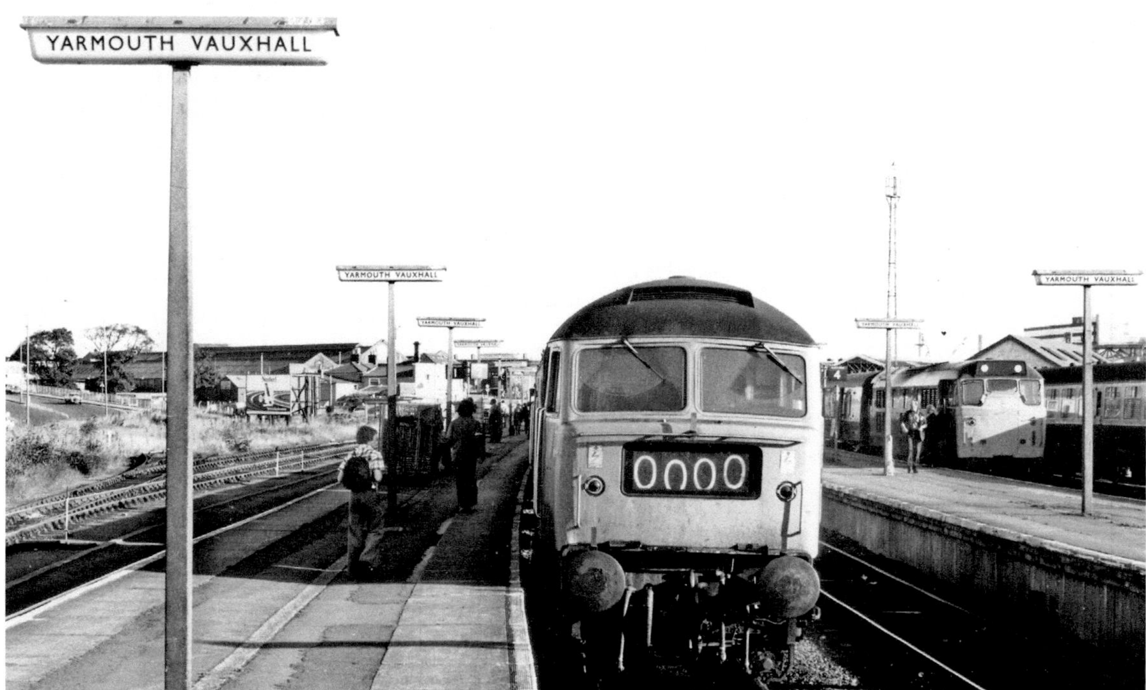

Yarmouth Vauxhall, Great Yarmouth, 28 August 1977.
Amongst an abundance of 1960s Eastern Region-style 'Yarmouth Vauxhall'-lettered fluorescent platform lamp shades are trains waiting to return with Merrymaker excursions. Thanks to these clearly lettered signs nobody could ever be in doubt that they had arrived at the seaside. It appears there were twice, maybe three times, as many as really necessary. It is the 1977 August bank holiday at Great Yarmouth, previously known as Yarmouth Vauxhall. On Merrymaker excursion duty, 47340 is waiting to depart for Manchester Piccadilly and 31269 is bound for Burton upon Trent; on the same day, 37263 brought in an excursion from Banbury. This trio made an interesting line-up, complementing the station's usual activity.

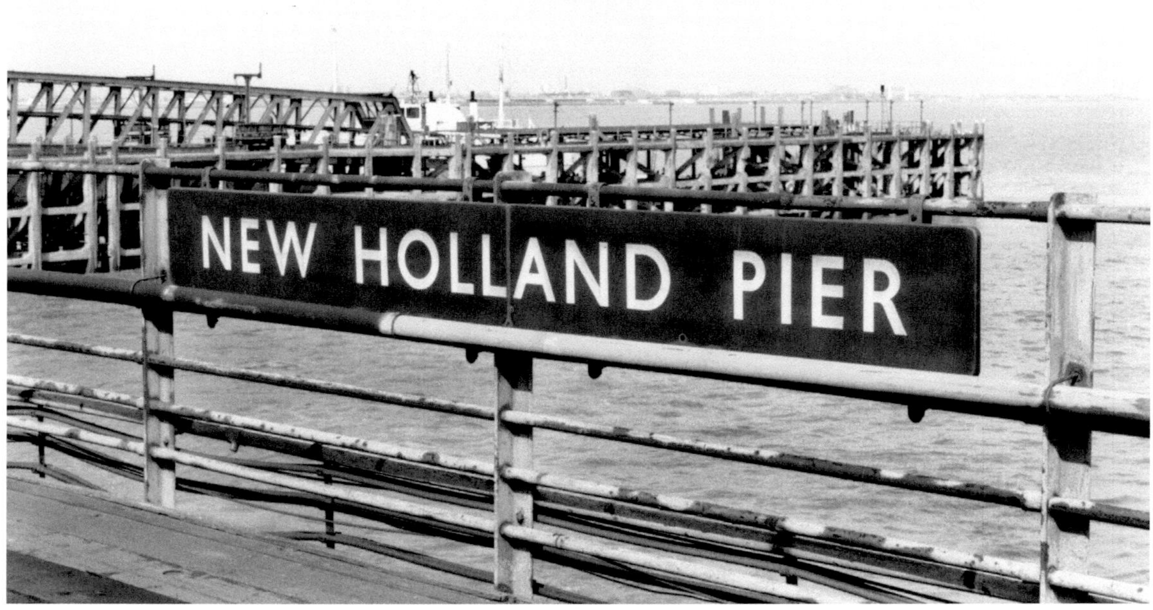

All at Sea, New Holland Pier, August 1980.
On my first visit to the Humber Ferry terminal railway station, I found it a rather odd experience, but my subsequent visits were always relished because of its quirkiness. This BR Eastern Region white-on-dark-blue sign gives an of idea why. It is surrounded by water, fixed to the rather decrepit pier station's fencing. The pier extended out into the Humber Estuary and had a regular passenger service serving the frequent British Rail Sealink ferry to and from Hull. It appeared very little had been spent on the wooden structure over the years. It had many vestiges dating back to LNER days: a real time warp of a place. Perhaps it is a good thing the opening of the Humber Bridge made it all redundant? I am not sure how much longer its structure could have kept carrying trains. For me, though, it is a shame it all came to an end on 24 June 1981.

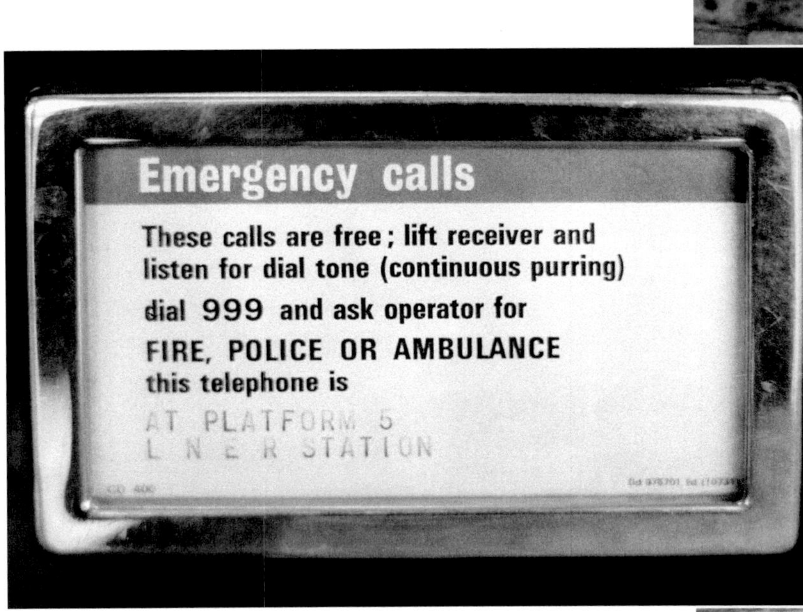

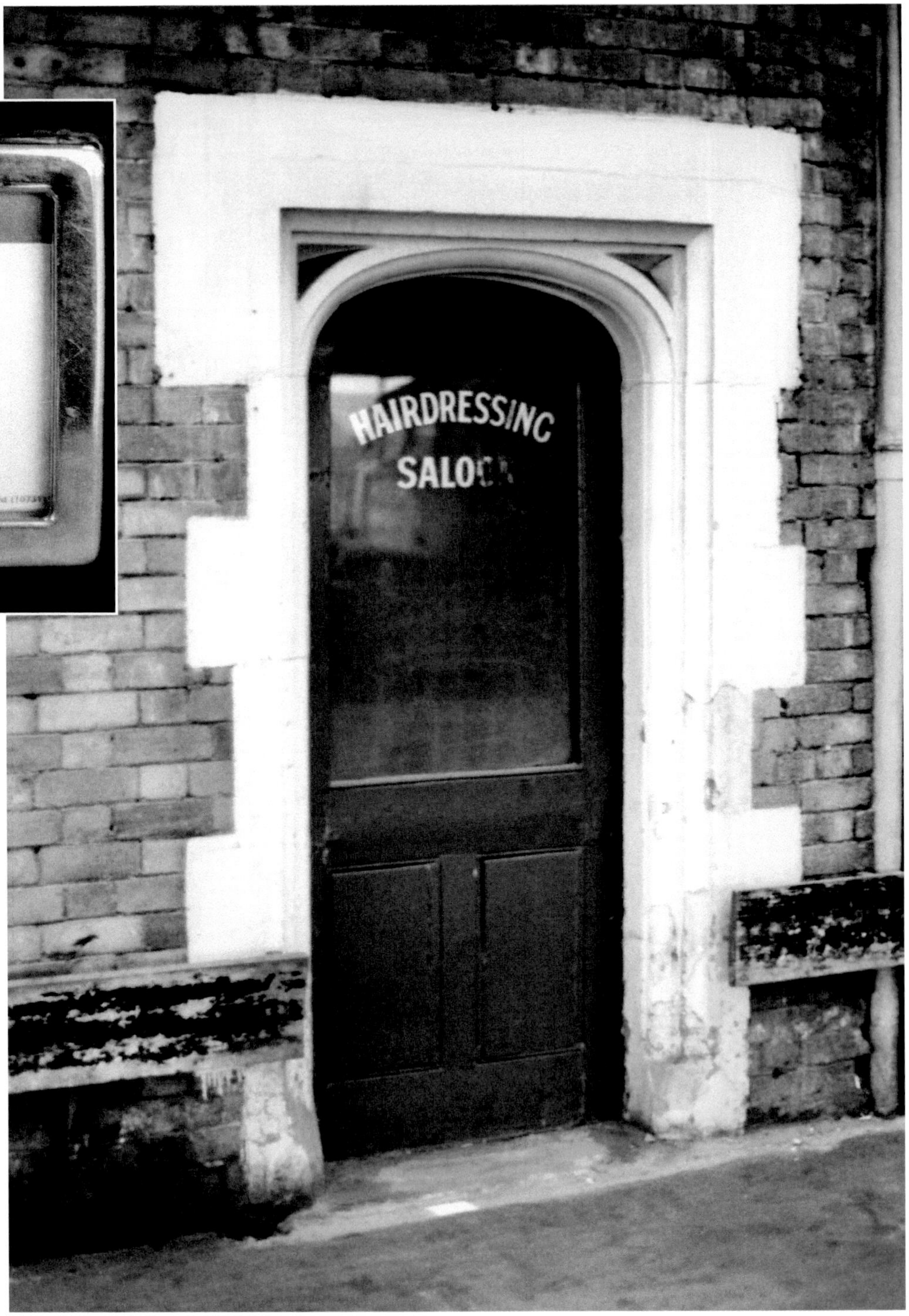

Above: GPO Call Box, Doncaster, August 1980.
This sign suggests Doncaster's GPO, later known as
British Telecom, did not recognise that the railway
system had been nationalised. By the time I took this
photograph, taken inside a station telephone box, it had
been thirty-two years since the LNER, became part of
British Railways. The cardboard sign appeared quite new
on a glorious summer's day during 1980.

Right: 'Haircut, Sir?' Stoke-on-Trent, Easter 1978.
This distinctly Edwardian-style sign and doorway must
have drawn in many a travelling gentleman. I could not
get inside to see if the vintage fixtures and fittings were
still intact. If they were I can imagine it would have
been like stepping back in time. I guess it must have
had regular customers as well as passing trade.
Not just for haircuts, but cut-throat razor shaves,
beard and moustache trims. I am presuming it was a
gentlemen's hairdressing salon, but it could have been
for ladies. Whatever the case, I found it rather intriguing
from the moment I noticed the doorway on one of
Stoke-on-Trent's platforms. Unfortunately, it was no
longer in use but many mainline stations still had such a
facility, albeit nowhere near as old.

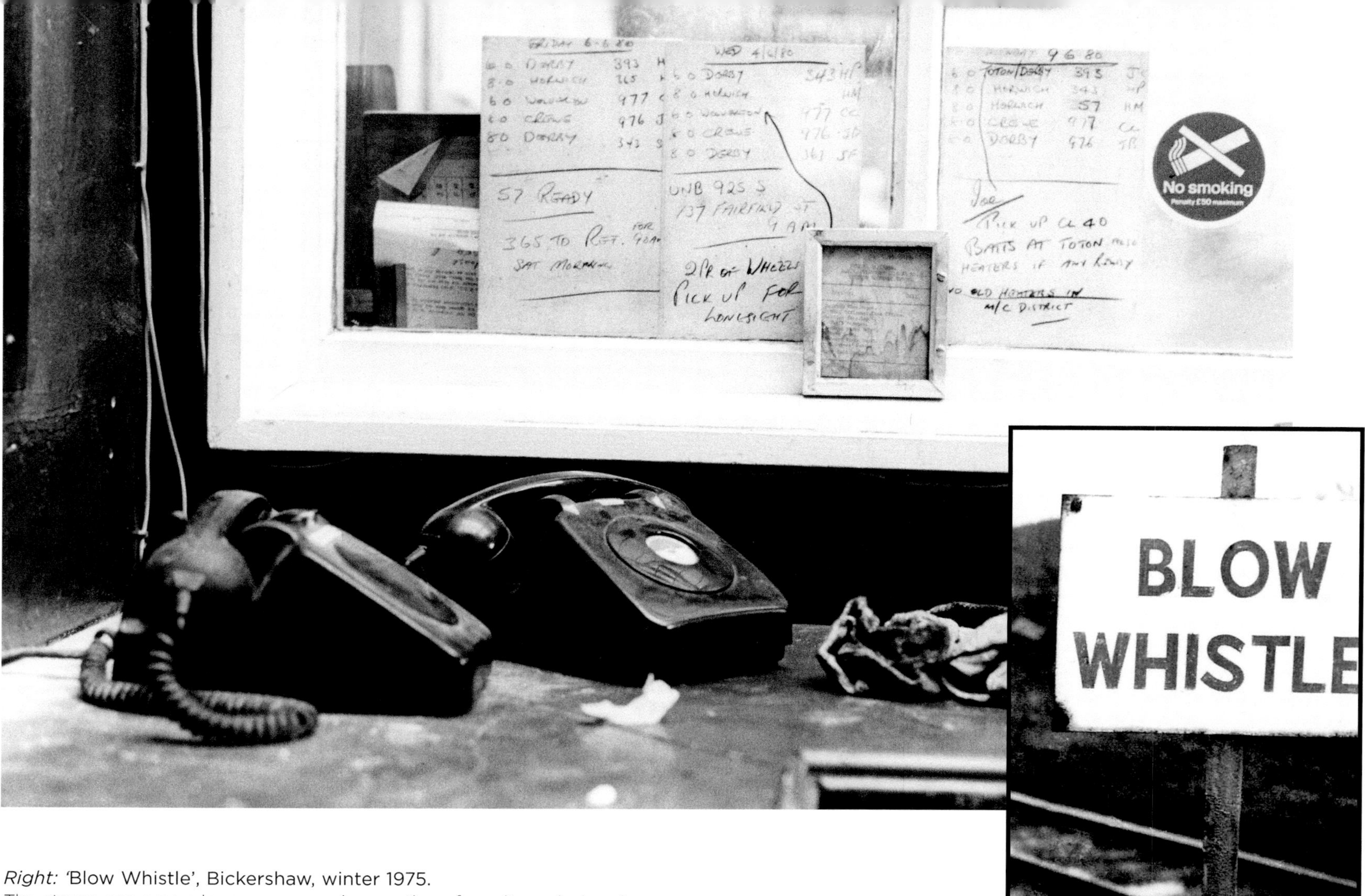

Right: 'Blow Whistle', Bickershaw, winter 1975.
The steam age was a long one, meaning vestiges from it carried on long after its demise. On the BR network lots of signs remained near crossings and tunnels instructing drivers to 'Whistle', even though modern traction couldn't whistle. Road signs for ungated crossings still depicted a steam loco – amazingly they still do. In the case of this shot, the sign was still applicable to steam locomotives. The drivers well and truly took heed of this sign. I can still hear the resulting haunting sound in my mind. This sign was close to a crossing on the outskirts of the National Coal Board (NCB) Bickershaw colliery system, which still used 'Austerity' saddle tank locos to haul wagons. On the day I took this photograph, the rails were wet and greasy. The loco doing the haulage was being worked hard on the incline out of the colliery, hauling heavy loaded coal wagons. The combination of sounds from the loco, gritty atmosphere and whistle being blown on the approach to the crossing was awesome. There was nobody there, other than the colliery workers and me; I felt like I was in a secret place, little or not even known to my fellow rail enthusiasts. Unforgettable!

Above: Truck Driver's Instructions, Reddish MPD, June 1980.
These handwritten job sheet tell us that Reddish Depot's lorries were kept busy running parts around. Destinations included Horwich, Toton and Crewe. Batteries for Class 40s were amongst the items to collect. The telephones were non-dialling direct-line types; someone out there will no doubt know where they connected to. Had somebody made or received a call shortly before I appeared and left their oily rag behind? Note, there was no smoking in this area – something probably appreciated by Angie the cat who liked to spend time sitting in this spot. A reader of one of my previous books told me the cat's name, via my Amazon feedback. It makes for enlightening reading getting answers to some long-unanswered questions via this facility – thank you readers!

'Tom Loves BM', Denton, February 1974.

Whatever happened to Tom and B.M.? Did they get married? Are they now grandparents? Did they split up? Do they still live in Denton? Did B.M. love Tom? Did she know that Tom loved her? One thing is for sure: Tom was in love with B.M. He also appeared to have no money to buy a spray paint canister to proclaim his love in Denton railway station's bus shelter-style waiting area. His graffiti looks like it has been scratched out with a penknife blade. The then regular passenger train service, which called at unmanned Denton, was a Paytrain linking Stockport with Stalybridge. Paytrain meant there was a guard who issued tickets to passengers boarding without a ticket. In theory, this meant the poster sign was not necessary. The guard on the two-car DMU should have easily copped anyone not intending to buy a ticket. Hiding in the toilet until he had passed by was not really an option.

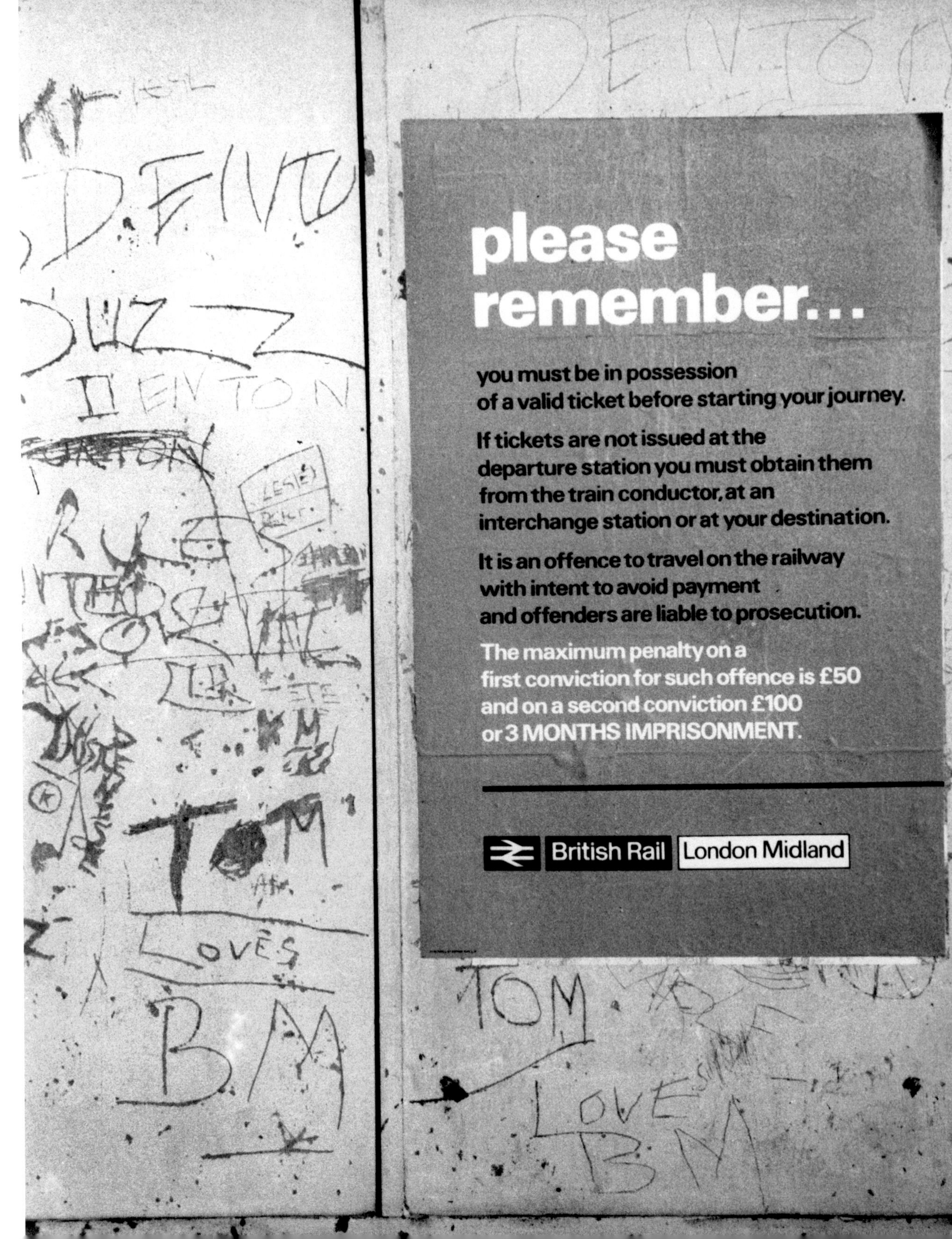

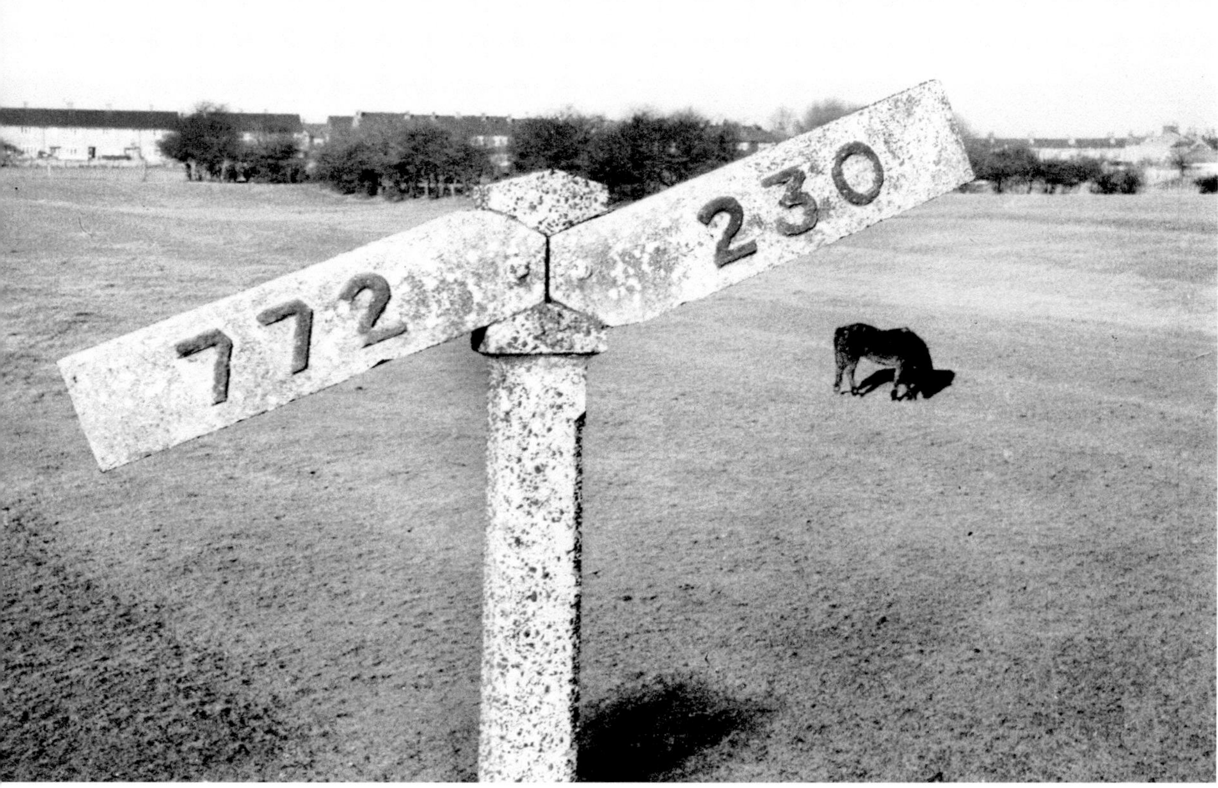

Uphill all the Way, Reddish, spring 1973.
This gradient post indicates that the climb to Denton is stiffening. Interestingly, the sign is made of reinforced concrete rather than the more common wooden examples. This was not unique: you could often see all sorts of signs, along with other important parts of the infrastructure, made of the same rough concrete-aggregate mix, such as fence and signal posts. Clearly the grazing horse is not at all interested in the gradient post or my presence. Soon after, I was apprehended by someone who questioned why I was on the lineside. When I explained that I was a railway photographer, they wished me all the best and went on their way.

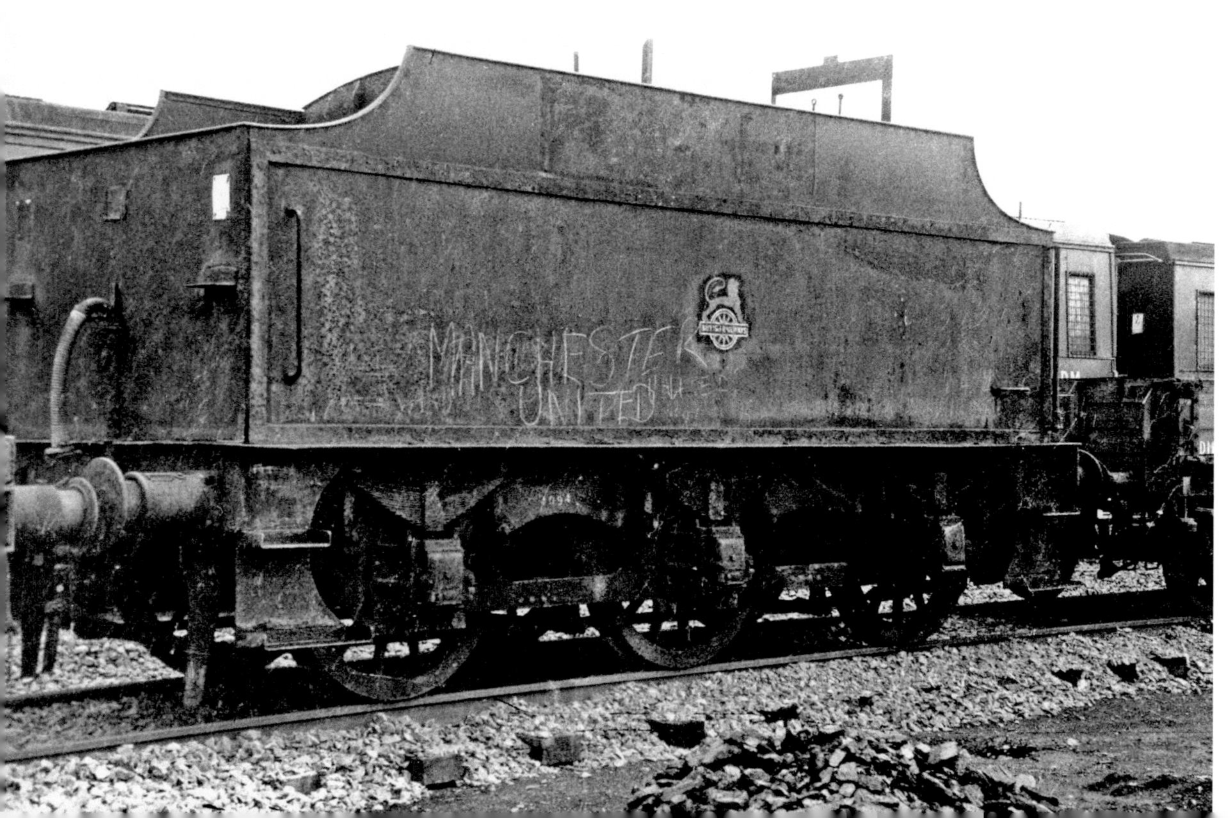
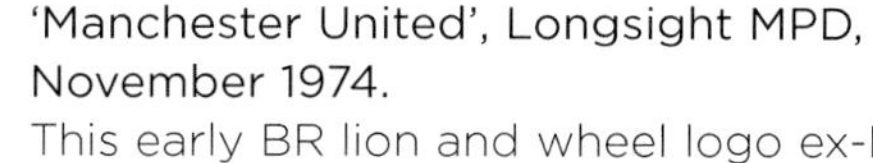

'Manchester United', Longsight MPD, November 1974.
This early BR lion and wheel logo ex-LMS 'Fairburn' steam locomotive tender was out of place amongst Longsight's electric and diesel locomotives. It was located in a siding within eyesight of the parallel A57 Hyde Road. I had seen it many times while riding on the top deck of a Selnec Mancunian bus. I wondered why it was there and had to bag a photograph of it. I guess it was a water carrier used by the engineers' department. This tender was a rare remnant of the once vast BR steam loco stock. It was still possible to occasionally see tenders in yards, even though locomotives had long since gone. I can remember seeing an ex-LNER B1 example on the other side of the Pennines. Clearly a rail worker or fellow rail enthusiast had thought this tender would benefit from the adornment of the chalked words 'Manchester United'.

Apapa, Reddish MPD, summer 1980.
Twenty-five Class 40s gained rather grand maritime-related names during their earlier years of BR service: the 133-ton 40035 *Apapa* was one of them. Sadly, they lost their superb nameplates during the early 1970s. After a few years of anonymity their names reappeared, thanks to enthusiasts using self-adhesive lettering. Some carried their names where the nameplates had once been affixed, others in the manner shown in this photograph. In some cases locos that had never been named gained unofficial ones using the same easy-to-apply sign-writing method. The chalked on 'DO NOT START' sign isn't in a very noticeable location. It is hoped nobody inadvertently started the loco because they didn't notice the instruction.

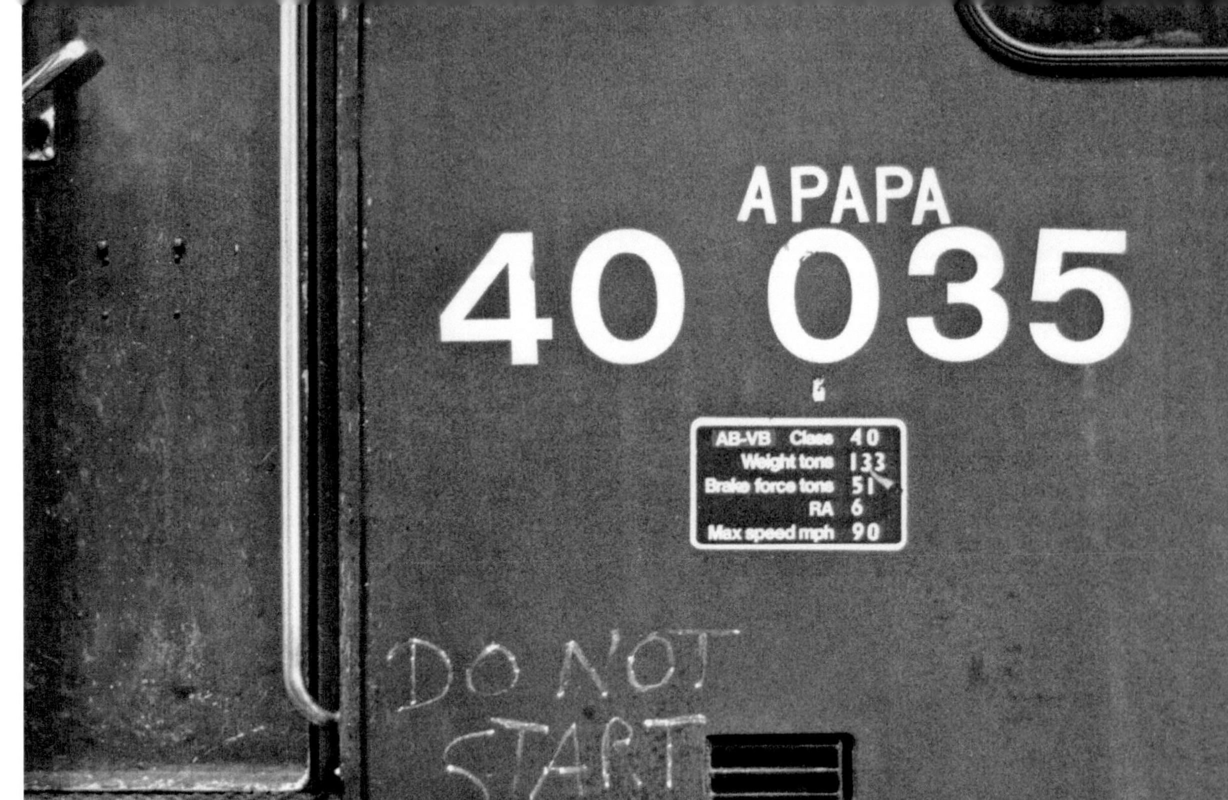

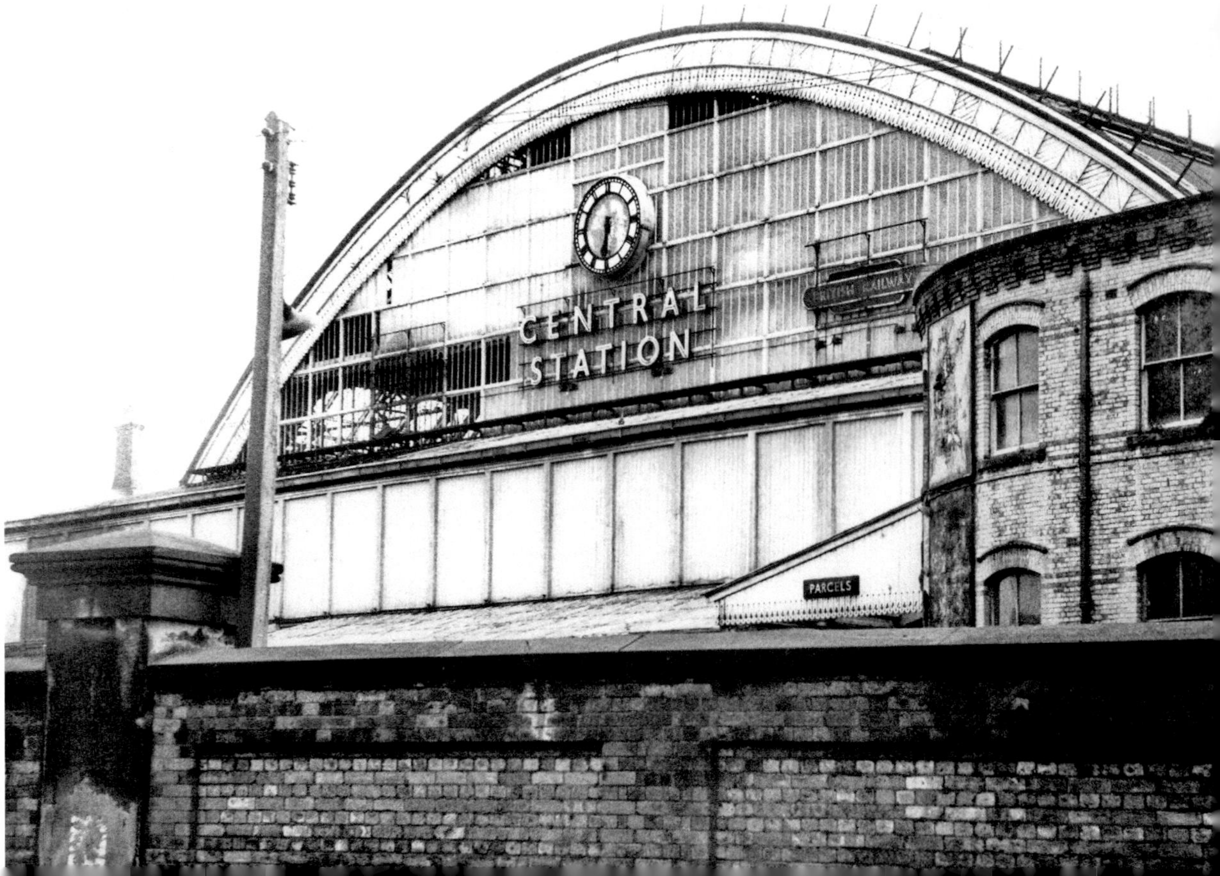

Central Station, Manchester, winter 1973.
A rather forlorn and partially fire-damaged Manchester Central station, which closed during May 1969. Part of the frontage had been badly damaged by a vagrant-caused fire in the station's celebrated cafeteria. Until then, there had been two giant British Railways neon totem signs adorning the frontage. The Central station sign and clock were also illuminated, until the station closed. The roof is the second widest unsupported iron arch in Britain. St Pancras has the largest. After a period of dereliction and use as a car park, the station was restored and then it became the Greater Manchester Exhibition Centre (G-Mex); it's now known as the Manchester Central Convention Complex, and is used for a wide array of large events, including party political conferences.

Speed Restriction, Guide Bridge, February 1979.
This speed-restriction sign, indicating 35mph maximum, seemed a little on the high side for this once-complex station area, which is now a fraction of its former self. Trains do now pass through what is left of it at greater speeds than 35mph. On this grim winter's day, a pair of Class 76s rumble through this fantastic old station. It was one of my favourite locations, being very atmospheric and jam-packed with railway interest. There is also an abundance of trains along with an expansive and well-used loco stabling point – superb!

Gentlemen and Waiting Room, Bury, January 1979.
Bury Bolton Street station is now the immaculate HQ of the East Lancashire Railway – a must-visit preserved railway. The station is now beautifully restored to 1950/60s British Railways London Midland Region maroon-era condition. When I took this photograph, it was in a semi-derelict condition and would soon be closed. It was replaced by a new bus and rail interchange in the centre of the town. BR maroon enamel signs were still very much in evidence; the station's imminent closure meant there was no need to replace them with modern ones. They looked worse for wear, just like the station. Even the Littlewoods billboard poster looks sad. Class 504 EMU M77165, at the tail of the two-car set, has just arrived with a service from Manchester Victoria.

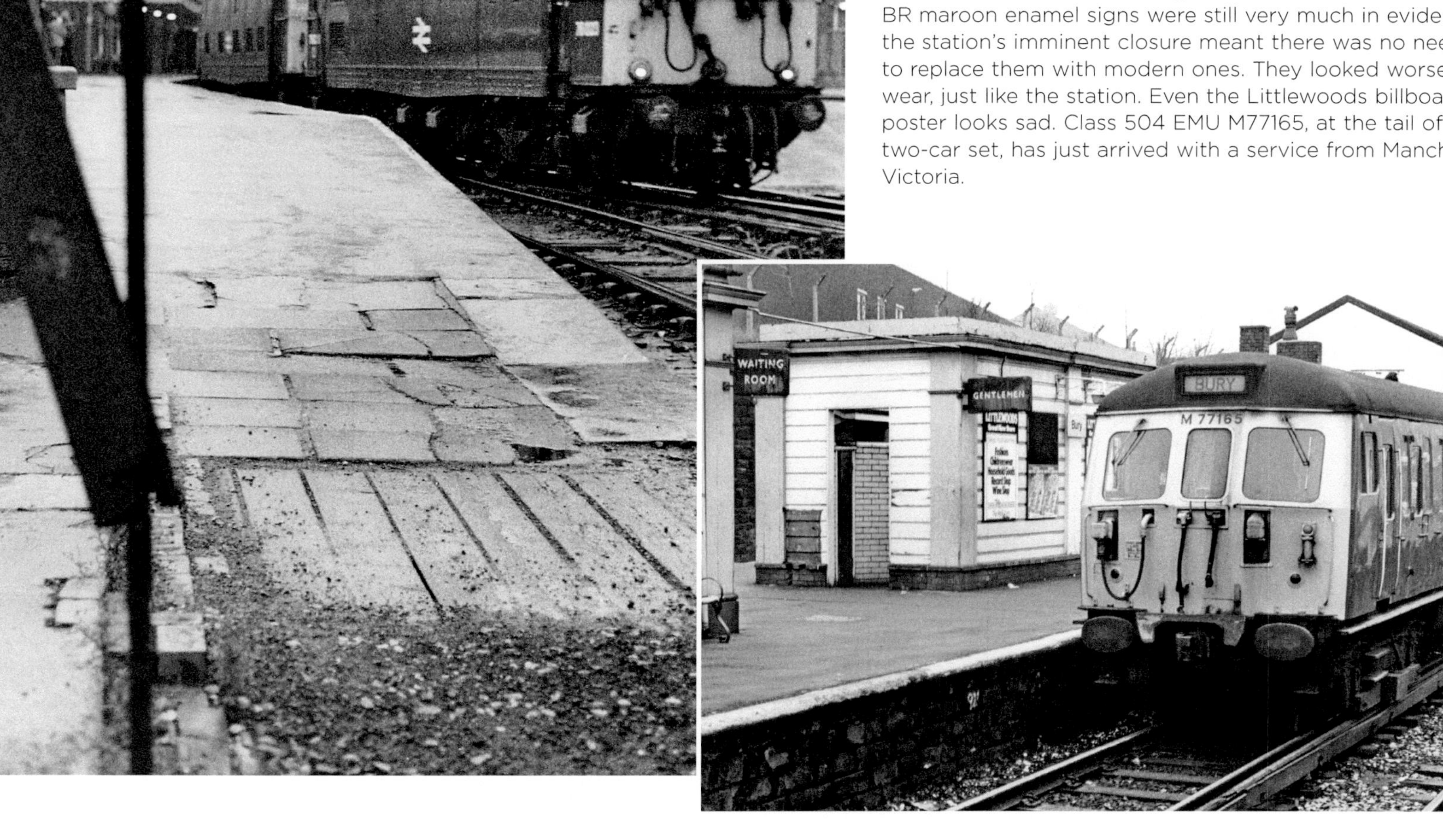

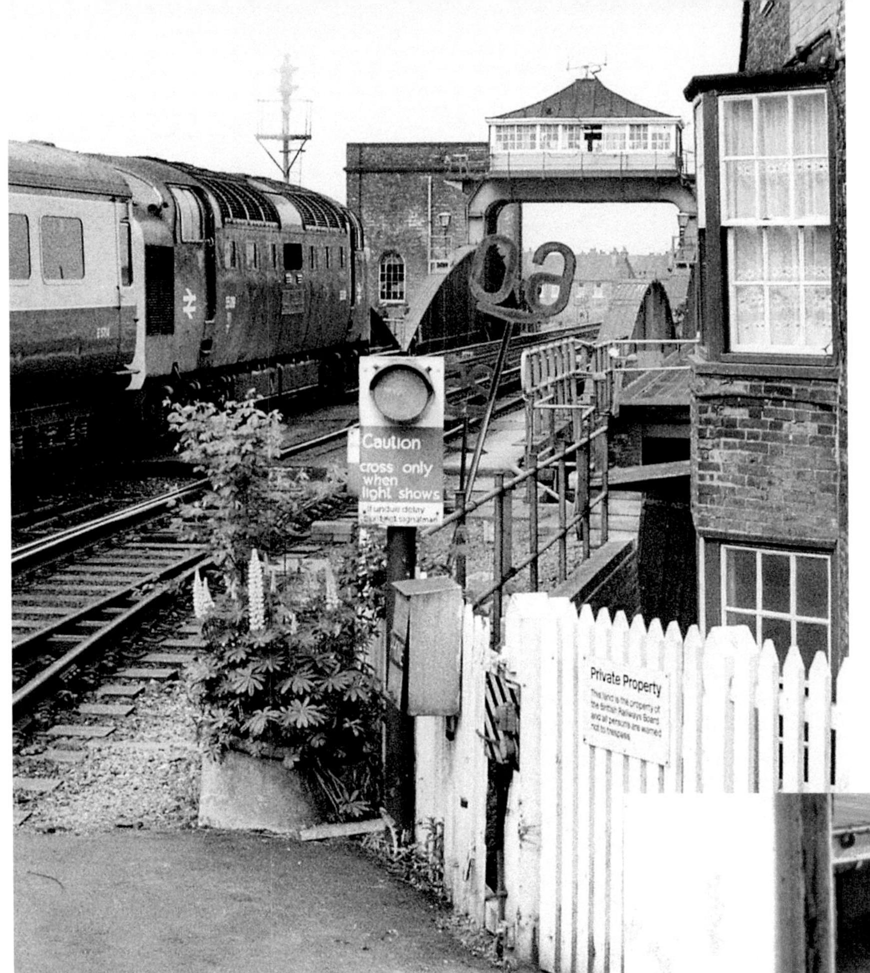

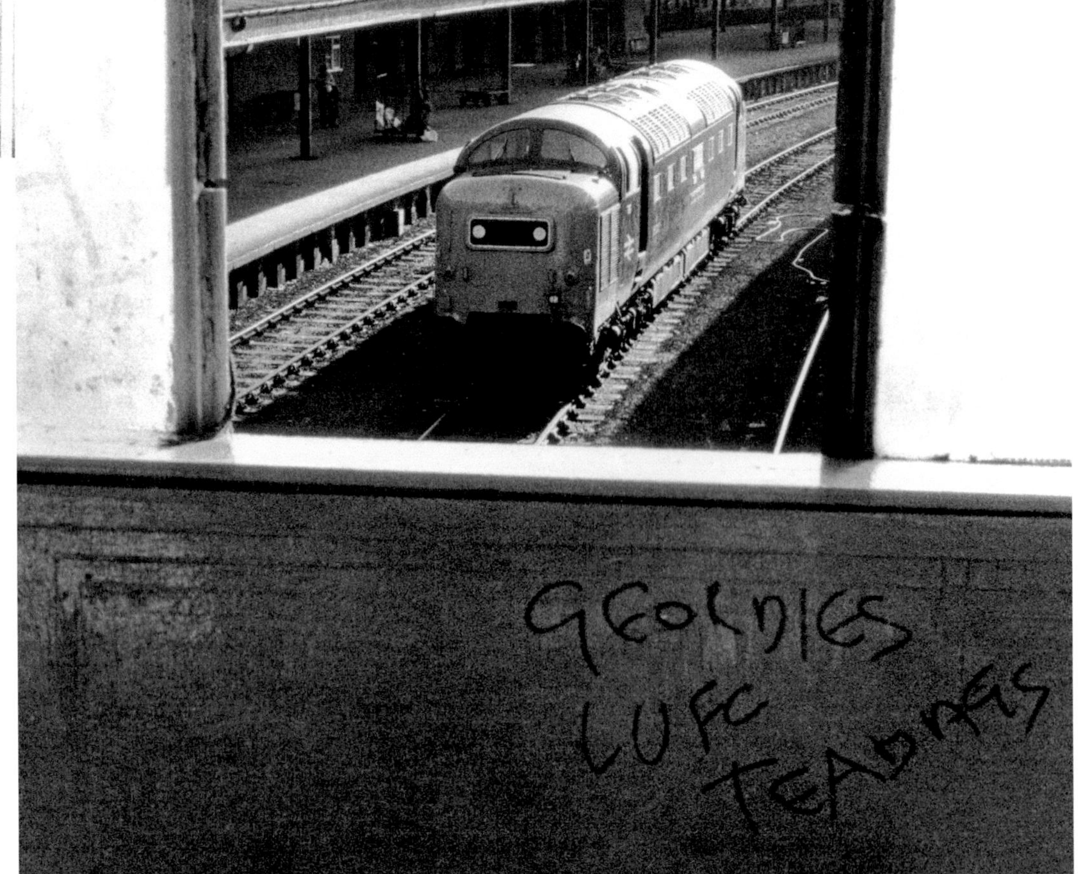

Below: 'Geordies LUFC Teabags', York, 20 March 1979.
Martin Walker/Beaver Sports now owns the fine loco 55022 *Royal Scots Grey*, visible through this perfectly placed footbridge window. A football supporter graffiti artist clearly couldn't resist the opportunity to make use of York station's footbridge to write a few words. It looks like a felt-tip pen has been used, rather than the more commonplace car paint aerosol. I can't decide whether it is the Geordies or LUFC who the sign writer is referring to as 'Teabags'. Graffiti adorning walls at railway stations is now quite a rarity compared with the 1970s. Car spares shops must have done a roaring trade selling cans of spray paint to budding artists – plus, stationers selling felt-tip pens, which back then came complete with a rather heady aroma. The 55 will soon be coupled up to a rake of Mark 2 coaching stock, which will form the 4.13 p.m. York–London King's Cross.

Above: 'Cross only when light shows', Selby, 9 June 1979.
55019 *Royal Highland Fusilier* leaves Selby with the 12.20 p.m. from London King's Cross to York on 9 June 1979. It is about to cross the distinctive 1891-built swing bridge, which spans the River Ouse. This little signage area featured a phone plaque, private property notice and cleverly illuminated crossing sign. It has been beautified with a neatly tended planter containing lupins in full bloom. The opening of the Selby Diversion meant that Anglo-Scottish, and other Inter-City trains, no longer crossed this swing bridge. To witness a 'Deltic'-hauled passenger train rumble across the bridge was indeed quite a sight.

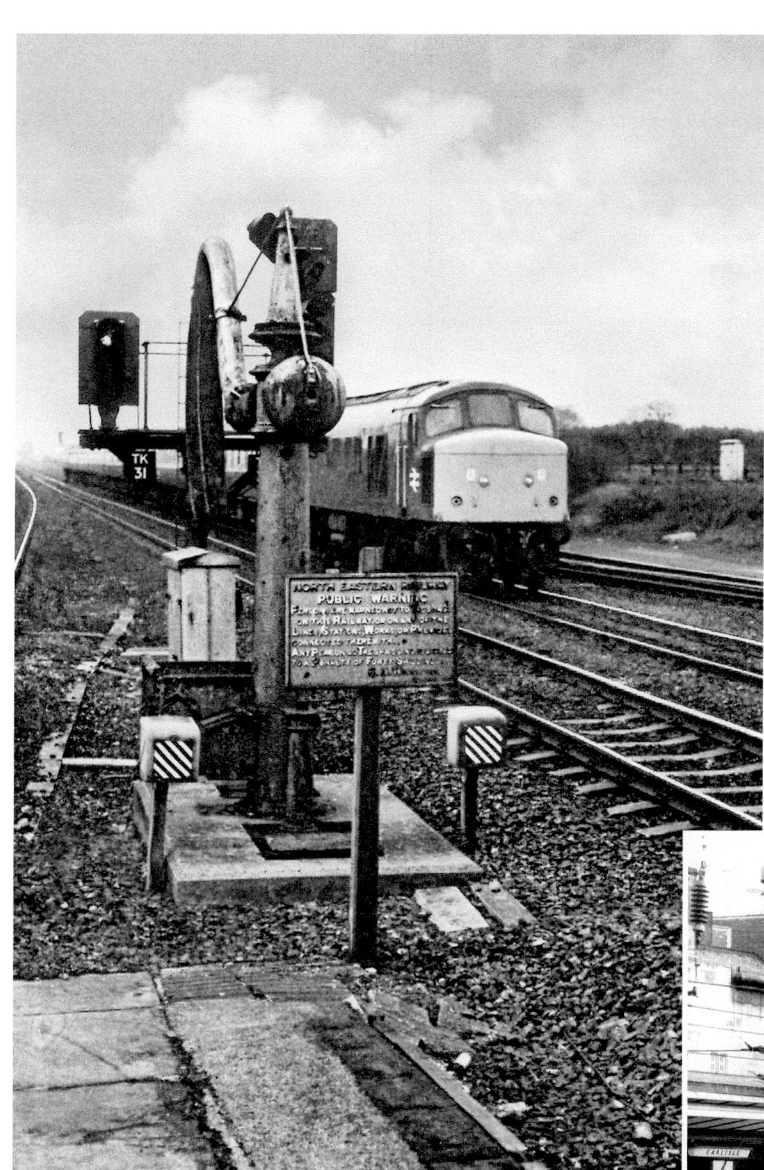

Public Warning, Thirsk, March 1979.

This North Eastern Railway cast-iron public warning sign was amongst an amazing array of steam age relics still at Thirsk. The water crane looks complete and still fully operational. It all looked very incongruous alongside this high-speed section of the East Coast Mainline. It would all be swept away when the line was electrified. Did any of it get saved? It would have been a preservationist or railwayana collector's dream. I had taken the train from York to Thirsk to photograph Class 55s speeding along the racetrack section either side of the station. I wasn't disappointed, as I bagged quite a few good shots. My favourite of the day is this one, though. The Class 46 is hauling a cross-country Inter-City train from Newcastle. Incidentally, in an area outside the station was a sports ground that had a Victorian grounded railway carriage being used as a pavilion. I must thank David Hey – take a look at his stunning and colossal website – for rescuing this image for me. All he had to work with was a contact sheet photograph.

Fluorescent Carlisle, May 1976.

This shot is one of my favourites. For some reason the combination of the London Midland Region 1960s fluorescent lampshade station sign and 45047 makes me want to run down the ramp and jump on the train. It is bound for Glasgow Central, via Dumfries. It had made its way from London St Pancras, via Sheffield, Leeds and the Settle & Carlisle route. The lampshade is different from the Eastern Region variant, but I prefer the London Midland version. Being from the North West, you could say I am biased.

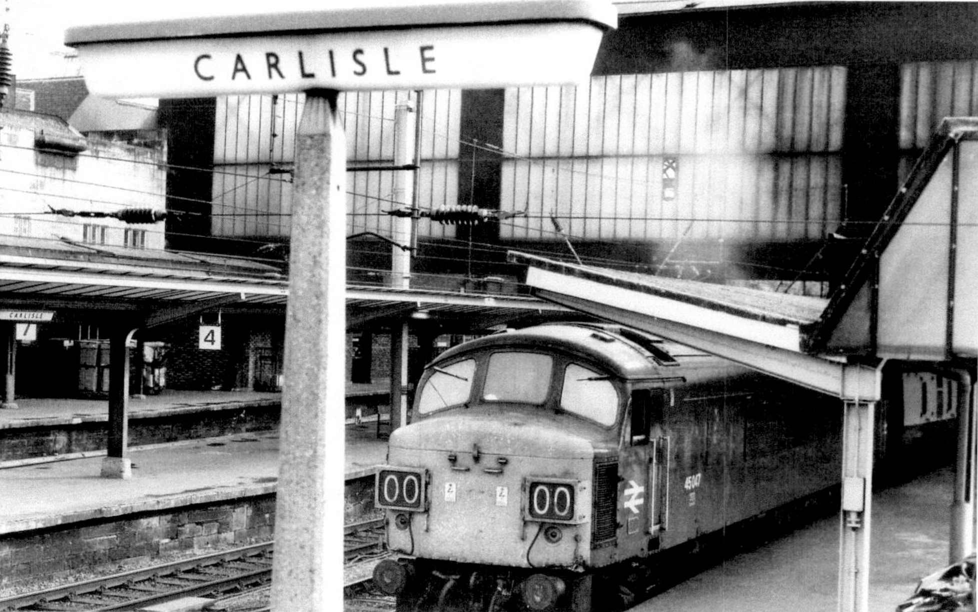

'Way out. To Skye Ferry', Kyle of Lochalsh, August 1981.
There is no longer a Skye ferry from Kyle of Lochalsh; a far less romantic-sounding road bridge has replaced it. I hope someone saved this nicely painted wooden sign. It would be a great addition to any railwayana collection. This Class 26-hauled train is bound for Inverness; it was the return working of the first train of the day from the Highland capital.

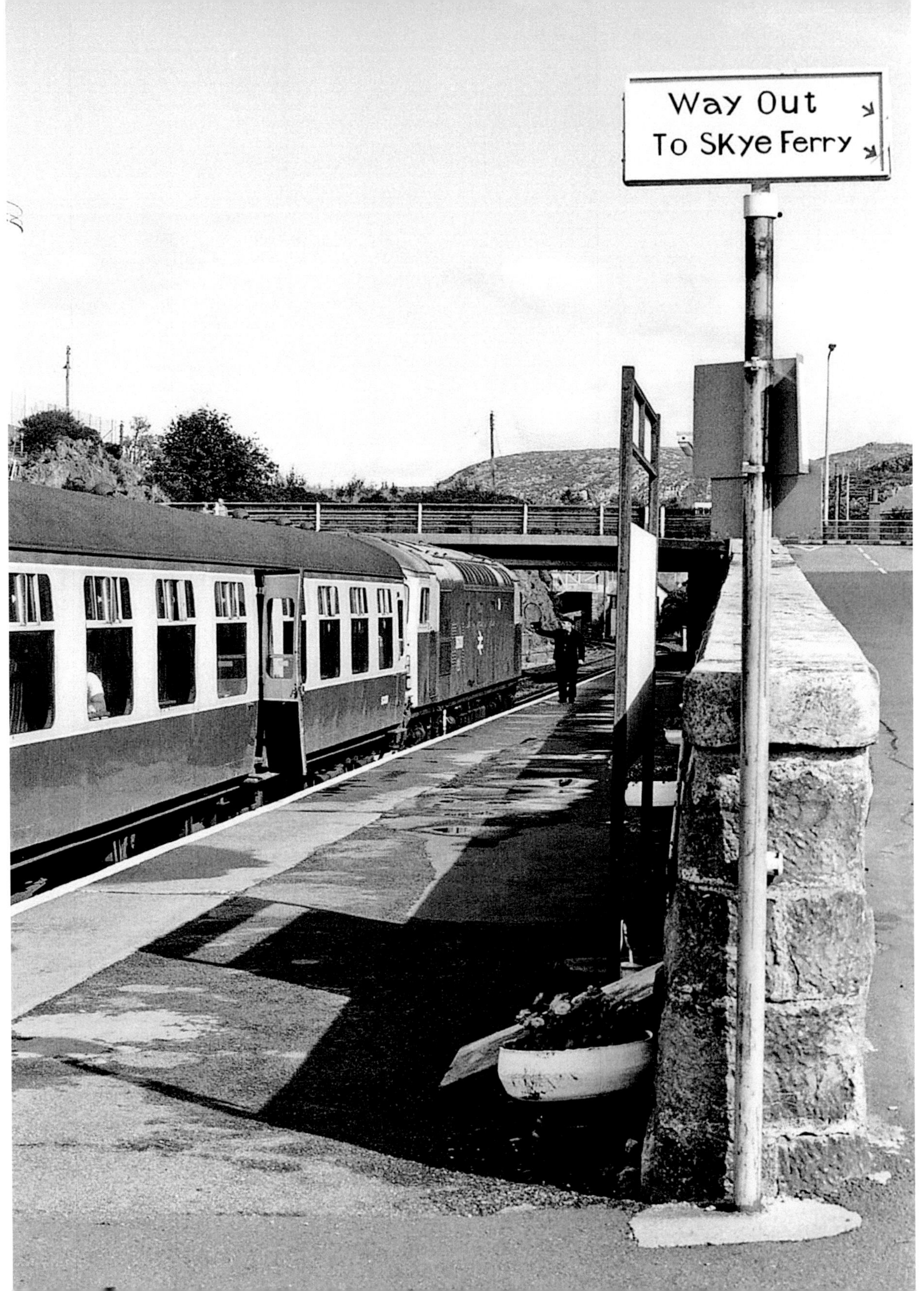

INTRODUCTION

Ever since I was a little lad watching steam-hauled goods trains passing Reddish North railway station I have been fascinated and intrigued by wagons. Where are they going? Where have they come from? What route did they take? What are they carrying? What are their contents used for? How old are the wagons? How much do they carry? Why are they the shape they are? Such a lot of questions – a lot harder to answer than those related to passenger trains. Back then, there was no Wikipedia or web pages to give an instant answer. The answers, if I could obtain them, often led to more questions. It was a great way of learning about industries, such as coal, power generating, engineering, manufacturing, oil and distribution, to name but a few. My curiosity took me to collieries, ports, sidings, steel works, cement works, distribution depots, chemical works, civil engineering yards, scrapyards and goods depots to photograph wagon happenings. In today's world it would be unthinkable that a teenager could have free and easy access to wander round them. I did them all and enjoyed every minute of it, learning lots of things along the way.

During the 1970s and early '80s, there was a mind-boggling array of wagons on the rail network. They were being used to transport goods and in departmental use serving BR's permanent-way gangs, plus its civil engineers. Significant numbers were built by pre-Nationalisation and even pre-Grouping railway companies. Similar to the 1960s changeover from steam to diesel or electric traction, this period was a period of transition for wagons. The old order, dating back to the birth of railways, was coming to an end. Small-capacity multi-customer or -destination wagons were giving way to the new order of 'Block Trains' and 'Railfreight'-branded medium-sized wagons. The efficient new era equated to large-capacity, fast, modern, quick-load and -discharge, air-braked wagons. Containerisation, bulk tankers, large-capacity vans and hopper wagons were now the name of the game. BR wagon workshops and private companies, such as Standard Railway Wagon, were receiving big purchase orders to build them as fast as possible.

During the 1970s and '80s, the new and old orders were working seemingly in a 'parallel universe' but on the same railway network. Fantastic to witness – I had even more wagons to ponder over than when I was a little lad. Well-used sidings, marshalling yards and goods depots were still very much part of the rail scene; this would not last much longer. Wagons were already going in mass numbers to be scrapped. Shunting locos and lower powered mixed-traffic locomotives, which had been used to haul the wagons, were also being withdrawn from service. Fortunately, they are ideally suited to preserved railways, resulting in quite a few examples getting a new lease of life.

'Block Trains', working direct from supplier to end user and back, were in sharp contrast to a few wagons or even just one making a protracted journey to its destination. However, in some cases their existence was far shorter lived than what they were designed to replace. The closure of collieries and coal-fired power stations would soon bring an end to many of them. The switch from oil-fired central heating to gas and the movement of oil by pipeline meant that quite a few bulk tank wagon trains were short lived.

Early Evening at Par, July 1974.
The driver of Class 52 D1049 *Western Monarch* waits for the signal to give him the all-clear to draw his lengthy train out of Par station. It is comprised of mainly short wheelbase vans, called 'Vanfits'. This is the land of long china clay trains: strings of small open wagons fitted with hoods known as 'Clayhoods'. Curiously there is only one of these wagons in evidence amongst this train. It is the first one, just behind the 'Western'. I can't remember for sure, but I have a sneaky feeling this train was destined for the nearby harbour. It was famous for being home to two low-slung steam locos. They were specially designed to negotiate the harbour railway's tight curves and bridge running under the BR mainline. They have been preserved. Their names are *Alfred* and *Judy*. The sight of these unusual little locos prompted Rev. W. Awdry to include them in his world-famous Railway Series children's books. I took this photograph while on the way back from Newquay to Torquay. I was on a day trip with my mum during a two-week family holiday to the 'English Riviera'.

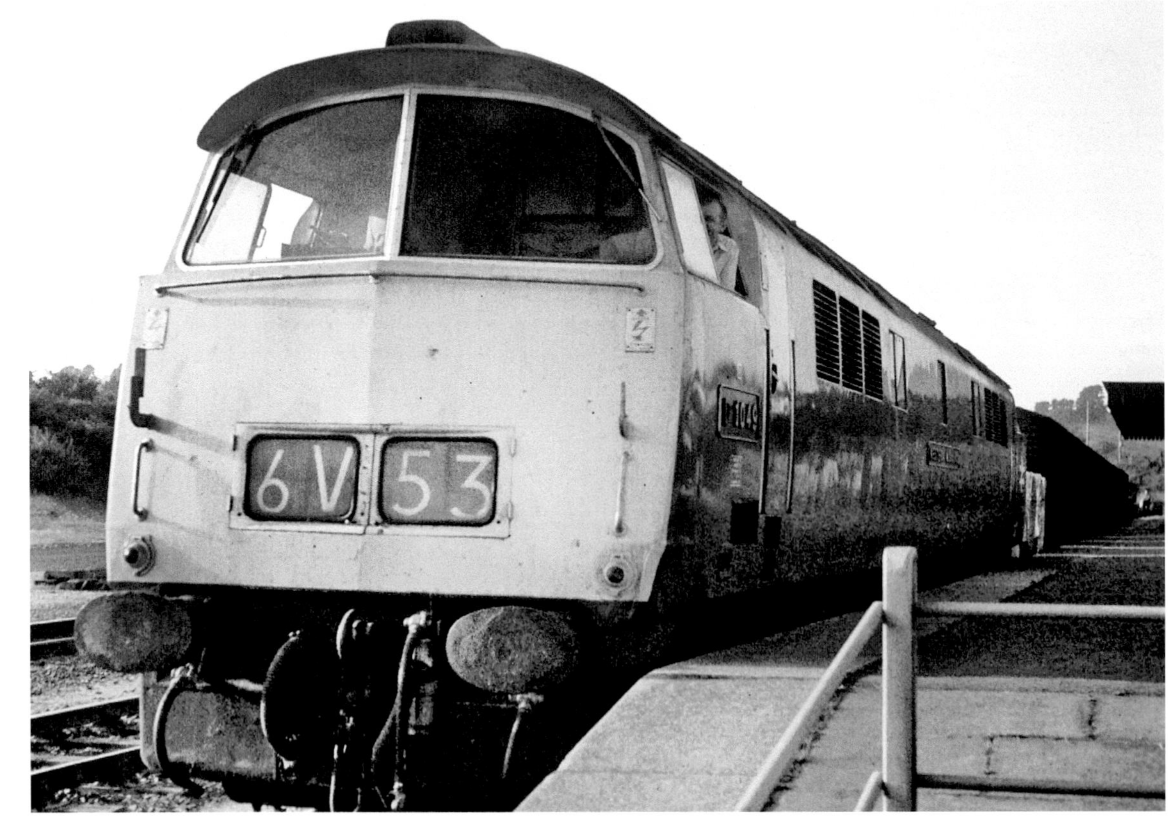

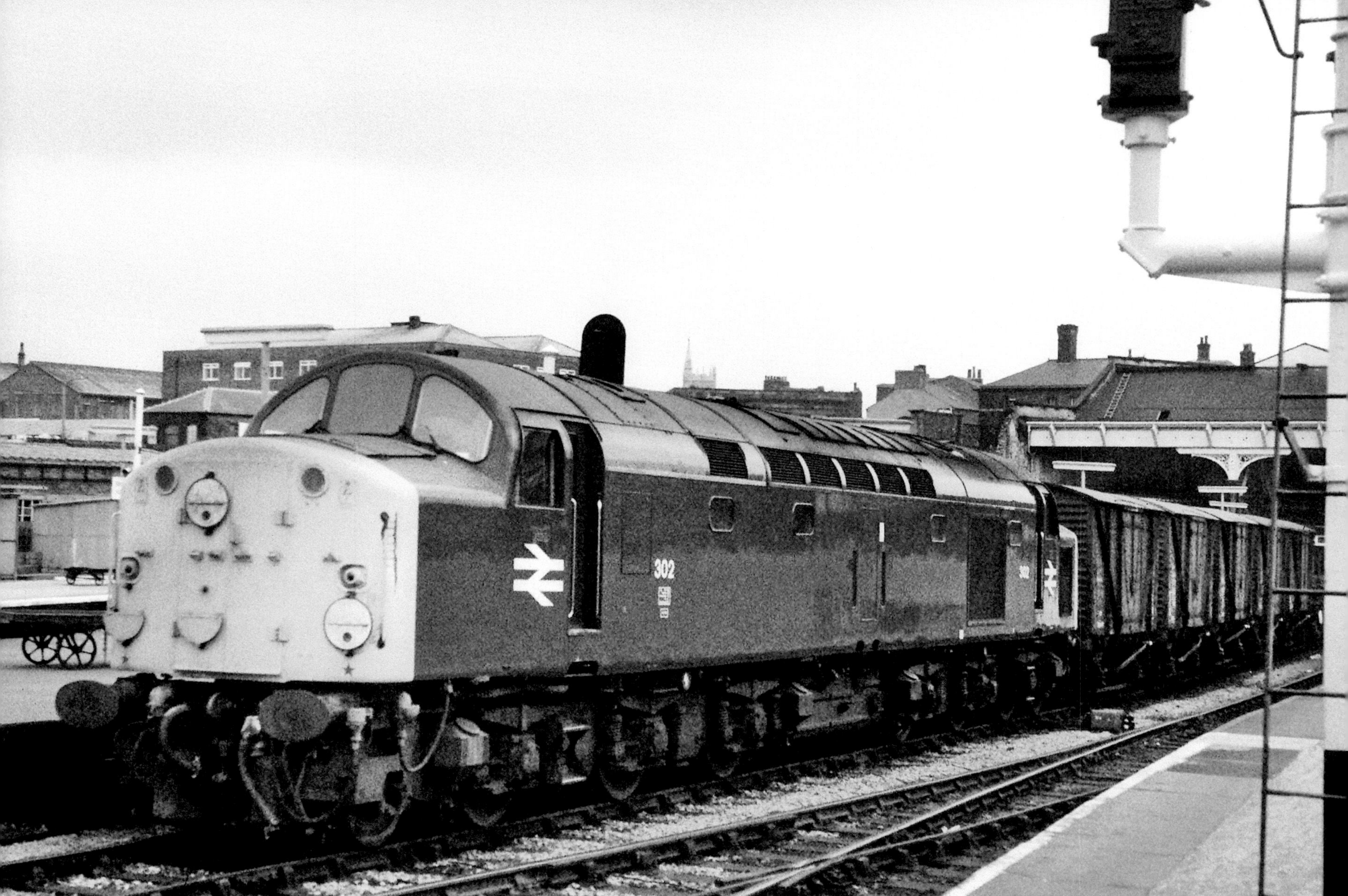

'Vanfits', Manchester Victoria, September 1973.
When I took this photograph of Class 40 number 302 (40102) hauling 'Vanfits', there were many small- to medium-sized factories and distribution depots that were still rail connected. Products such as car parts, electrical goods, paint, paper and tins of food were typical payloads. This meant small-capacity vans such as the 'Vanfit' were ideally suited. At the time, the age-old practice of being rail connected was rapidly declining. Not surprisingly, companies preferred the versatility of road transport, especially as the motorway system was largely complete. BR had, since the 1960s, been shying away from this type of traffic, because it often made little or no money. In addition, the BR goods depots were on limited time; they used both open and van wagons to ship single items or batch loads. Consequently, the 'Vanfits' days were numbered – a huge amount were scrapped. However, quite a few of their bodies found their way to farmers' fields, making great storage sheds. You can still see them in use now.

Mixed Freight, Wellington, July 1974.
On a very wet summer's day a Class 47 powers past Wellington's Platform 2, heading in the Wolverhampton direction. Immediately behind the loco is a steel open merchandise wagon (ZGV) carrying what looks like a large sheeted-over electrical component. Behind it is an earlier built wooden-bodied ZGO open wagon carrying electrical switch boxes. Behind them are two ferry vans. Following up is a string of empty HTO 21-ton hopper wagons. I remember feeling cold and damp when I took this photograph. In a bid to reinstate my feeling of well being, I grabbed a cup of tea from the Travellers Fare Buffet on Platform 2 soon afterwards. Then I resumed my wait for a Metro-Cammell Class 101 DMU, which took me to Shrewsbury.

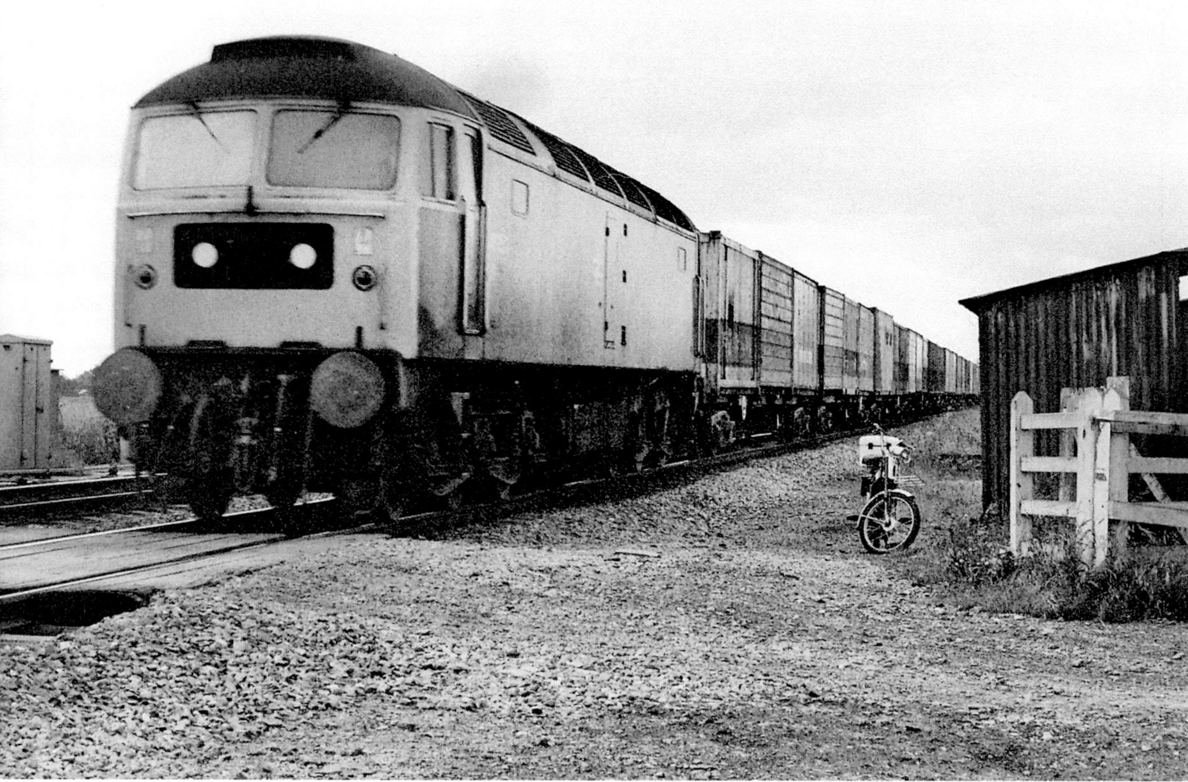

'Funky Moped', Chat Moss, August 1979.
I remember my mates used to like playing Jasper Carrott's 'Funky Moped' on the jukebox at the Lord Nelson in Gorton. I can see them now laughing along with it. Some of them used to have 125cc and 250cc bikes, so they thought mopeds were naff. I reckon this one looks pretty good. Incidentally, the Class 47 is hauling a Holyhead–Manchester's Longsight Freightliner terminal container train. The 'Freightliner' was BR's cure to the expensive transhipment of goods and as such it radically improved ease of handling. These trains eradicated many low-capacity wagons from the network. Containerisation became global and massive. Despite this, the Holyhead (for Ireland) and Longsight terminals have long since closed.

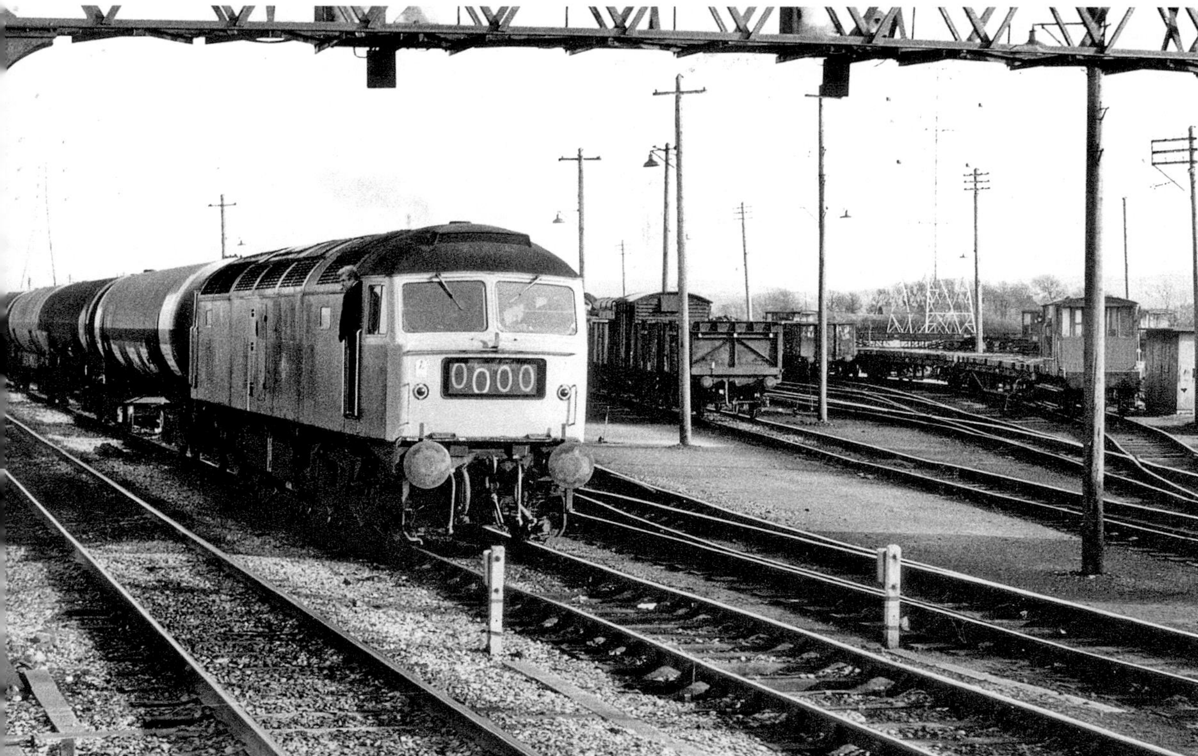

Milford Haven Oil, Llanelli, 19 February 1977.
Still in superb two-tone BR green livery, 47185 is held waiting for a green signal at Llanelli with a Milford Haven oil refinery train. This working comprises BR's successful new freight era 'Block Train' 102-ton-capacity bogie tank wagons. It is easy to see why such trains were far more cost effective than small-capacity wagons strung together destined for a variety of destinations. By the time I took this shot scrap yards were being filled with no-longer-viable small wagons awaiting the cutter's torch. Despite this, the adjacent sidings, seen in this photograph, are still very much in business handling traditional freight trains.

Vital Oil Supply, Lincoln Central, August 1980.
The wagon tagged on to the back of 03034's match truck is fuel for the DMUs and locos operating out of Lincoln. Hence, it was a vital supply. The match truck, which normally accompanied the 03, was an ex-small container wagon. It had the capacity to take three, usually containing cement. It was intended to help with braking and ensure track circuits worked correctly as the small wheelbase loco went about its business. Despite its fine-looking appearance, sadly this handy little loco was withdrawn during February 1983. Fortunately, quite a few examples have made it into preservation.

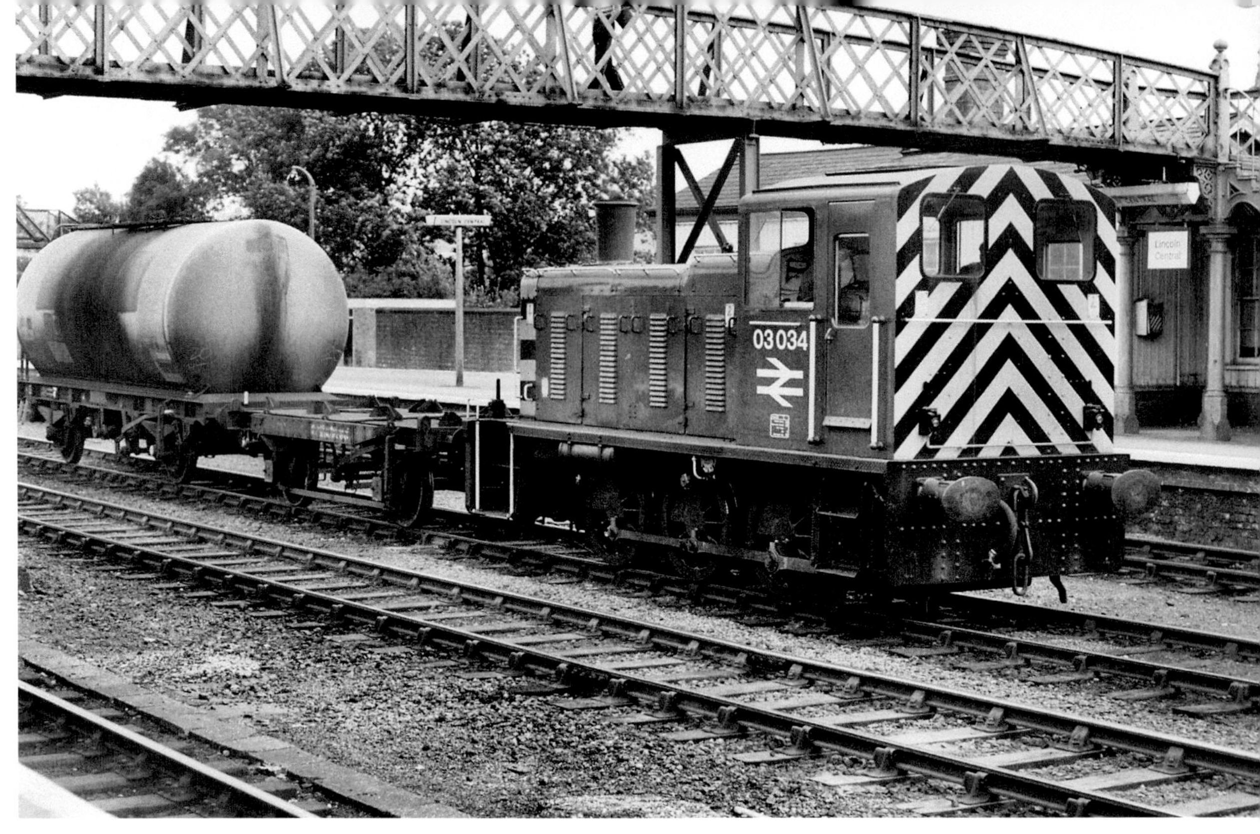

ICI Tanks, Earlstown, June 1978.
On a very hot and sunny day, 40104 powers along the West Coast Mainline with a long train of Imperial Chemical Industries-liveried tank wagons. ICI was once a household name and the UK's largest chemical manufacturer. From 1991 it began to be broken up, and the name gradually disappeared from our vocabulary. In turn the distinctive logo vanished from its large fleet of tank wagons. They carried a wide variety of ICI products such as anhydrous ammonia, caustic soda, methanol and sodium carbonate. They would run as 'Block Trains', as seen in this photograph, or as part of a mixed train. The wagons ran between ICI plants, and to supply end users.

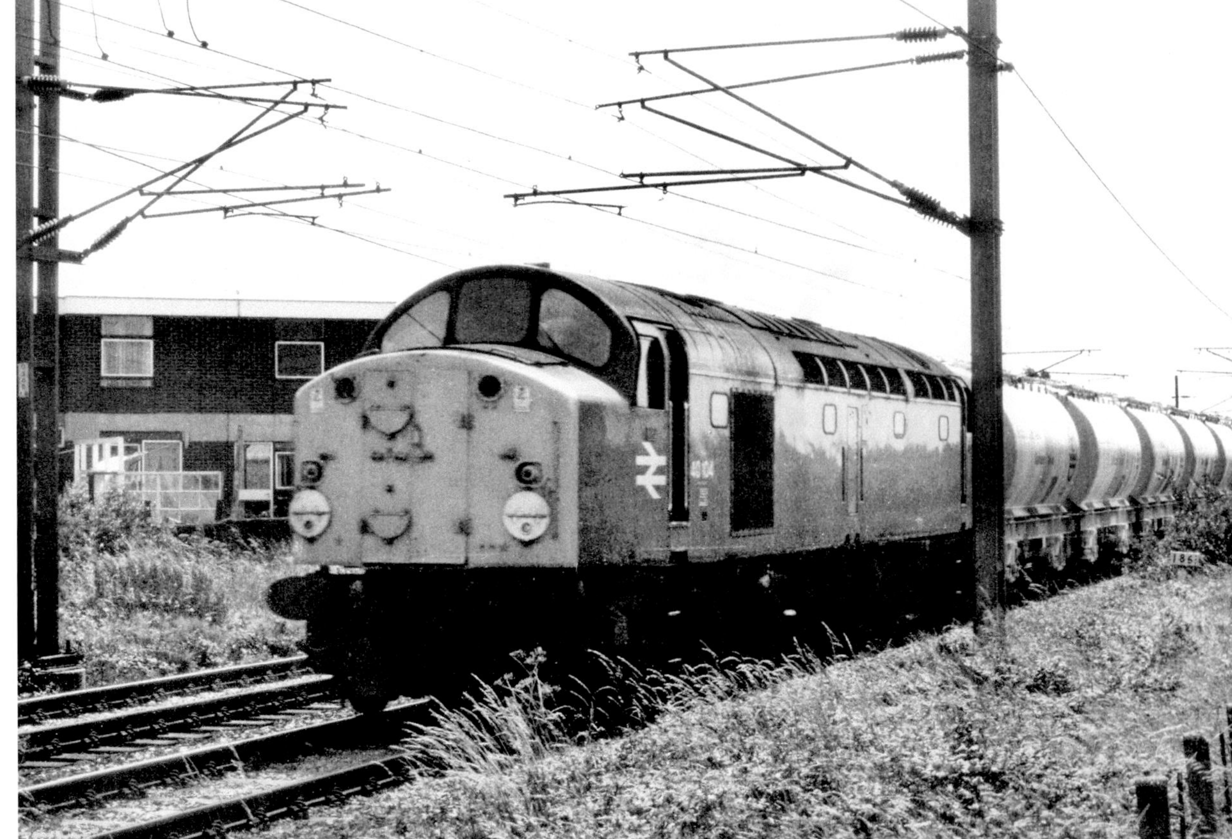

Below: Gone West, Exeter Riverside, May 1975.

Just as London Midland Region Class 50s replaced Class 52s, Class 25s travelled from the North West to fill the gap left by withdrawn Class 35 'Hymeks'. I only ever saw two of the Beyer Peacock Manchester-built Class 35s in BR service: once at Taunton and once at Bristol Bath Road Depot. They had been introduced to haul the Western Region's less demanding mixed-traffic duties, previously the forte of 'Hall' and 'Manor' Class steam locomotives. Sadly, like all the Western Region's diesel hydraulics, they only had a short service life. When I took this shot at Exeter's still busy Riverside yard there was plenty of old-style mixed-freight traffic, just the purpose for which the 25s and 35s had been built. This unidentified class member is marshalling a train, which included three-axle milk tank wagons. These curious wagons had for many years served country dairy plants, which latterly tended to be on truncated branch lines. For example, the Hemyock branch line stayed in operation until 31 October 1975, serving the town's dairy. The line's final months of operation were entrusted to the Class 25s. The 25s' life on the Western Region was far shorter than the Class 35s, being quickly usurped by ex-Eastern Region Class 31s.

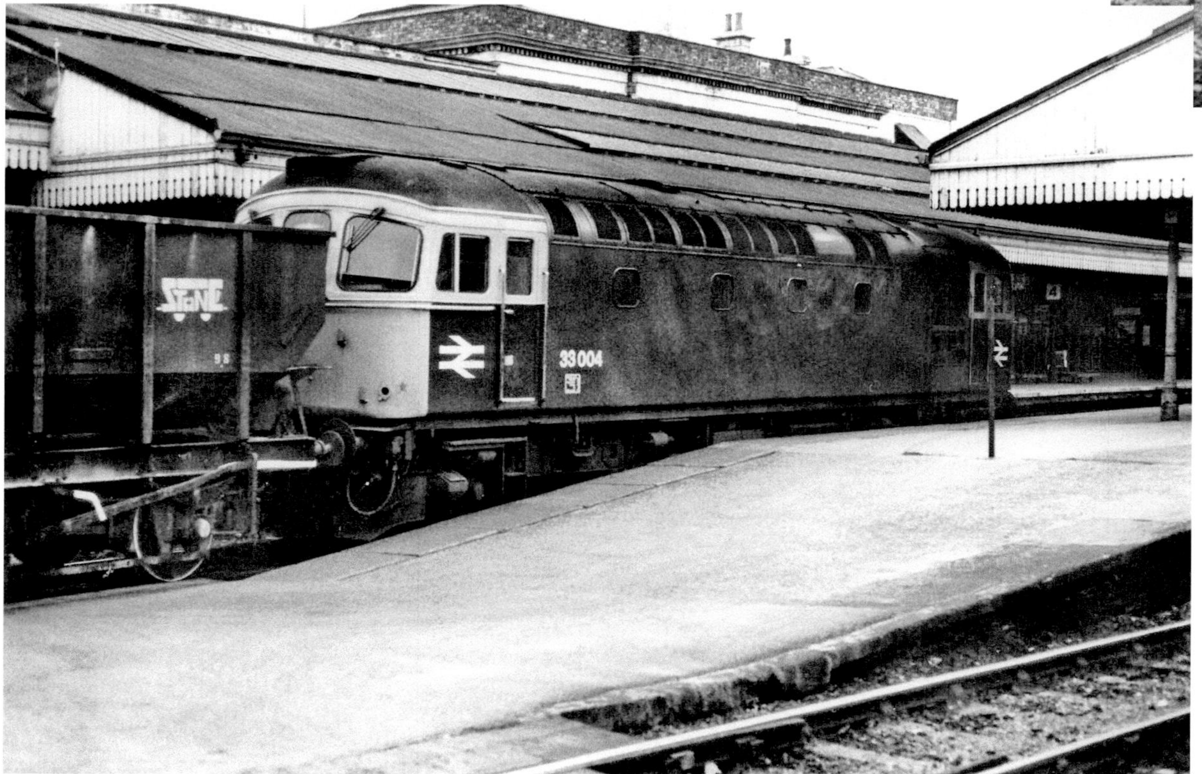

Above: Yeoman Stone, Salisbury, 26 March 1977.

As a youngster I always associated Yeoman with steak-pie fillings. They were regularly seen on TV and on my dinner plate. I can recommend them – lovely! Apparently they are no longer available – what a shame. The 1986 introduction of Foster Yeoman's Class 59s to haul their high-capacity stone wagons alerted me to another company called Yeoman. I understand this 33004-hauled freight is a Yeoman stone train. Unlike their super high-capacity freight wagons of the 1980s, this train comprises old HOP21 vacuum-braked ex-coal hoppers.

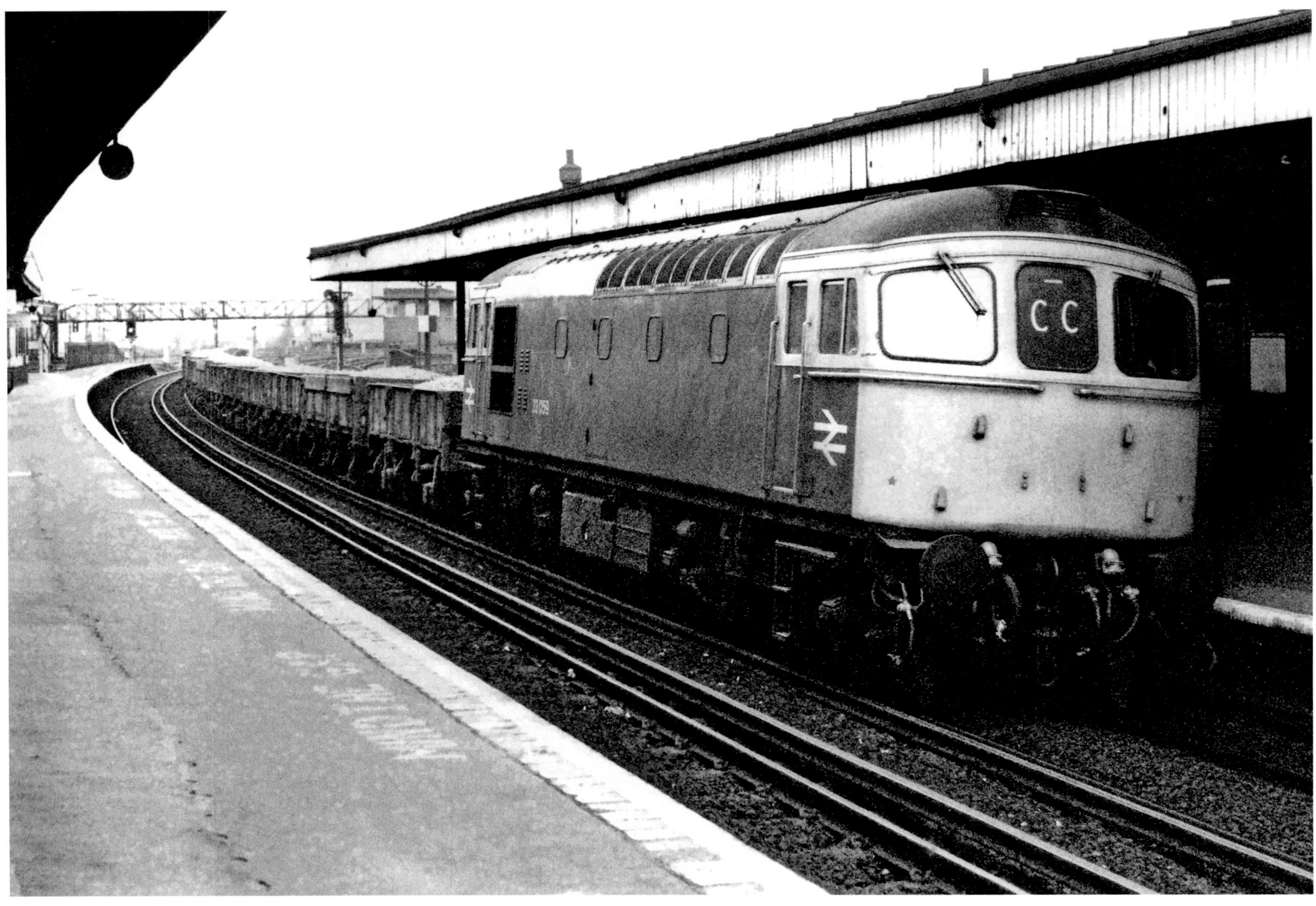

Southern 'Grampus', Clapham Junction, May 1980.
Loco 33059 hauls a loaded permanent-way engineer's ballast train through Clapham Junction. The lengthy train is made up of BR departmental 'Grampus' wagons. This permanent-way/civil engineer part of BR's vast empire had a wonderful array of wagons, most of which were curiously named after sea creatures. I can't help but wonder why. I must admit to having to consult Wikipedia to find out what a grampus is – a dolphin-like creature. Part of the array included names such as 'Cod', 'Sturgeon', 'Turbot' and 'Whale'. Many of the wagons were quite aged, which made them even more interesting to me. They came in a wide variety of guises, including flats, hoppers, drop-sided and brake vans. Fortunately, many lasted long enough to avoid being broken up by scrap men. Instead, they were snapped up by preservations, their designs making them must-have additions to a preserved railway's fleet, often being used for the purpose they were designed for.

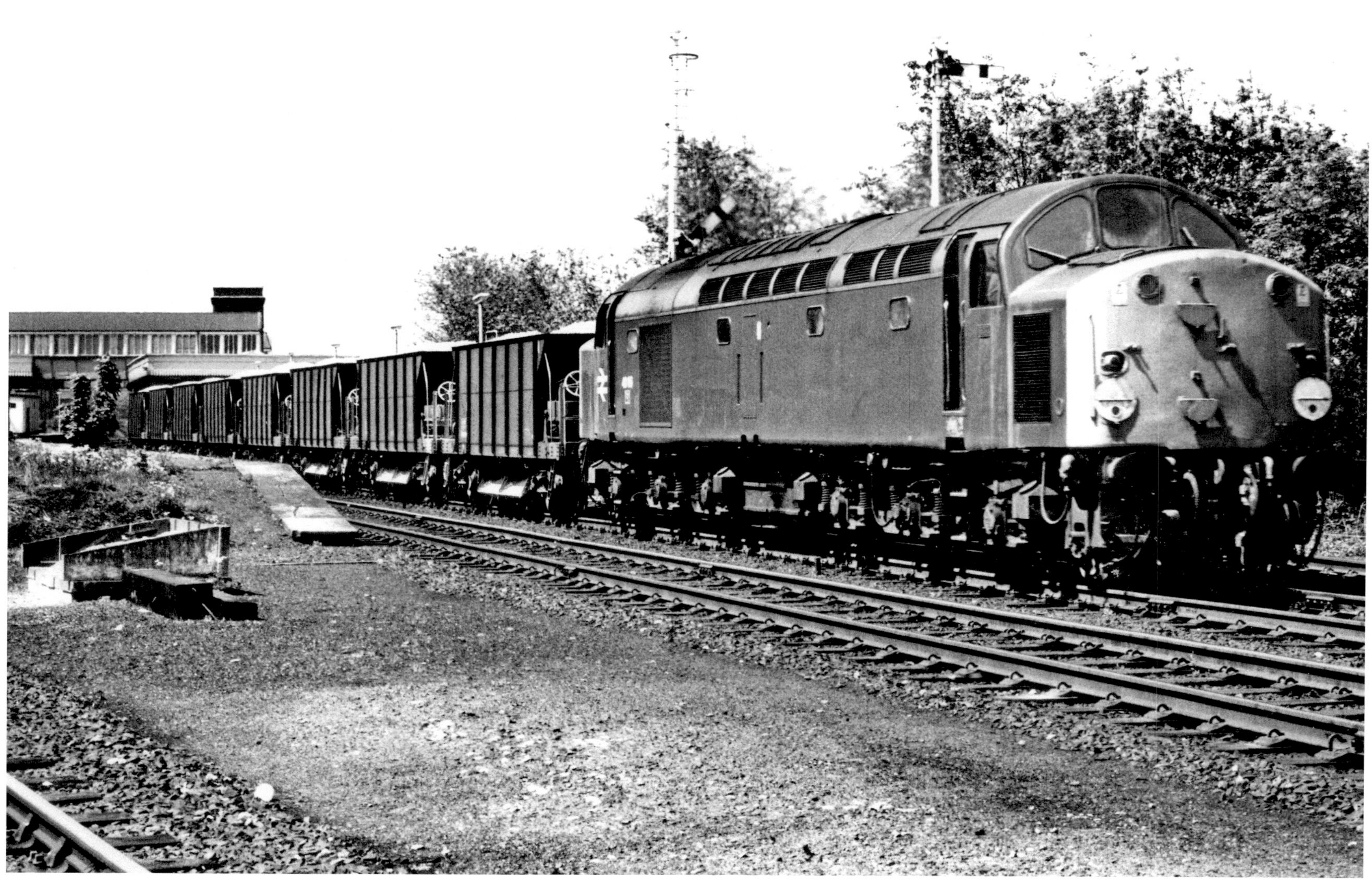

Sea Lions at Colwyn Bay, 1977.
No. 40111, complete with telltale welded-up nose doors, roars through Colwyn Bay with a fully loaded rake of 40-ton-capacity BR departmental 'Sea Lion' ballast wagons. These wagons were introduced in 1970, being a welded version of the Southern Region's riveted 'Walrus' wagon. They gradually replaced many of the smaller wagons, such as the 'Grampus'. They improved the process of getting plenty of fresh ballast to the permanent-way gang dramatically. This train gained its fresh load from the Penmaenmawr quarry a few miles west along the North Wales Coast Line.

BR Steam, York, July 1975.
No. 08705 heads up a departmental train of wagons including this 3-ton safe working load (swl) steam-powered crane and ex-LMS runner wagon. I bagged this photograph at York, while on a family holiday in Scarborough. Many people think steam was eradicated from the BR stocklist on 11 August 1968. In fact, it lived on well into the 1970s. Steam-powered cranes were still in evidence, dotted around the network. They included the massive heavy-lift cranes based at loco depots. Fortunately, due to their extended life on BR, several examples made it into preservation. Better still, some are in operational condition.

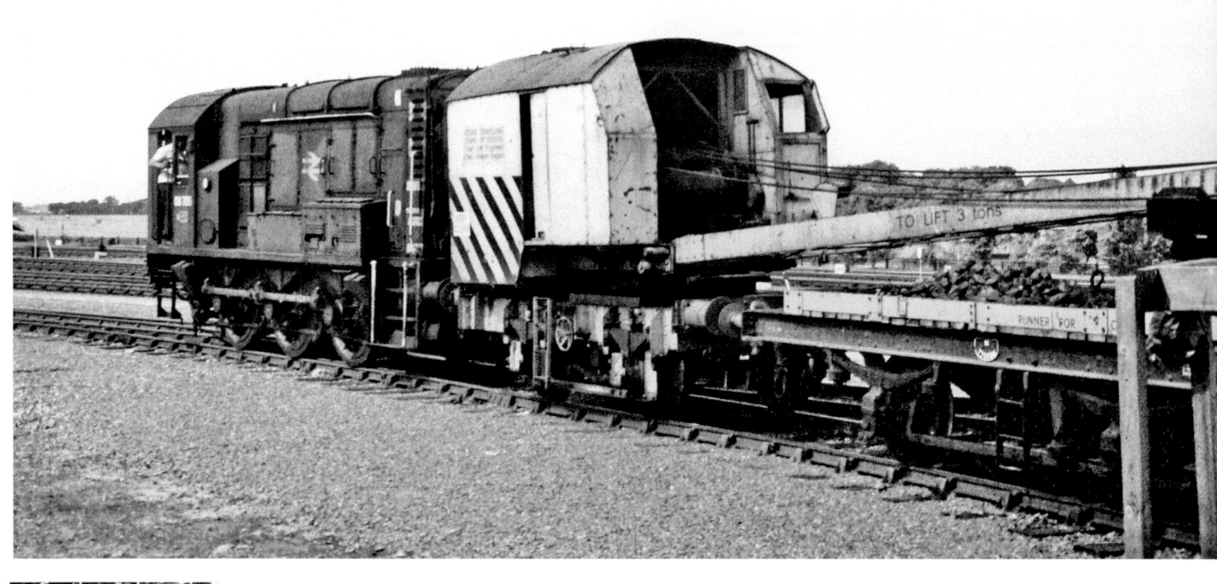

Block Cement, Oxford, August 1979.
No. 47157 heads north past Oxford's distinctively GWR-designed wooden signal box. It is hauling a rake of twelve 'Block Train' 'Double Dimple' high-capacity dry powder cement wagons. Their odd shape aided the rapid and thorough discharge of the powder through the underslung hoppers. Just like the new-era 102-ton-capacity oil tank wagons, these carried the same amount of dry powder cement. They were known as PDA and built by Metro Cammell between 1969 and 1972. They were built to serve the newly opened Northfleet cement works, then the largest in Europe. The site has now closed and been cleared. When it was operating these wagons they were kept busy supplying Blue Circle Cement terminals with Northfleet's product. These wagons could also be seen working for the company's Hope Valley works. This train might have been heading there.

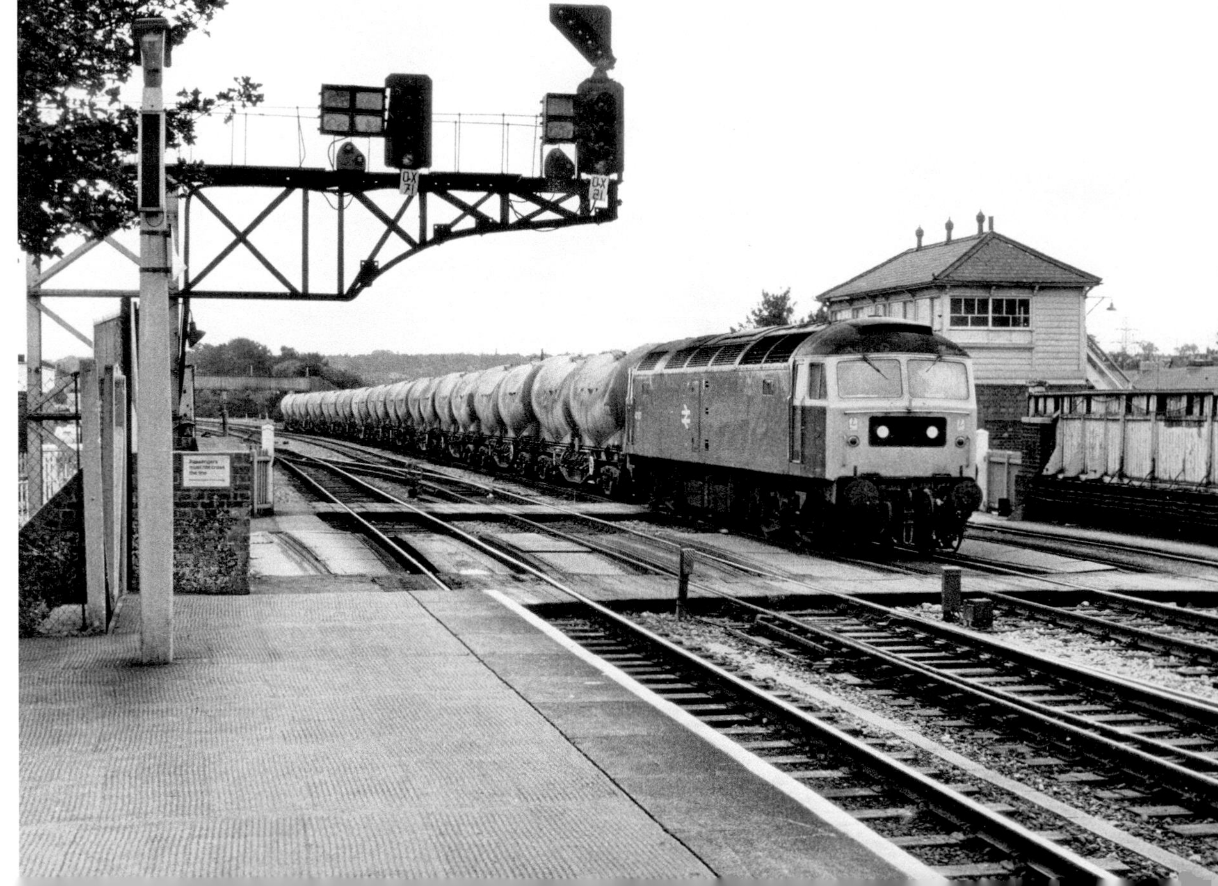

Right: Accra Cruises By, Guide Bridge, October 1973.
Class 40 number 234 (40034) cruises through an atmospheric Guide Bridge with a train of empty CPV 'Presflo' cement wagons. These small wagons will be familiar to railway modellers. They have been popular products of the many OO-gauge specialist companies ever since the days of Hornby-Dublo and Airfix kits. This train is heading back to Blue Circle's Hope Valley plant via Earles Sidings.

Below: Didcot-bound 'Merry-go-round', Oxford, August 1979.
Brand-new Doncaster-built 56060 hauls a long train of fully loaded HAA 'Merry-go-round' wagons through Oxford. It is bound for the now closed Didcot power station. These trains were designed to supply large coal-fired power stations with as much of the black stuff as they needed. They plied full between an NCB colliery and a CEGB power station, then empty back to the colliery – a highly efficient cyclic working that was soon acquired its apt 'Merry-go-round' nickname. The Class 56s were designed and ideally suited for this work. Unfortunately with the demise of Britain's coalfields many became redundant. Some examples later found work in mainland Europe. Plus, there are still a few working on our modern rail network. 56060 managed to dodge the scrap man rather well.

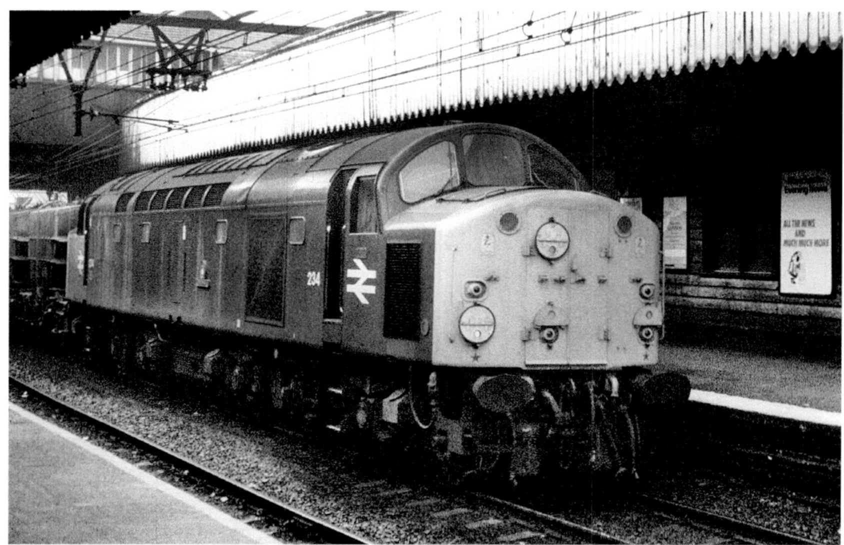

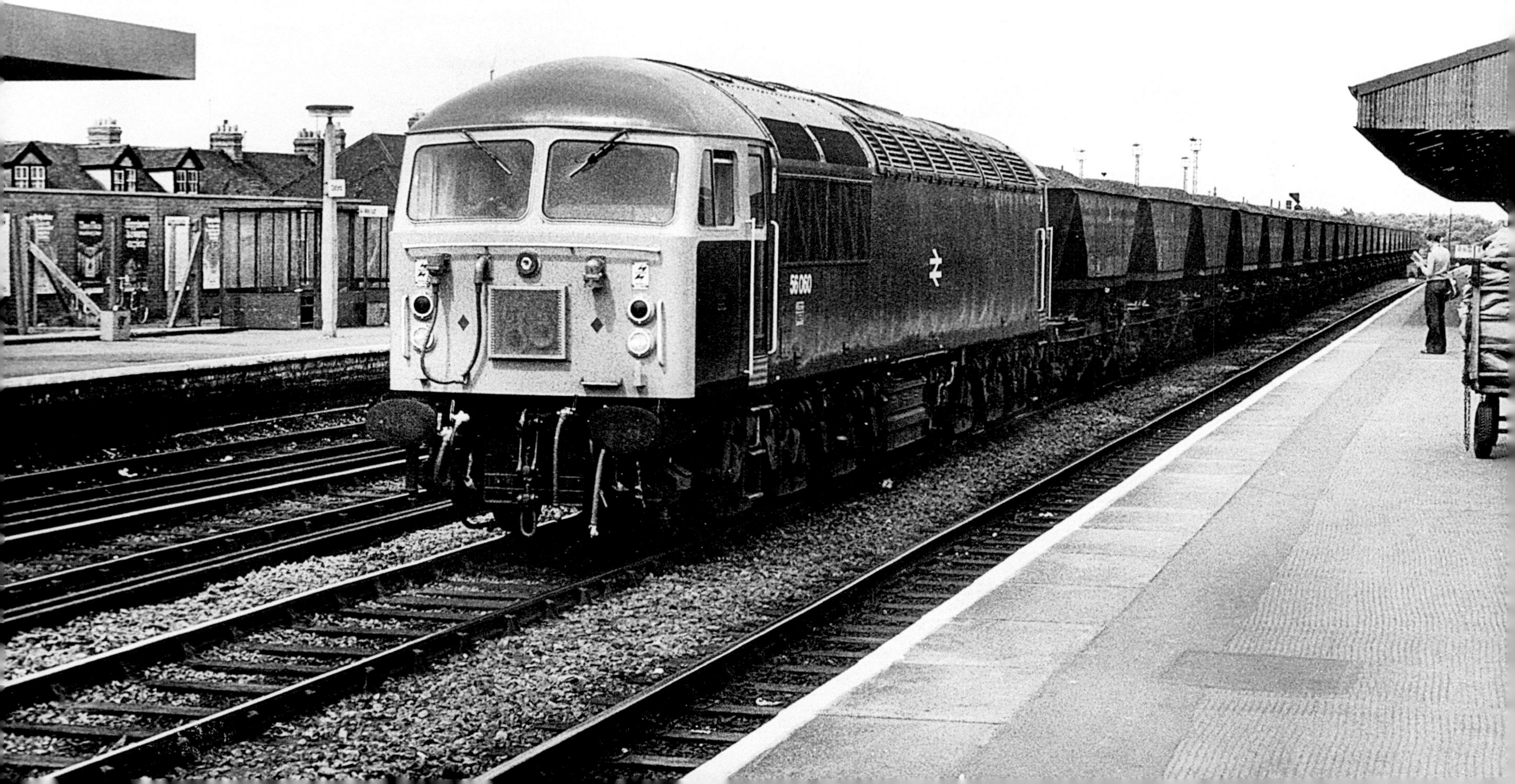

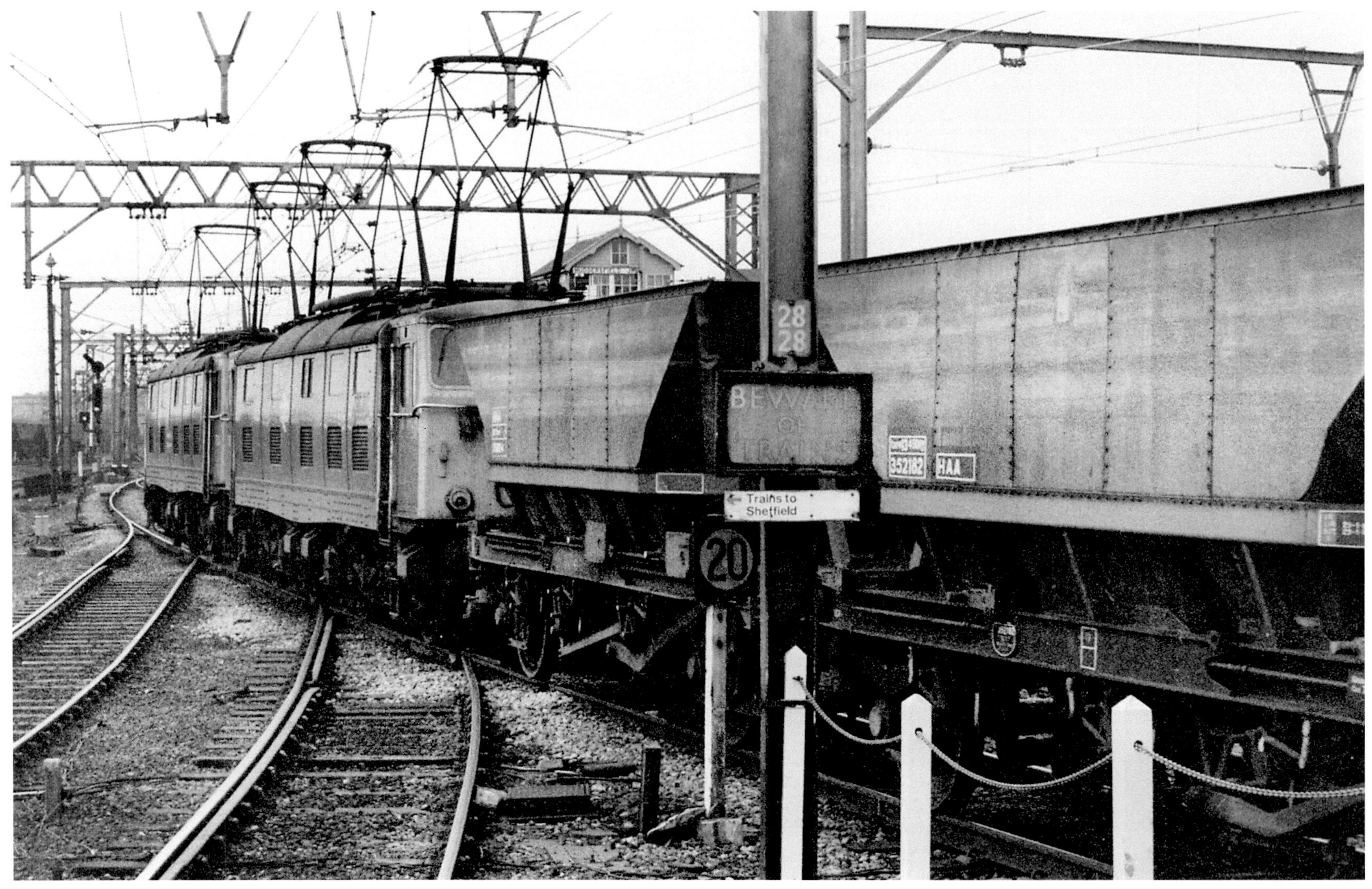

Penistone 'Merry-go-round', May 1980.

This is a business-like shot of a pair of Woodhead-route Class 76s powering through Penistone with a train of empty HAA coal hopper wagons. It suggests BR had got it right with the efficient movement of coal from source to end user. A seemingly perfect combination of electric traction hauling modern freight wagons amidst relatively new infrastructure. The line was fully modernised during the 1950s and the permanent way appeared to be kept in tiptop condition. For example, continuous welded rail abounded. The scene belies the fact that the route had been declared unviable and would close one year later. The expensive infrastructure would be swept away and the locos scrapped.

Could it have been because the route's main purpose, the movement of coal from the Yorkshire pits, would have soon ceased anyway? Gradually, after the bitter 1984 Miners' Strike, all the Yorkshire pits would close. Was it all part of an already laid-out big picture? Despite this, the HAA wagons saw many more years' service, the last being used to serve the Hope Cement works. The survivors ran until 2010. The under frames from a thousand HAAs and their derivatives have been reused as part of a new fleet of MHA box spoil wagons. The train in this photograph is returning from CEGB Fiddlers Ferry power station for reloading.

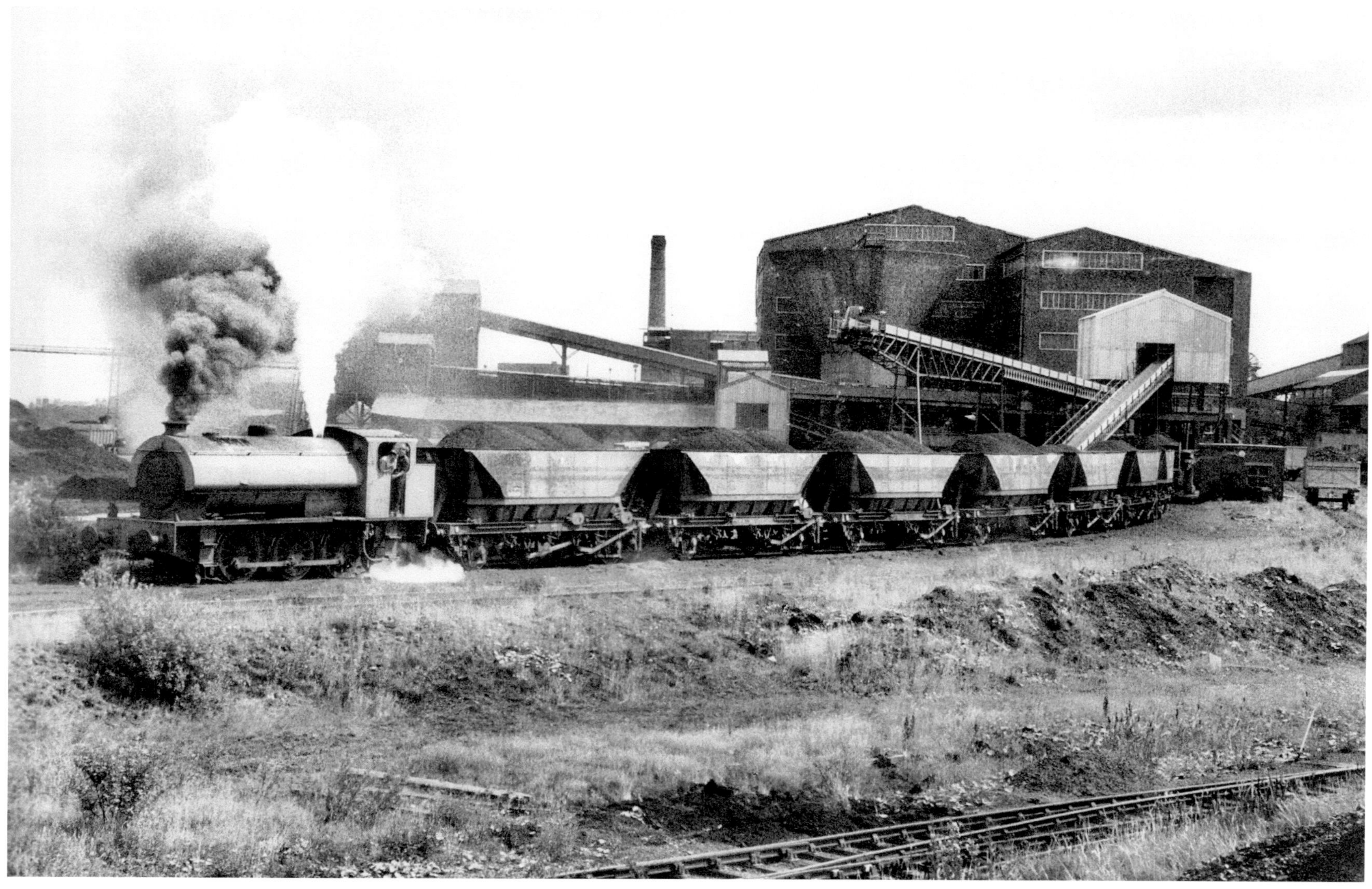

The Source, Bickershaw, near Wigan, August 1975.
The NCB's 1940s and '50s-built fleet of 'Austerity' steam locos were originally intended to haul rakes of small wheelbase wagons. These included BR's ubiquitous 16-tonners. The widespread introduction of the HAA wagon meant that the saddle tank locos were worked to their limit moving far heavier trains to and from the pit head. Their job was to collect and drop off the wagons from the BR and NCB exchange sidings. It was quite a spectacle watching these locos going about their work: spine-tingling stuff when they were attacking a heavy incline with a heavy train on wet rails. The age of the industrial steam loco was far from over when I took this photograph. Every region of the NCB still used them, as did the CEGB, plus many other enterprises. Their ruggedness and the ready supply of coal did have a bearing on their extended life. In this shot, this fresh out of the NCB's Walkden workshops 'Austerity' is about to ascend the steep incline from Bickershaw colliery. Steam locos were still used at Bickershaw during the 1980s; the pit closed in 1990.

Coal from the Valleys, Llanelli, 19 February 1977.
An unidentified Class 47 at Llanelli, with a string of 16-ton coal wagons fully loaded with what the Welsh Valleys are famous for. The deep coal mines of South Wales were once in abundance; as in other parts of the UK, they are now all gone. It is likely the coal emanated from one of mines linked by spurs off the lower reaches of this route. Curiously, even though by this time the practice of displaying the train reporting number as a headcode had ended, this 47's blinds are displaying 4C28. I am not sure if it was the correct one or had been from a working some time previously. If it is correct, the 4 indicates it is an express freight, with vacuum braking on 90 per cent of the train; the C suggests it is bound for Bristol or the West Country. There is a fair chance the headcode might well have been correct if the 16-tonners were vacuum-brake fitted. The loco's driver might have liked using the blinds and continued the practice long after it had been abandoned. I would have. They remind me of bus destination and number blinds. On the way to school, my mates and I used to change them. We could easily access them on Manchester Corporation open-back buses. I guess we must have misled a few would-be passengers as the bus made its way to its destination.

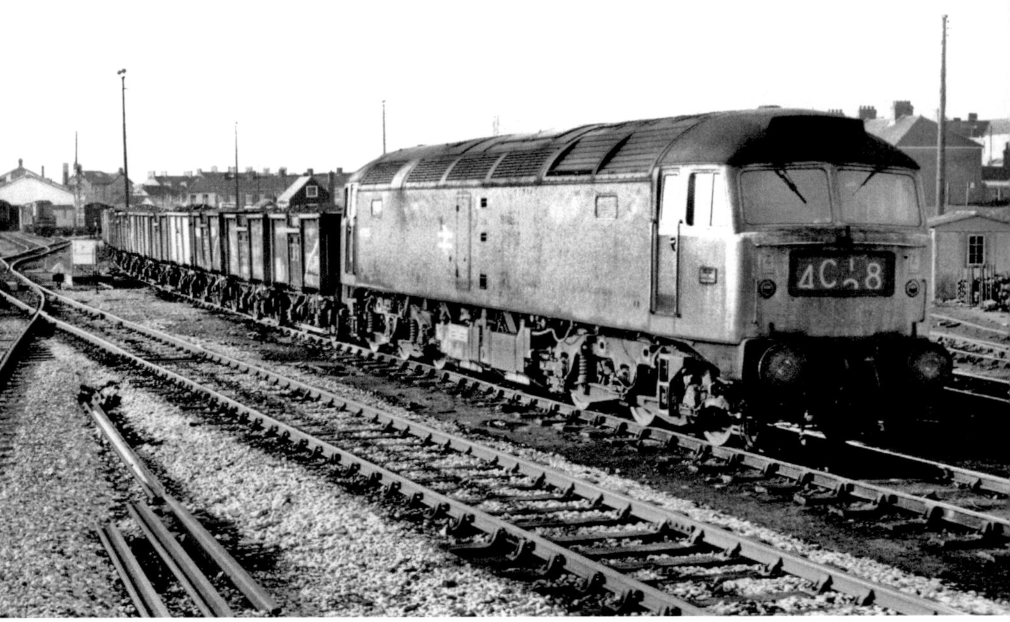

North Wales Coal, Wrexham, January 1974.
Quite a few people would only associate coal mining with South Wales, not North Wales. I was one of them until the latter part of the 1970s. When I took this photograph I presumed this 'Windcutter' (long train of 16-ton-capacity steel-bodied coal wagons) had made its way through Hereford and Shrewsbury from the Welsh Valleys. I was wrong. It had come from nearby Bersham colliery. During the latter part of the 1970s, a series of steam excursions ran past the colliery, which I had learnt still employed a steam loco. One Saturday, I decided to do some strategic linesiding. My intention was to photograph one of the excursions and then visit the colliery. Unfortunately, the steam special didn't run and the colliery's 'kettle' was nowhere to be seen; I came away, with no photographs. I had driven to my supposed ideal location in my ailing VW Beetle, whose exhaust system blew on me while driving home. Not a good day. I rather like this atmospheric, but slightly grim, photograph. It is full of interest: a parcel train being loaded, lower-quadrant semaphore signals, the deserted areas and the sense of movement. The 7 headcode indicates this is an express freight, not fitted with a continuous brake. The letter F indicates it was bound for Nottingham or Liverpool. In this case it is likely to be heading for Liverpool.

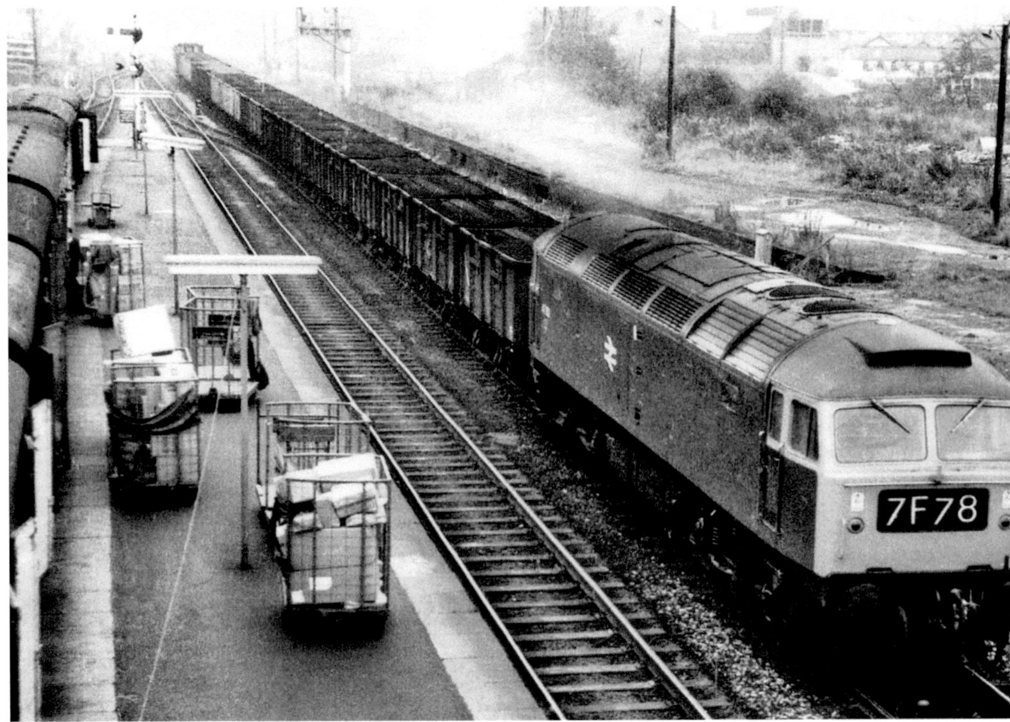

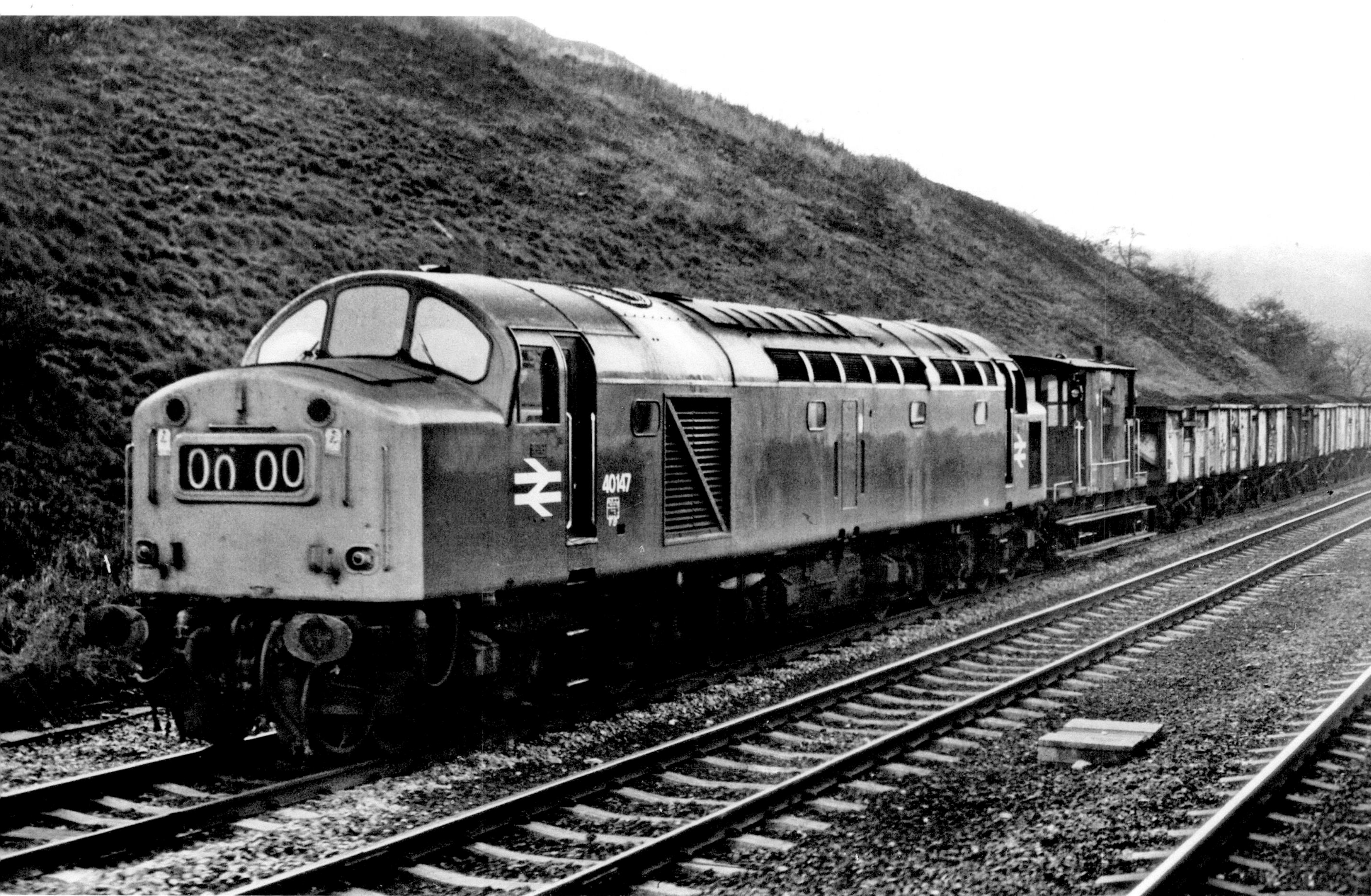

Saturday Working, Micklefield, 20 November 1976.
Wakefield's Healey Mills-allocated 40147 heads up a coal train, which I believe emanated from the nearby Peckfield colliery. The pit was an early closure of the 1980s decimation of Yorkshire coal mines. It closed on 21 October 1980. I can vividly remember bagging this shot while passing on a Class 47-hauled Liverpool Lime Street–Newcastle service. The train was running late because the 47 had to be summoned to replace the train's defective Class 46 at Leeds. The 46 was promptly despatched to nearby Neville Hill Depot for attention. I was excitedly bound for York, where I was going to see and photograph 1023 *Western Fusilier*. The Class 52 had hauled the 'Western Talisman' railtour from London King's Cross. It certainly brought out the crowds that day.

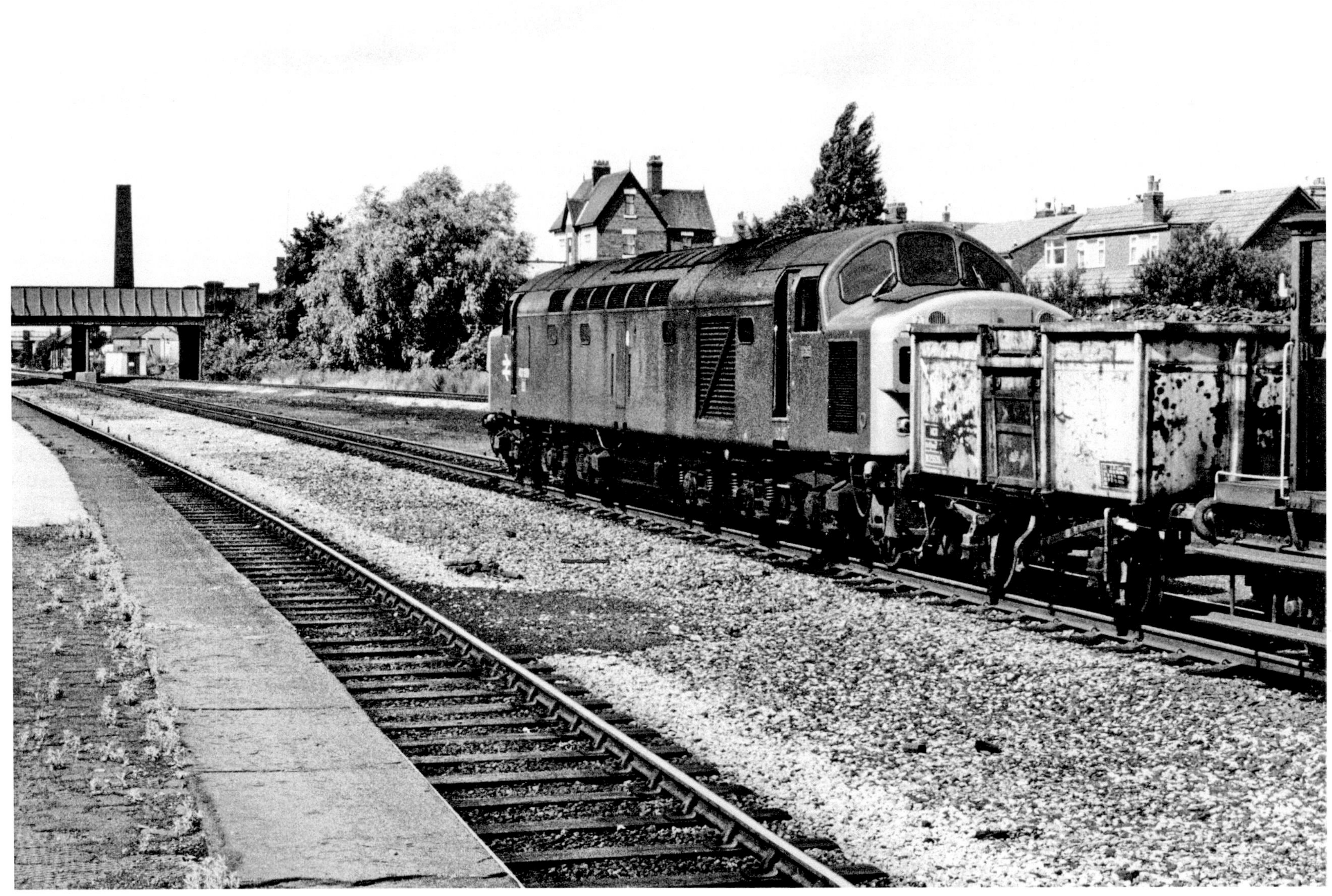

16 Tons of Coal, Poulton–le-Fylde, August 1978.
Super power for such a small freight train, 40139 is about to be routed on to the truncated Fleetwood branch line at Poulton-le-Fylde. The branch was kept alive serving ICI Hillhouse, ICI Burn Naze and Wyre power station. This small delivery of coal could have been bound for any of the three industrial locations. The photograph is a little misleading: behind the brake van are eight ICI tank wagons and another brake van. This suggests the train would be split in two. A photograph of it, looking towards Preston, appears on p. 155 of *British Rail Northern Scene* (my first book). The rail-connected industrial concerns ensured most of the track remained in situ long after the passenger service to Fleetwood came to an end. The Poulton & Wyre Railway Society are now trying to reopen the line for passenger trains. They have already restored Thornton and Cleveley's station in readiness.

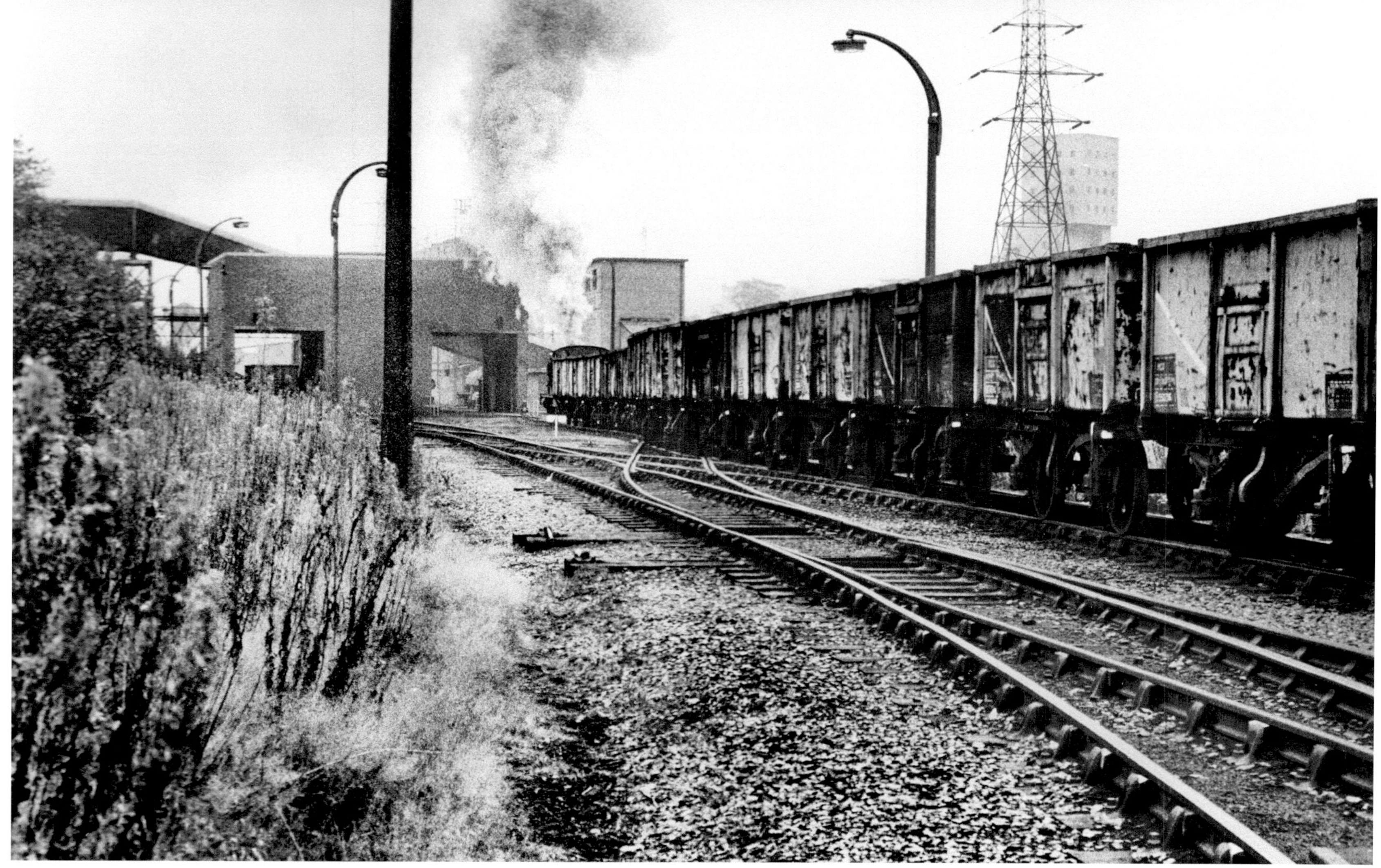

End User, Agecroft, October 1976.

I spent many a happy afternoon at CEGB Agecroft power station – not everybody's way of wistfully remembering their teenage Saturday afternoons. No kidding, it was really good. I used to gain access through the fence separating its coal wagon storage sidings and the football field close to Clifton station. I would arrive on the hourly Manchester Victoria–Blackburn service. The power station had a fleet of three small 'Robert Stephenson' and 'Hawthorn' 0-4-0 saddle tanks. They were named *Agecroft 1*, *Agecroft 2* and *Agecroft 3*, all of which have been preserved. Each day one of the locomotives would push long strings of 16-ton coal wagons through the tippling plant. One by one each wagon would be discharged and its contents would cross the Manchester–Bolton railway line, via conveyor, to feed the power station. This operation was controlled by a red and green light, which would tell the driver when to stop and then push the next wagon in line through the tippler. This process was quite lengthy, allowing me plenty of time to spend in the loco cab or to photograph proceedings. Once the process was complete the empties would be push to the far end of the site. In this shot that's what is happening. At the other end, beyond the A6044, was NCB Agecroft colliery, where the coal trains were supplied from. The little locos would return the empties and bring in another supply. It was a terrific example of integrated working, which worked really well until either the miners or power station workers went on strike. This became a commonplace occurrence during the 1970s and early '80s and resulted in widespread power blackouts and short-time working. The little locos continued doing their jobs into the 1980s, after which they were replaced by a new conveyor system. Agecroft colliery closed in March 1991 and the power station was switched off two years later. The site of the power station is now occupied by HM Prison Forest Bank.

Sand for Rockware Glass, March, 28 August 1977.
No. 31177 hauling a train of empty 'BIS Sand for Rockware Glass Ltd'-emblazoned hopper wagons. Held at the signal near March, it's bound for the large British Industrial sand quarry at Middleton Towers in Norfolk. Once there, it will be reloaded with glass-making sand for one of the Rockware Ltd factories at Doncaster, Worksop or Knottingley.

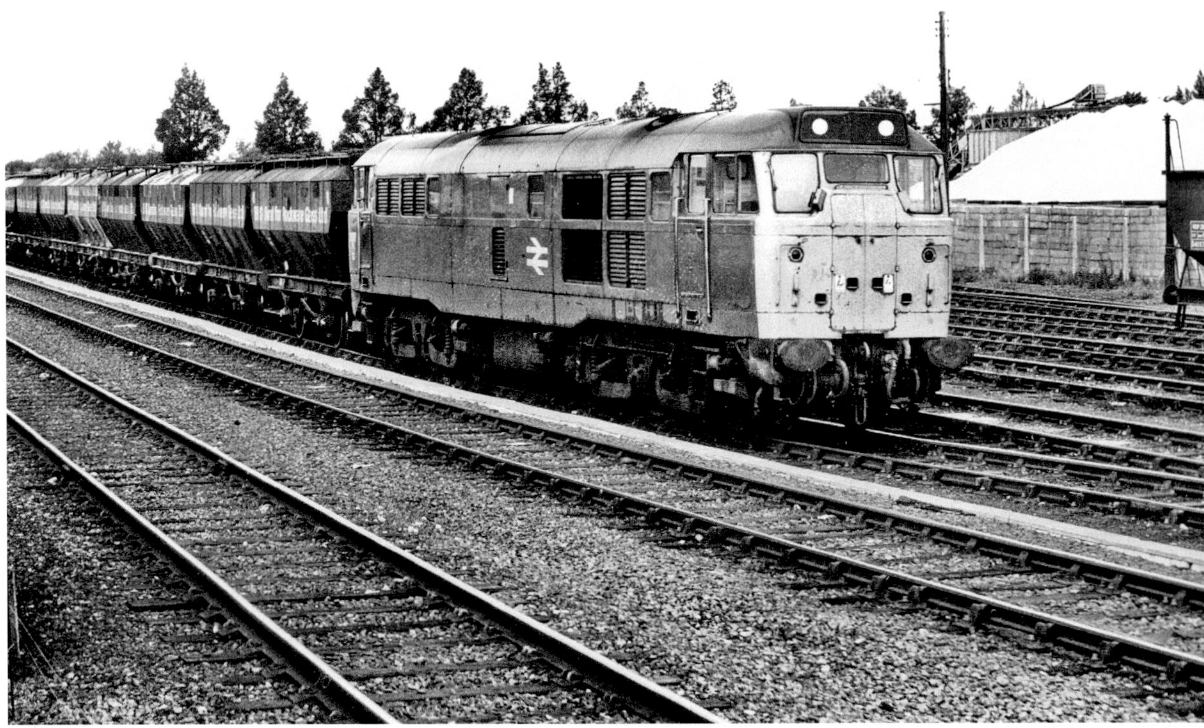

Walls, Godley, September 1973.
No. 76057 motors eastwards through Godley with an empty steel train, made up of pre-Nationalisation bogie bolster wagons. It appears they have been adapted to carry a certain type of steel section, maybe tubes or girders. I have tried to research them, without success. I'm sure someone out there will remember them. The train is passing the Walls factory – bacon, sausages and pies were its speciality. The numbering on the loco had fairly recently modified from E26057 to 76057; it was one of the first 76s to receive a TOPS number.

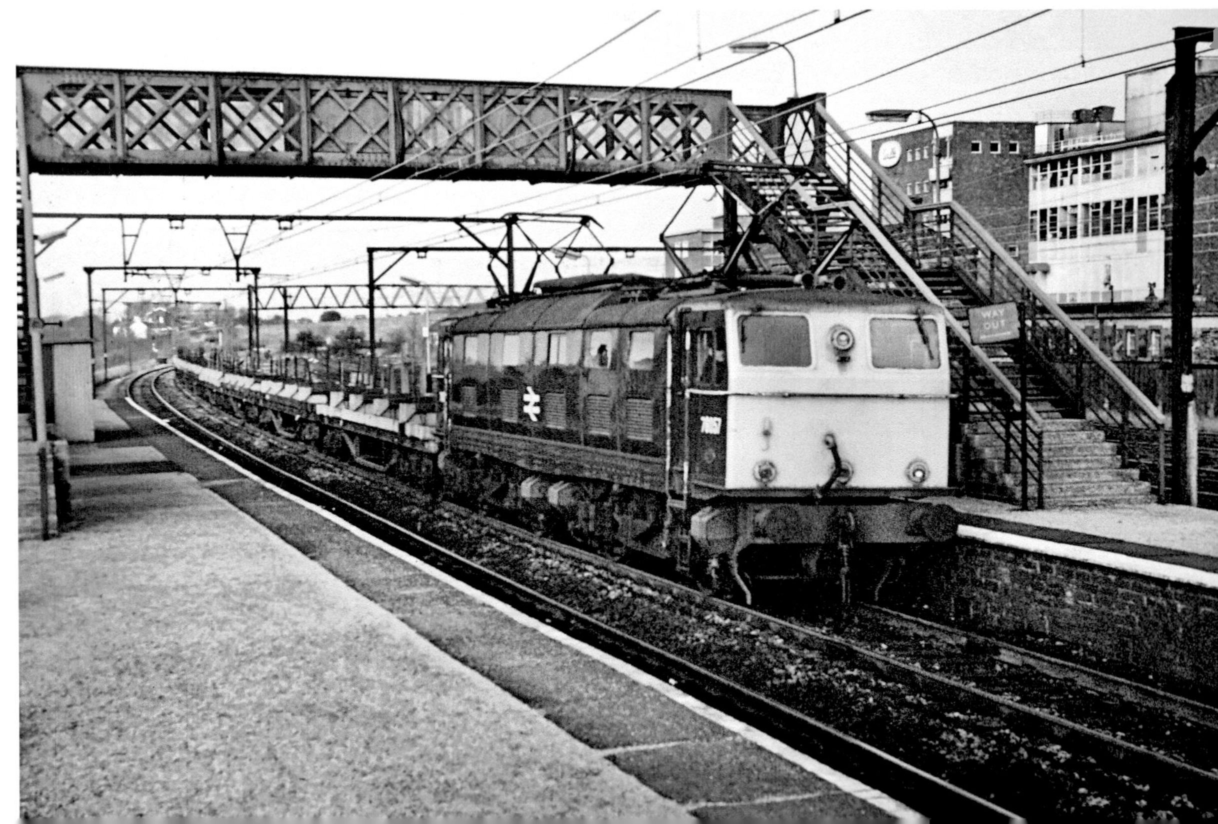

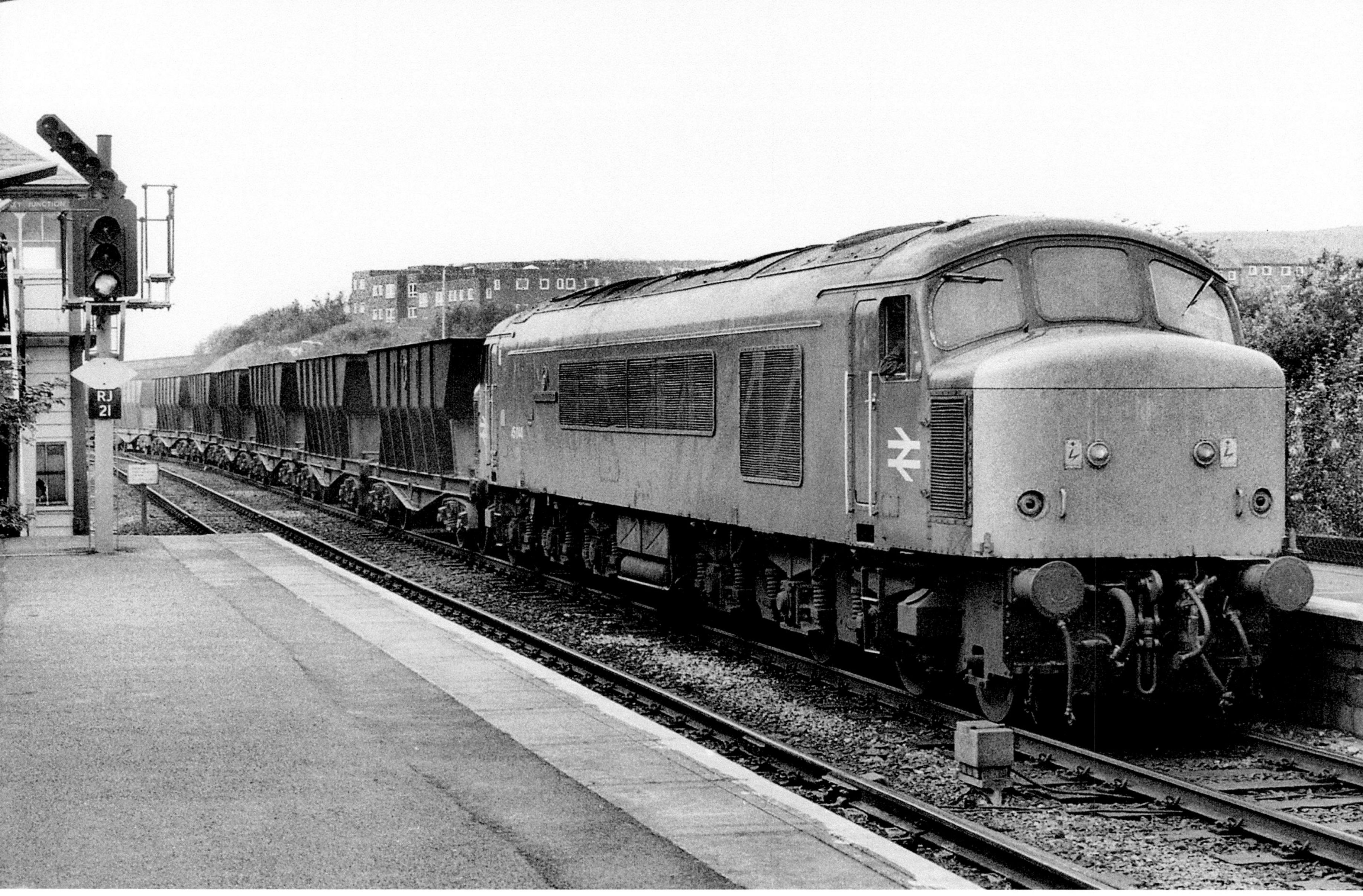

Peak Freight, Marple, July 1980.

No. 45044 *Royal Inniskilling Fusilier* looks out of place approaching Romiley station with its train of empty ICI hopper wagons. It would have looked far better powering along with a rake of Mark 1 blue- and grey-liveried coaches in tow. Displacement by Class 47s and later on HSTs meant that these fine-looking locomotives were increasingly being demoted to freight work. In turn, they were displacing Class 25s and Class 40s. The ICI hopper wagons were introduced during the 1930s to work between the Buxton area limestone quarries and ICI plant at Northwich. They are one of the earliest examples of 'Block Trains'. Their use and operation was highly efficient. In fact, they continued in use until 1997, making them a definite success story. A few still survive, some in preservation.

5 END OF THE LINE

INTRODUCTION

'End of the line' sounds very final; in some cases it is. In others it's the precursor for something new or perhaps a return journey. Maybe it's the start of an adventure or new experience? It could be the changeover point on part of a longer journey. In some cases it can be the enforced stopping point on a truncated route somewhere. This selection of photographs covers quite a few of these possibilities and perhaps show a few more I haven't considered.

Unfortunately, the 1970s and '80s days of mass scrapping of rolling stock and locos did often mean that I regularly came across the negative side of the phrase. Yards and depots were littered with forlorn hardware waiting for the scrap men. In some cases this hardware was relatively new. The BR Western Region diesel hydraulics were prime examples – in particular the Manchester-built 'Hymeks'. The effects of Dr Beeching's rail network cuts meant that all too often a line would end far short of its original destination. Truncated lines serving rail-linked industrial concerns, such as coal mines, milk plants and chemical works, were plentiful. These downgraded freight-only lines snookered the Beeching's plans a little. Now they have long gone, as a result of the places they served closing. Truncated passenger lines were also dotted about, serving places deemed worthy to still have a railway station. Barnstaple immediately springs to mind. I remember taking photographs at the station and in the town when the infrastructure was tantalisingly still in place. It was a clear reminder of the recently closed section of the route to Ilfracombe. A group of preservationists had a plan to save the line to the seaside town, but sadly it failed. In addition, lines ran off from the freight-only line down to Meeth, which were all once part of the Southern Railway's 'Atlantic Coast Express' crack train service. Fortunately, the line from Exeter to Barnstaple – the Tarka Line – still survives.

There were two down-at-heel end-of-the-line stations that were definitely not meant to survive beyond the early 1980s: Clayton West and Bury Bolton Street. I, of course, just had to take lots of photographs at each place. Miraculously both have found new leases of life. Clayton West is now the terminus of the excellent Kirklees Light Railway. Bury Bolton Street is the HQ and hub of the superb 1950s, '60s and '70s time-warp East Lancashire Railway. The complete environment is so well done, with the result that my recently taken photographs on the railway could pass as being from the 1970s.

The more upbeat aspect of the end of the line was busy terminus stations: the gateway to town, city or seaside destinations.

Favourites of mine were the capital and holiday destinations such as Blackpool and Scarborough. Back in the 1970s and '80s seaside destinations featured heavily on BR Merrymaker excursion train itineraries. They were usually loco-hauled and brought all sorts of welcome sights to seaside towns. Class 20s, 25s, 31s, 37s, 40s, 45s, 47s, 50s, 52s and 55s all had a part to play bringing train loads of townies to the nation's seaside destinations. They are also the gateway to a new journey, the start of a new chapter. I have my fingers crossed that you enjoy this one.

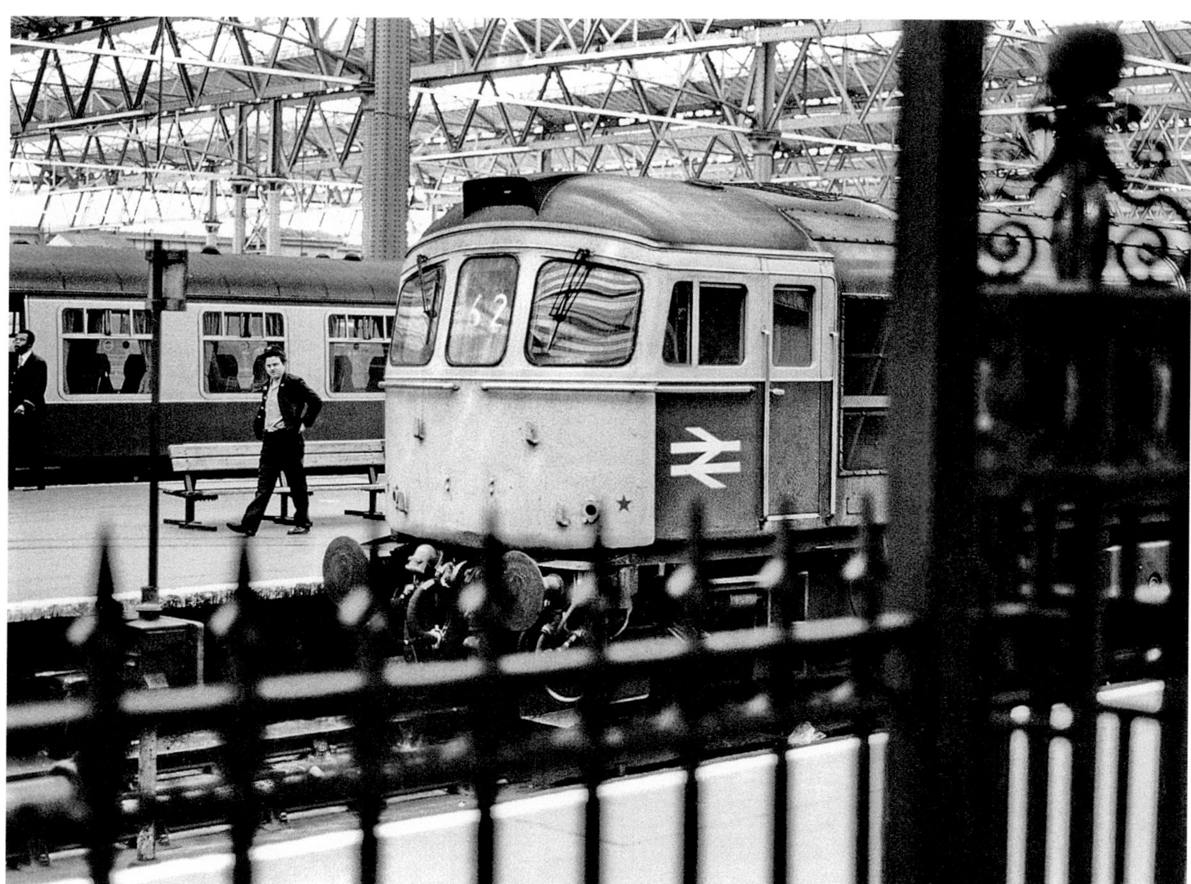

'Who are you looking at?' London Waterloo, April 1978.
I caught the station worker's eye as I snapped this over-the-fence photograph. I wonder what he is thinking? He has probably seen lots of other photographers taking shots at this handy vantage point. Since it was erected, millions of people must have peered over this superb iron fence. It's a brilliant place to watch the station's bustling activity and simply look at the trains – particularly watching them arrive and depart. It is also ideal for waving someone off or looking out for somebody who has just arrived. The Class 33, seen in this photograph, has recently pulled up a safe distance away from the buffer stops with an afternoon working from Exeter St Davids, via Salisbury.

Waterloo Reflections, April 1981.
The day's intermittent April showers are very much in evidence in this end-of-the-line bay platform photograph of 73110. The puddles on the platform are creating plenty of incomplete reflections of the versatile electro-diesel loco. I am guessing it is between station pilot and 'Thunderbird' duties. This class of loco has fared very well: a sizeable proportion have either been preserved or remain in service on the modern railway network. The Great Central Railway Nottingham helped to preserve 73110 by providing a home for it.

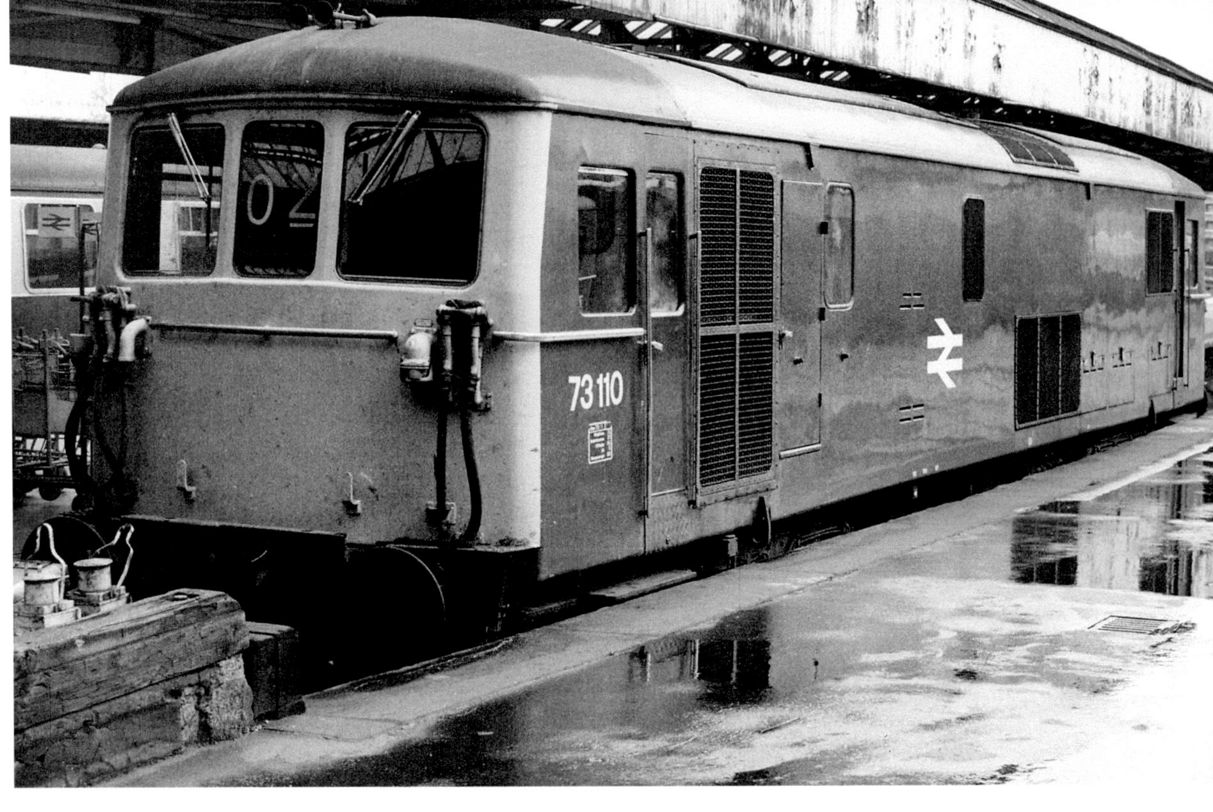

Read All About It, London Paddington, May 1979.
This chap is so engrossed in his newspaper he hasn't noticed me taking this photograph. Standing at the buffer stops of London Paddington's Platform 5 is 253034. Alongside on Platform 6 is 253003. By 1979, the highly successful Inter-City 125 Class 253 sets had become well established on the Western Region's principal mainline routes, usurping the Class 50s. This has remained the case well into the twenty-first century, bearing testament to their great design – without doubt, one of BR's best ever rolling-stock investments.

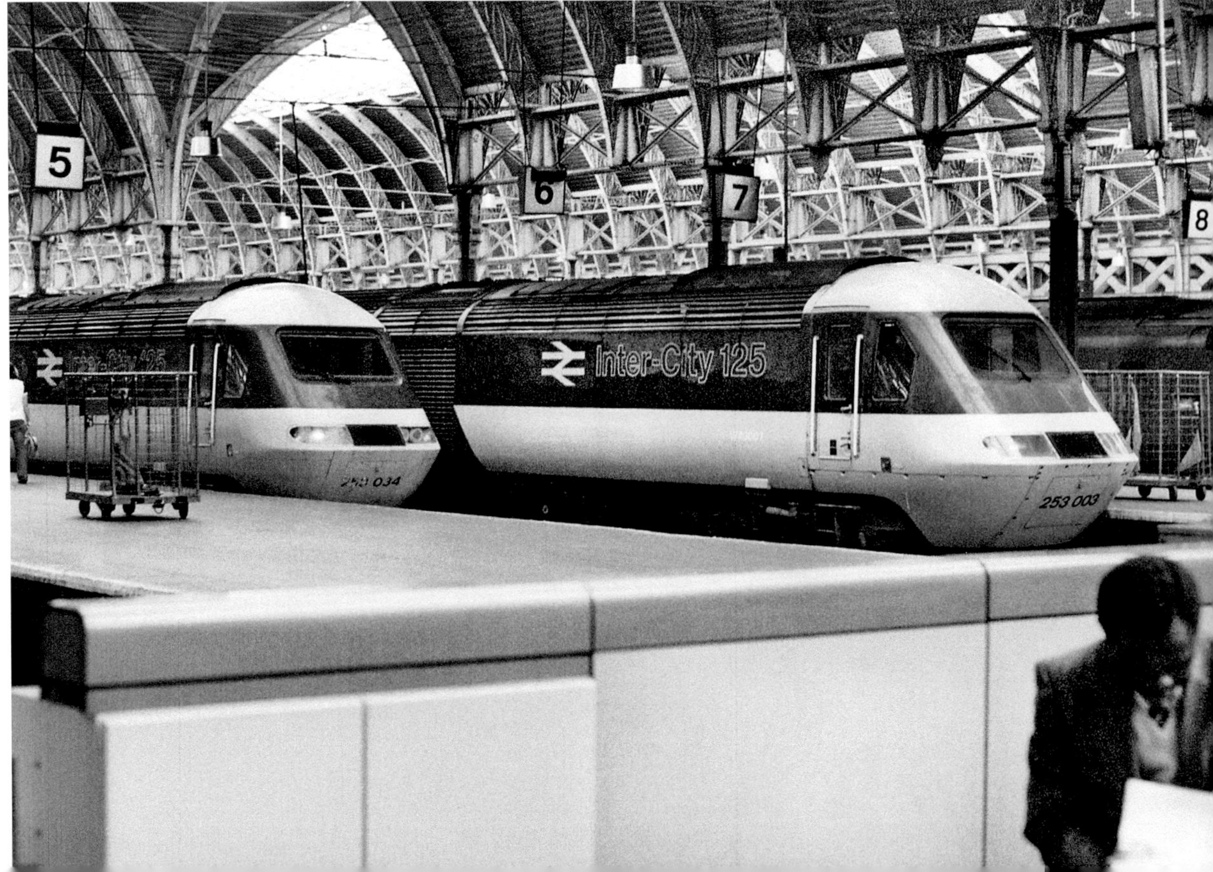

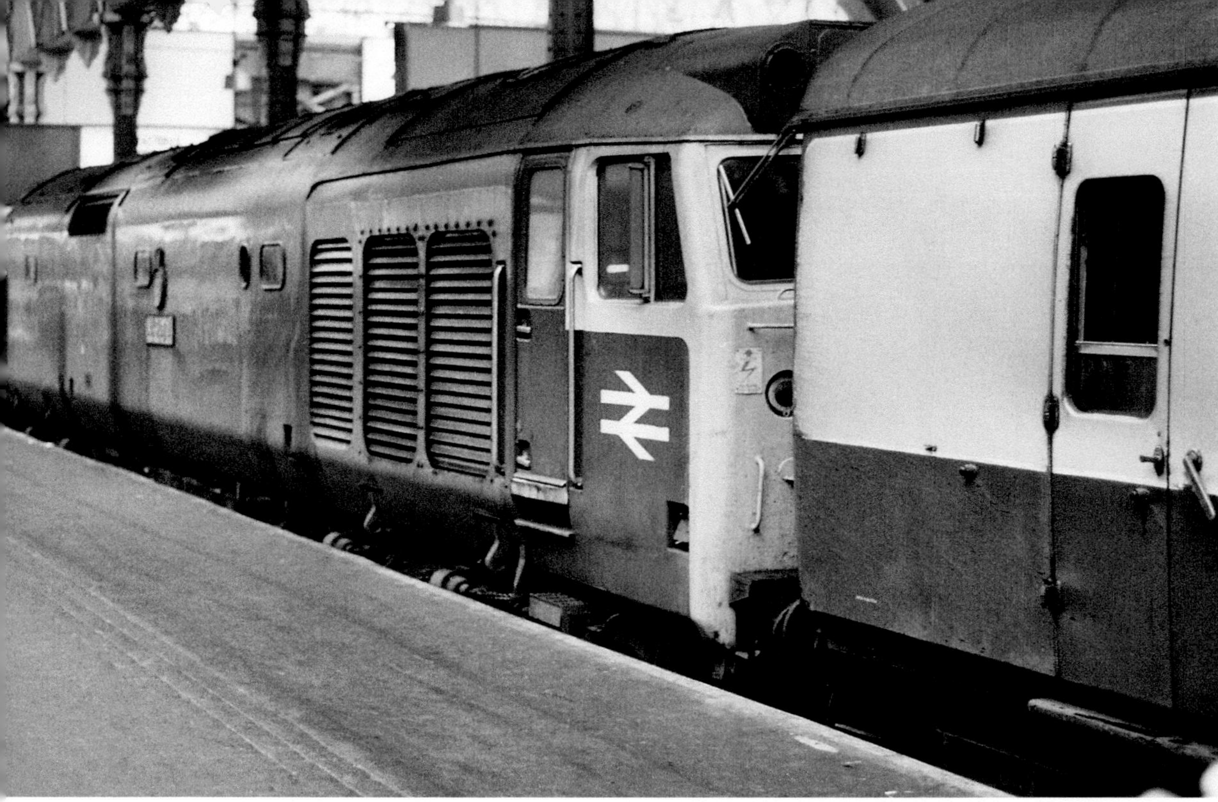

Ark Royal, London Paddington, May 1979.
Despite their supremacy on the Western Region mainlines coming to an end, Class 50s were still commonplace at Paddington when I took this photograph. 50035 *Ark Royal* has been brought to a stand close to the buffer stops after arriving with a train from the West Country. It will have made a splendid sight viewed from the busy station concourse. The loco was withdrawn on 3 August 1990 and then preserved by The Fifty Fund. It was handed over to the preservation group during the 1991 Old Oak Common Open Day. It has since had spells hauling trains, principally on the Severn Valley Railway.

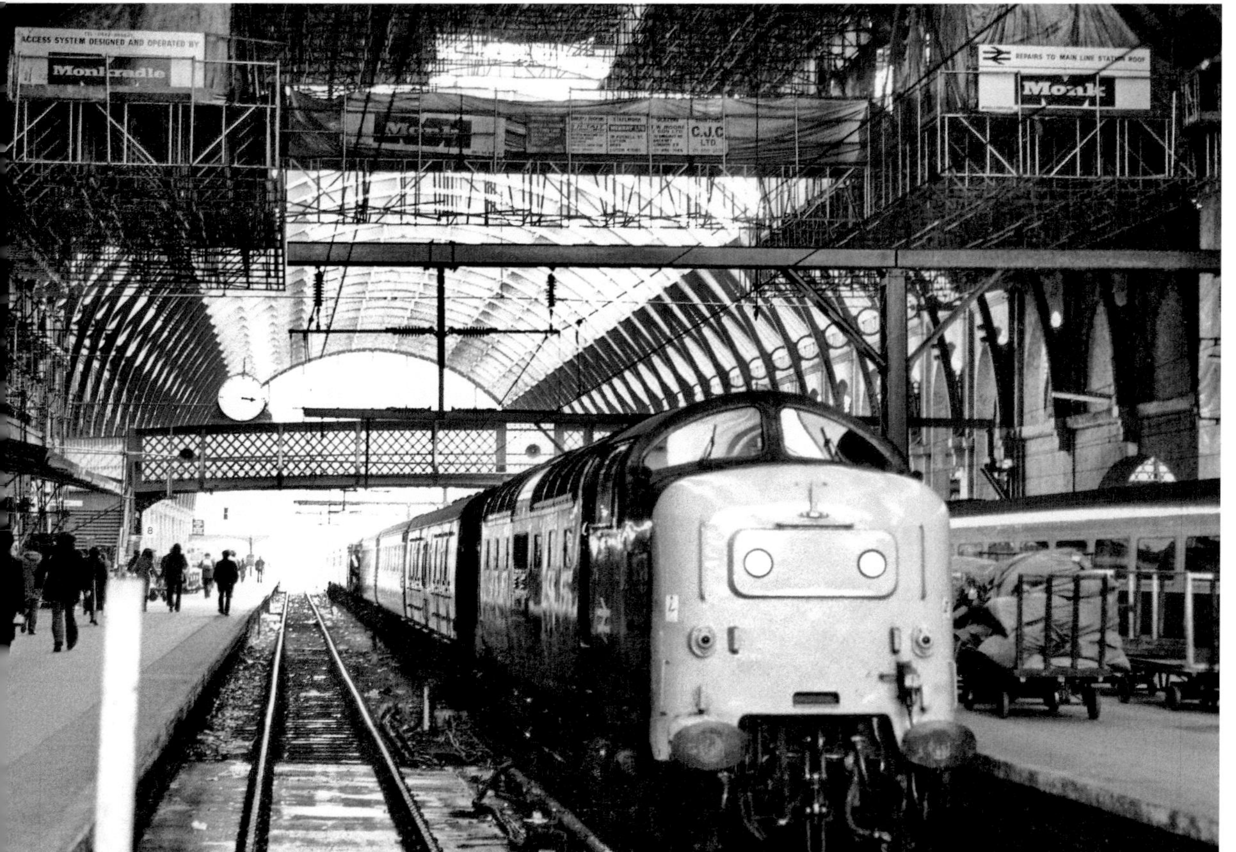

'Deltic' Arrival, London King's Cross, March 1980.
A classic buffer-stop view of King's Cross station, made all the better for the presence of the 'Deltic'. Midway down the train somebody appears to have a carriage door open and is about to climb down on to the track. Hopefully, it is a rail worker. Above the train there's plenty of repair or refurbishment being undertaken to the station's roof. The signs tell us it has been sub contracted by BR to Monk. They are using their specially designed 'Monkcradle' to assist in their sizeable task. There are plenty of passengers walking away from my camera, along Platform 8. Presumably, they will be boarding a yet-to-arrive mainline train on that platform or are going to catch a suburban or outer suburban train. Did they notice the scaffolding high above them?

Lord Nelson at Euston, London, April 1979.
On the day I took this photograph, Lord Nelson was being remembered at Trafalgar Square and Euston. 87018 *Lord Nelson* had arrived at London Euston, Platform 7 a few minutes earlier with a service from Manchester Piccadilly. I was on it. I ran up the ramp to take this photograph, just in case the train was quickly drawn out of the station as empty stock. I needn't have bothered as it would later form a return working to Manchester. Could the two mailbags haphazardly lying on the platform have fallen off a platform trolley? There are few neatly parked nearby. It wasn't the best of photographic conditions in the confines of the 1960s-built station – very similar to Birmingham New Street. This photograph was a handheld, wide aperture, slow shutter-speed job.

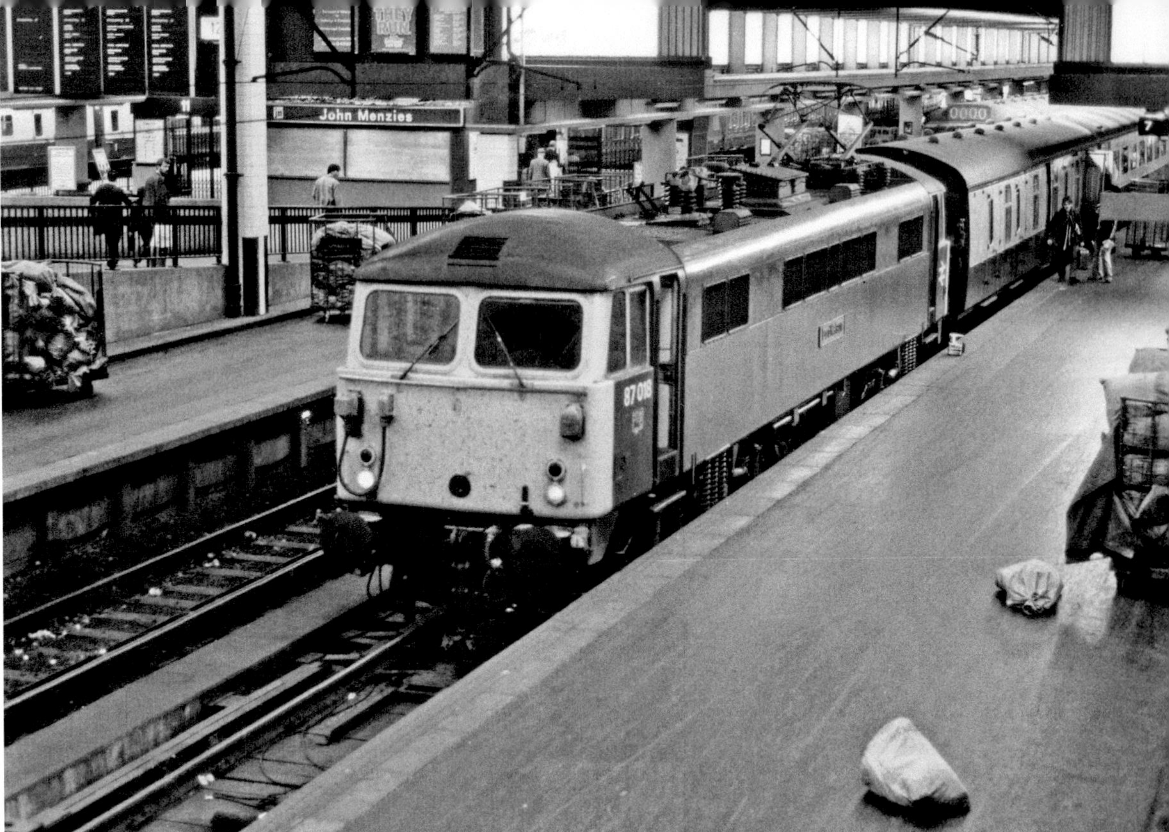

Isle of Wight Tube, Ryde Pier, May 1976.
End of the line at Ryde – any further and the train would be in the Solent. This superbly vintage ex-London Underground Standard Tube train dates from the 1920s. BR's Stewarts Lane Depot refurbished six four-car Class 485 sets and six three-car Class 486 sets during 1966 and 1967, after which, they crossed the sea, by ferry of course, to the Isle of Wight. They were destined for use on the island's newly electrified and truncated railway system. Class 485 number 043 makes a rather odd sight waiting to depart from Ryde Pier. It would soon pull away, once the ferry passengers from the mainland had boarded the train. Working close to the sea, these EMUs suffered quite badly from salt-induced corrosion. Nevertheless they provided good service, the last being withdrawn during 1992. The whole fleet was replaced, with more ex-London Underground Tube stock being introduced during 1989. The new incumbents are two-car sets known as Class 483s. Two trailer cars from the withdrawn Class 485/486 sets were saved for preservation. They now form part of London Transport's operational 'Standard Stock' museum train.

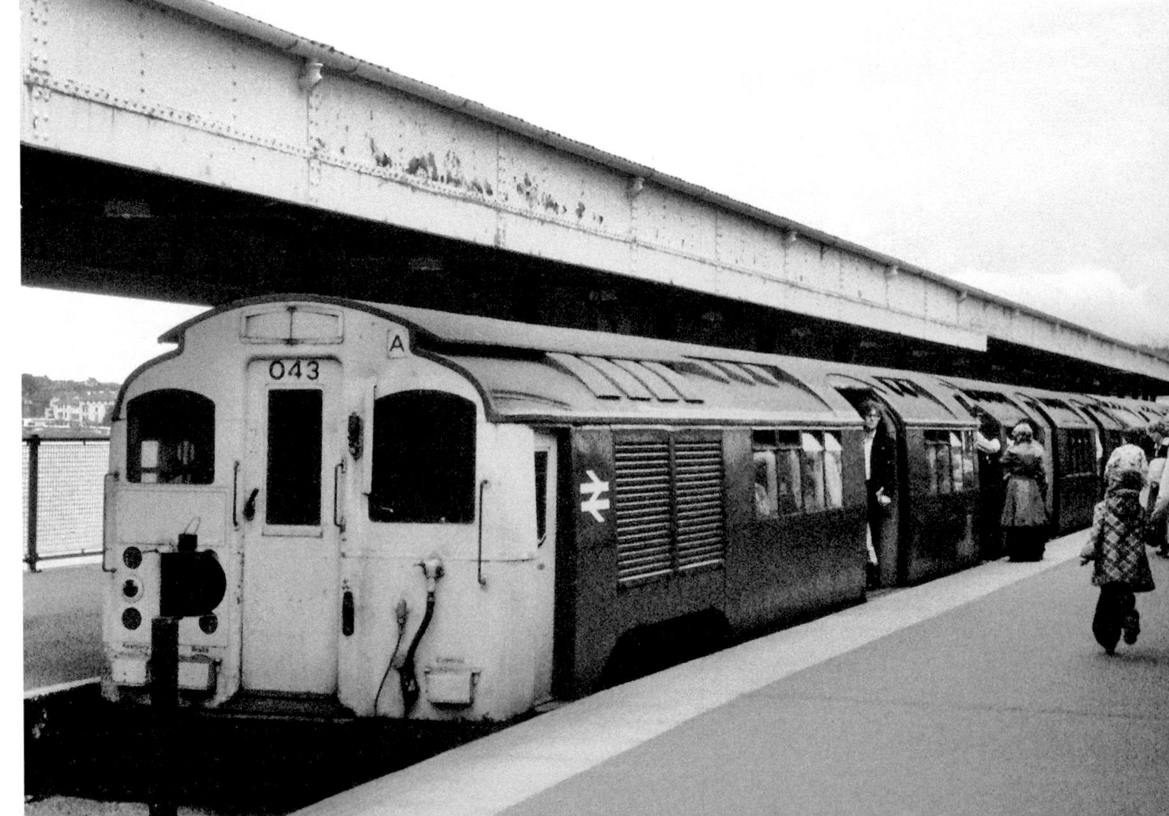

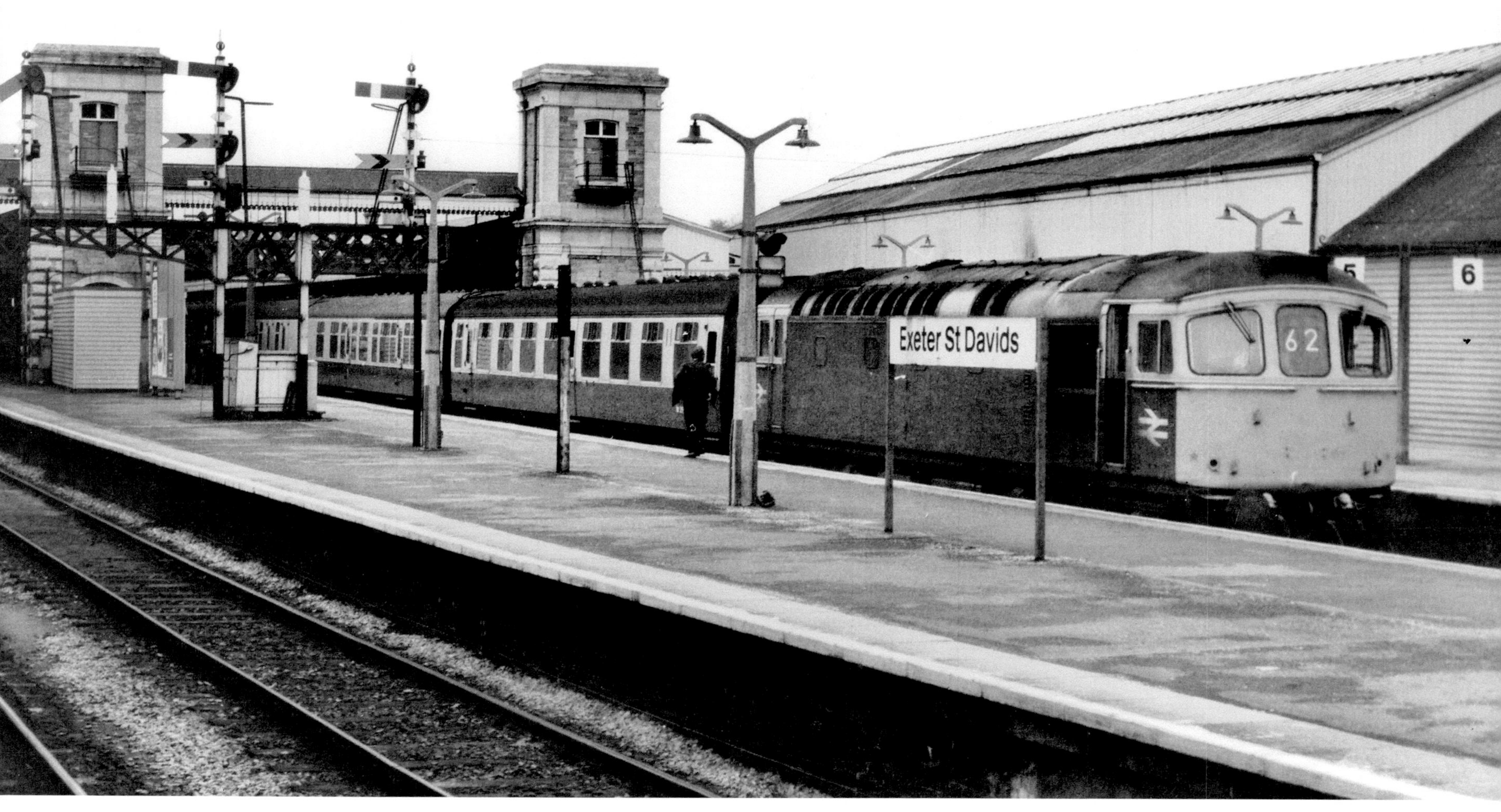

Southern in Great Western Heartland, Exeter St Davids, March 1974.
The first time I visited the West Country, during the summer of 1973, I found it odd to see a Southern Region train at Exeter St Davids. The Class 33 in this photograph has just arrived there with a morning train from London Waterloo. I still think it looks a little out of place standing amidst the station's vast array of ex-GWR paraphernalia. It hadn't dawned on me that the Southern's London Waterloo passenger services had called there on their way to and from North Devon, Plymouth and Cornwall for decades. By the time I took this photograph, while aboard a BR excursion from Manchester, these services were being terminated at St Davids. The Beeching cuts had decimated the ex-LSWR North Devon routes, leaving just a few freight-only lines and the passenger service from Exeter to Barnstaple. Ten years later Class 33s were travelling miles away from their Southern strongholds. I would never have dreamt that they would one day be regularly hauling trains to and from Manchester Piccadilly.

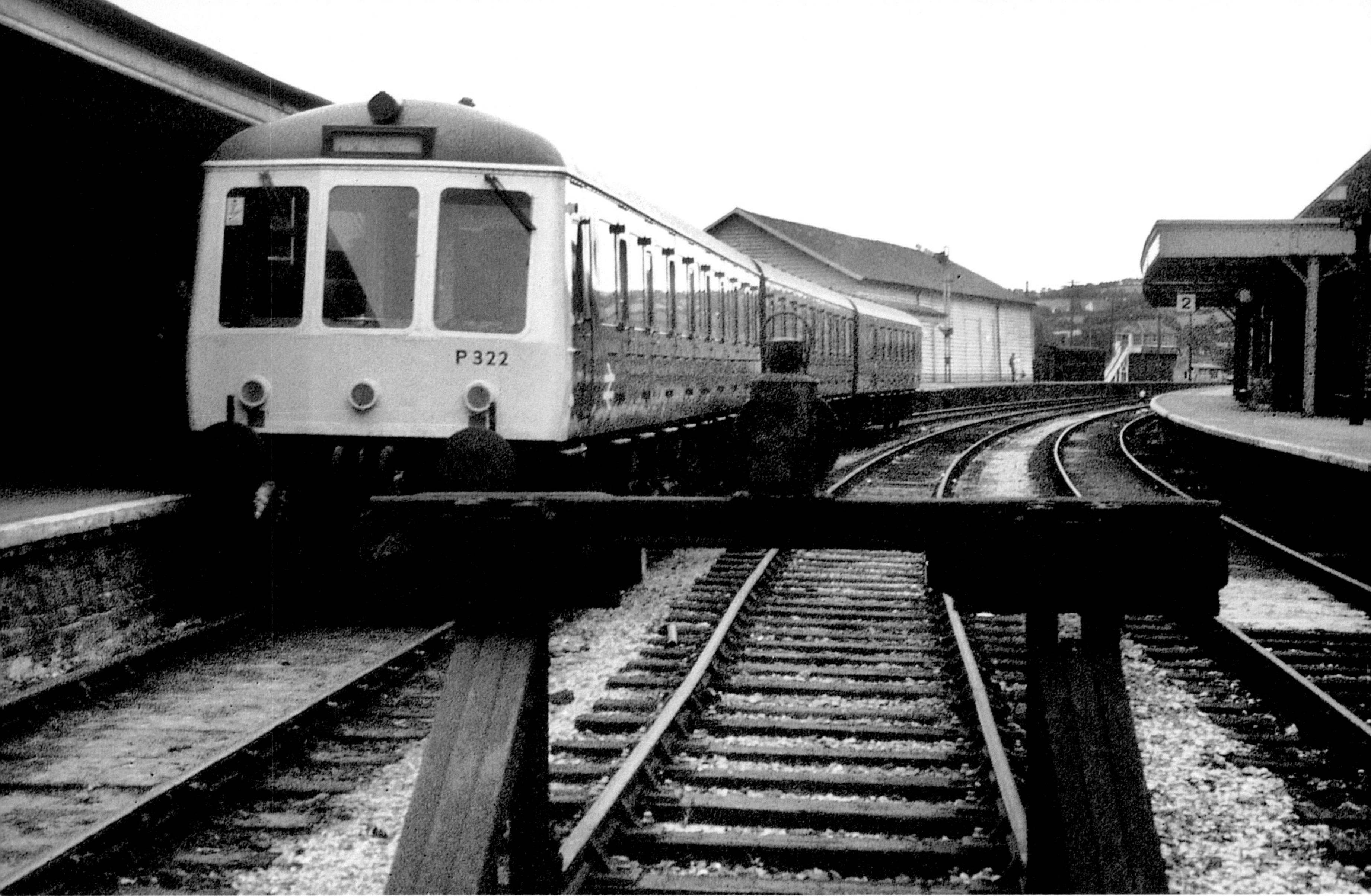

Truncated 'Withered Arm', Barnstaple, August 1974.

The 'Withered Arm' was the very apt name given to the ex-LSWR amazing array of lines built to infiltrate the Great Western's Devon and Cornwall kingdom. I guess the railway company had hoped their North Devon destinations, such as Bideford and Ilfracombe, would become as popular as the GWR's South Devon 'English Riviera'. Sadly it didn't happen and so during the 1960s and early 1970s they were axed from BR's passenger service map. This photograph is of Plymouth-based suburban three-car DMU, formation number P322, which has just arrived at Barnstaple from Exeter St Davids. The station is largely intact, still waiting for the 'Atlantic Coast Express' to arrive from London Waterloo. It would never arrive, having last ran ten years earlier. It would have had portions for Ilfracombe and Torrington, which split and met at Barnstaple. Part of the remaining infrastructure included the still operational goods depot and signal box. The platform to the right still had freight trains passing through serving Bideford, Torrington and Meeth. The freight service ended in 1982. The lines were lifted and the track bed became the popular 'Tarka Trail'. This then made Barnstaple the end of the line for the truncated 'Withered Arm'. It now just has one platform and track.

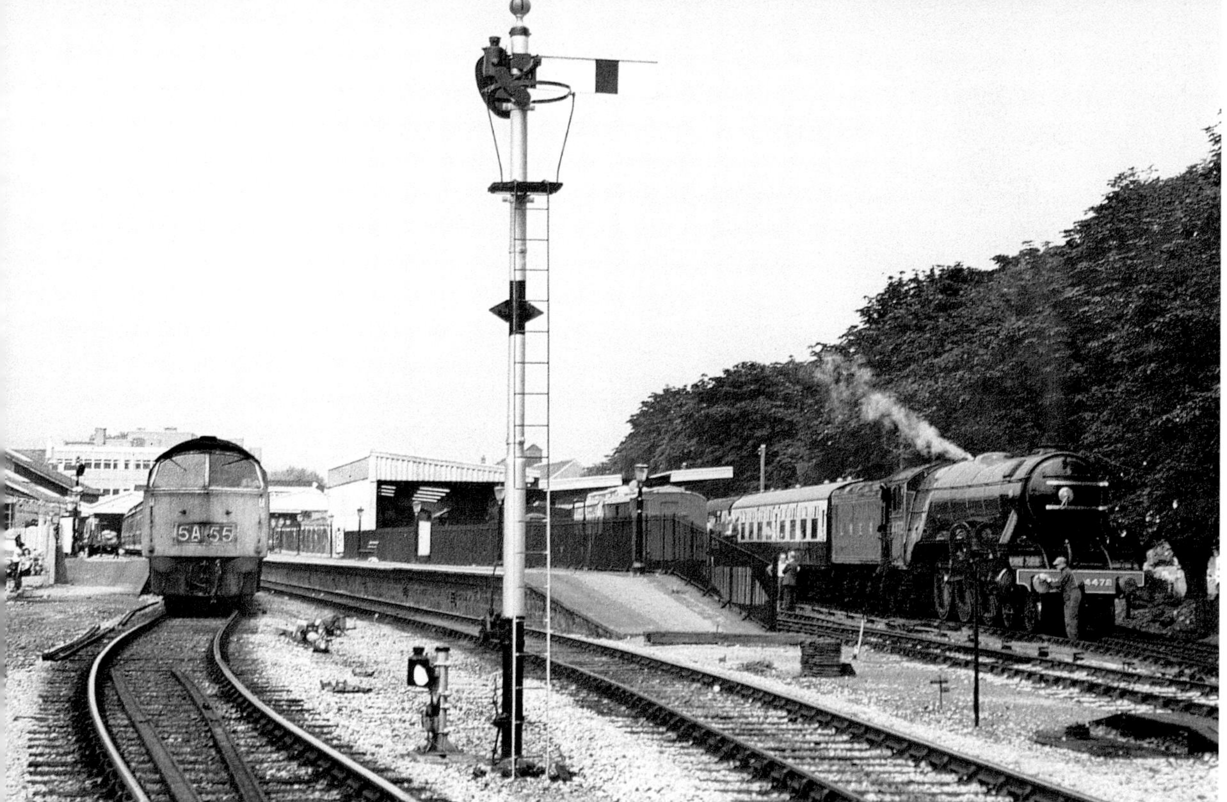

The Start and End of the Line, Paignton, July 1973.
Until one year prior to me taking this photograph, BR ran passenger services through to Kingswear. A beautiful place on the River Dart, the line down to Kingswear has stunning scenery – making it a must-do train trip. I can't understand why BR decided to truncate their line from Newton Abbot at Paignton. Anyway, by the time I took this photograph, on a glorious July day in 1973, the end of the line was Paignton and the Dart Valley Railway had taken over the line to Kingswear. This shot shows a Class 52 'Western' waiting to take empty coaching stock to the carriage sidings. Alongside is the new Torbay Steam Railway station, from where the steam railway's trains departed for Kingswear. Recently repatriated from America and restored to working order 4472 *Flying Scotsman* is waiting to depart with a morning working. During the summer of 1973 the world famous loco shared haulage of services with the railway's preserved ex-GWR steam locos.

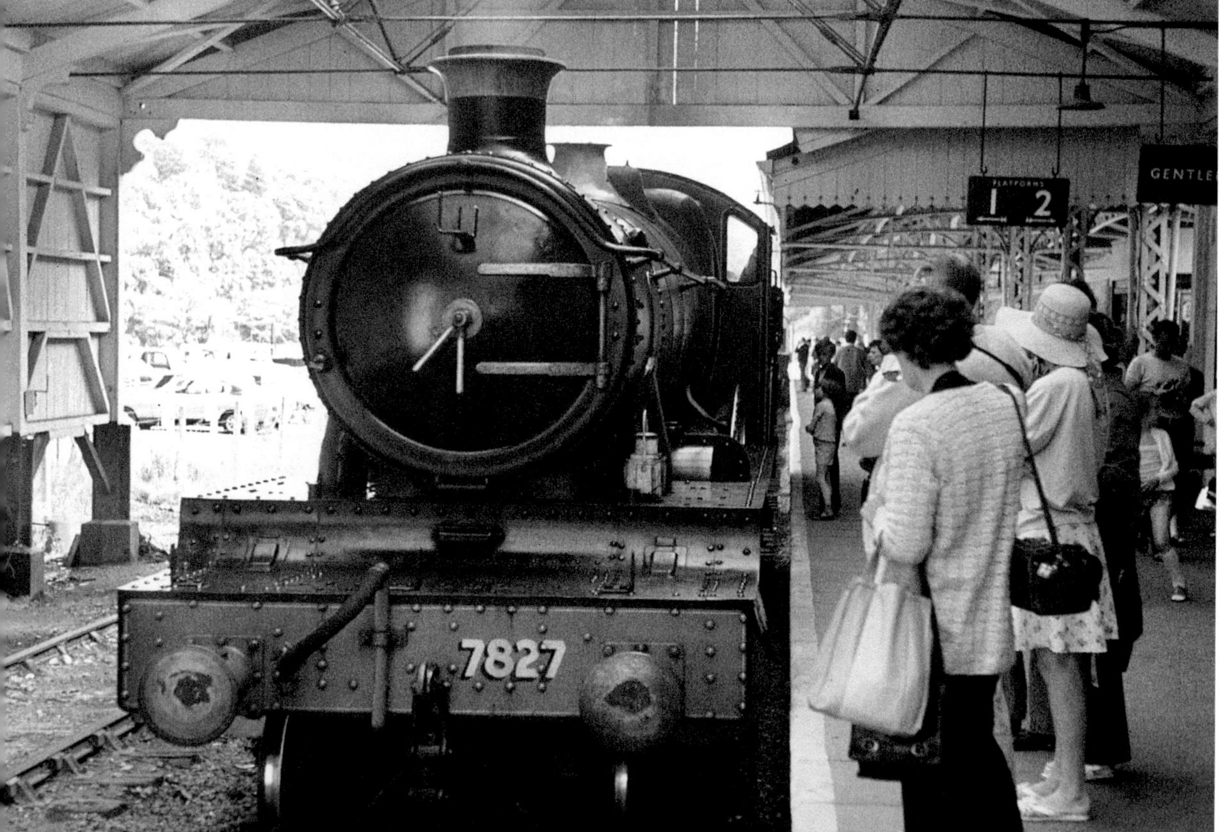

End of the Line, Kingswear, July 1973.
While being the end of the line from Paignton, and once upon a time from London Paddington, this shot taken on the newly reopened line signifies a new beginning. The station is very much how BR left it one year earlier, complete with Western Region enamel signs. The loco, 7827 *Lydham Manor*, was built by BR in 1950 and was withdrawn just fifteen years later. It went to Barry scrap line, then rescued and restored by the Dart Valley Railway in readiness for the reopening of this route. It is strange to think that back then the GWR-designed steam loco was only 23 years old. The onlookers, including me, probably thought it was much older. The line has thrived ever since it was taken over from BR and the loco still hauls trains on it.

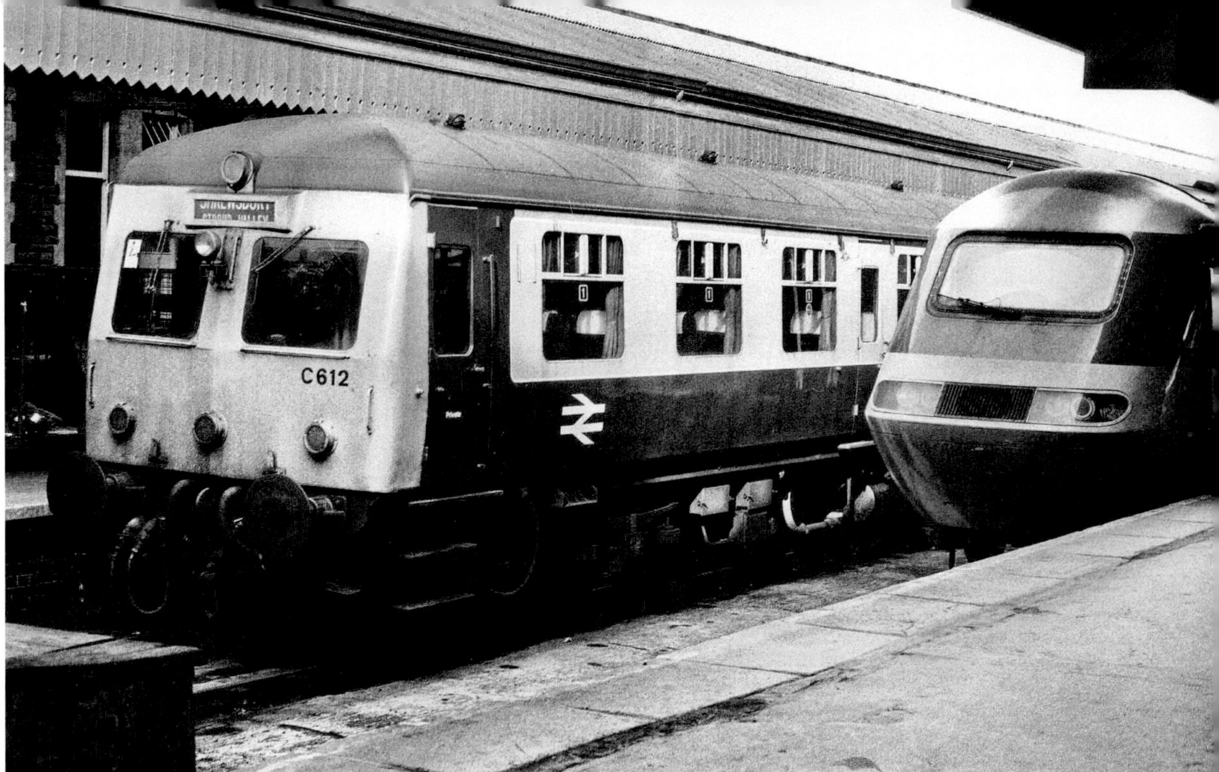

Journey's End, Swansea, 19 February 1977.
I took this photograph shortly after arriving at Swansea on an unusually sunny February afternoon. Using a Round-Robin ticket from Manchester to Swansea and back, I travelled south via the Mid Wales Line and back home using the Central Wales Line. I travelled on this HST (253003) from Cardiff Central to my journey's end. Alongside it, at the buffer stops, is my return train, which would take me to Shrewsbury. It wasn't much dearer to buy a first-class ticket, so I did. You can see the first-class part of the homeward-bound Class 120 DMU in which I travelled in luxury on a very enjoyable and interesting day out, at an amazingly cheap price. Thank goodness the Central Wales Line survived the Beeching cuts – it is wonderful. You can still buy Round-Robin tickets in certain areas – they are well worth investigating.

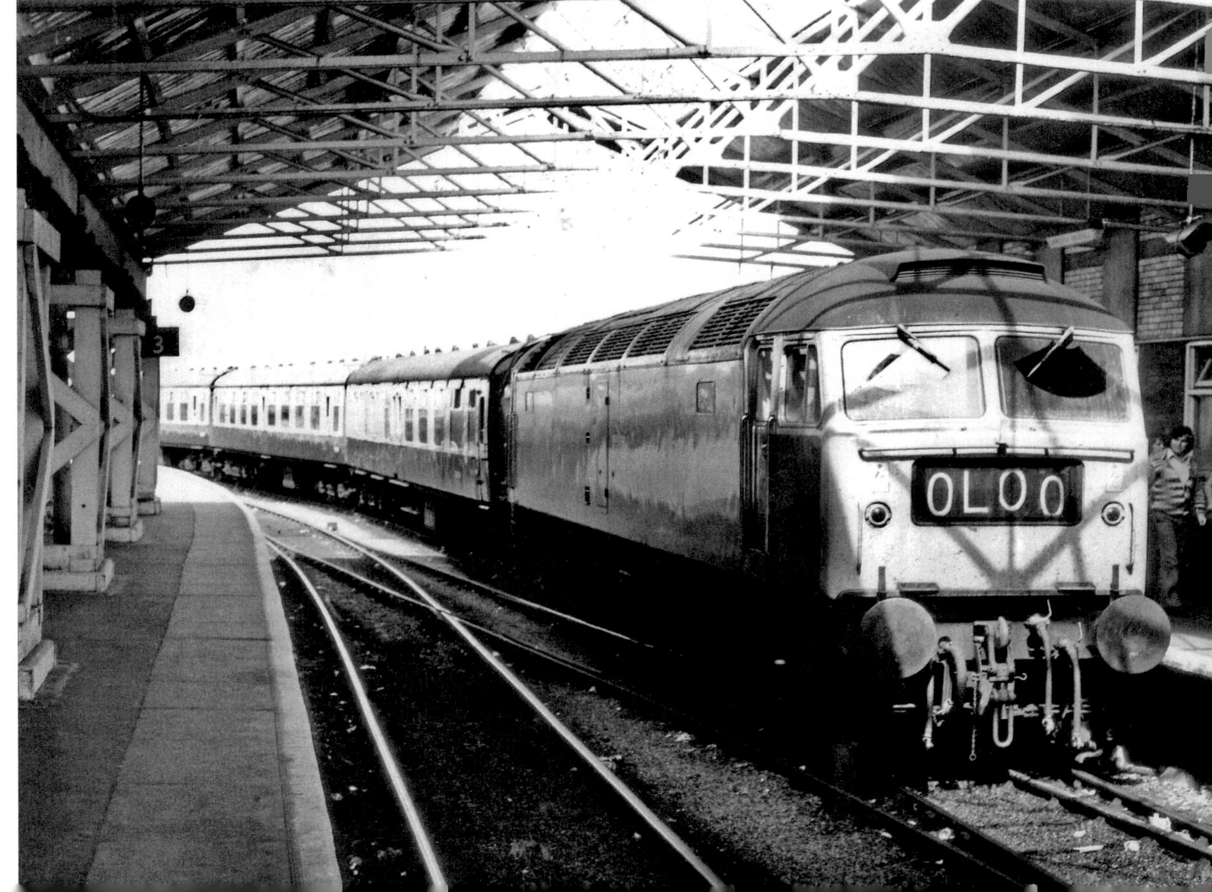

An Afternoon at the Seaside, Great Yarmouth, 28 August 1977.
Great Yarmouth's curiously short overall roof must have only been meant for small trains, such as the two-car DMUs. 47340 and its train accentuate the petiteness of it. The train has just arrived with an excursion from Manchester Piccadilly. I was on it. The loco would soon be uncoupled and then draw forward to the buffer stop. After that move, it would reverse over the cross over and then run alongside Platform 3 to the far end of the station. This would be followed by the loco coupling up to the rear of the train and then shunting it backwards so that it would stand close to the buffer stops. It spent the whole of the afternoon there. It is a good job it wasn't raining, because the two-car DMUs that shuttled to and from Norwich had to use the roofless Platform 1, while the big train was in town.

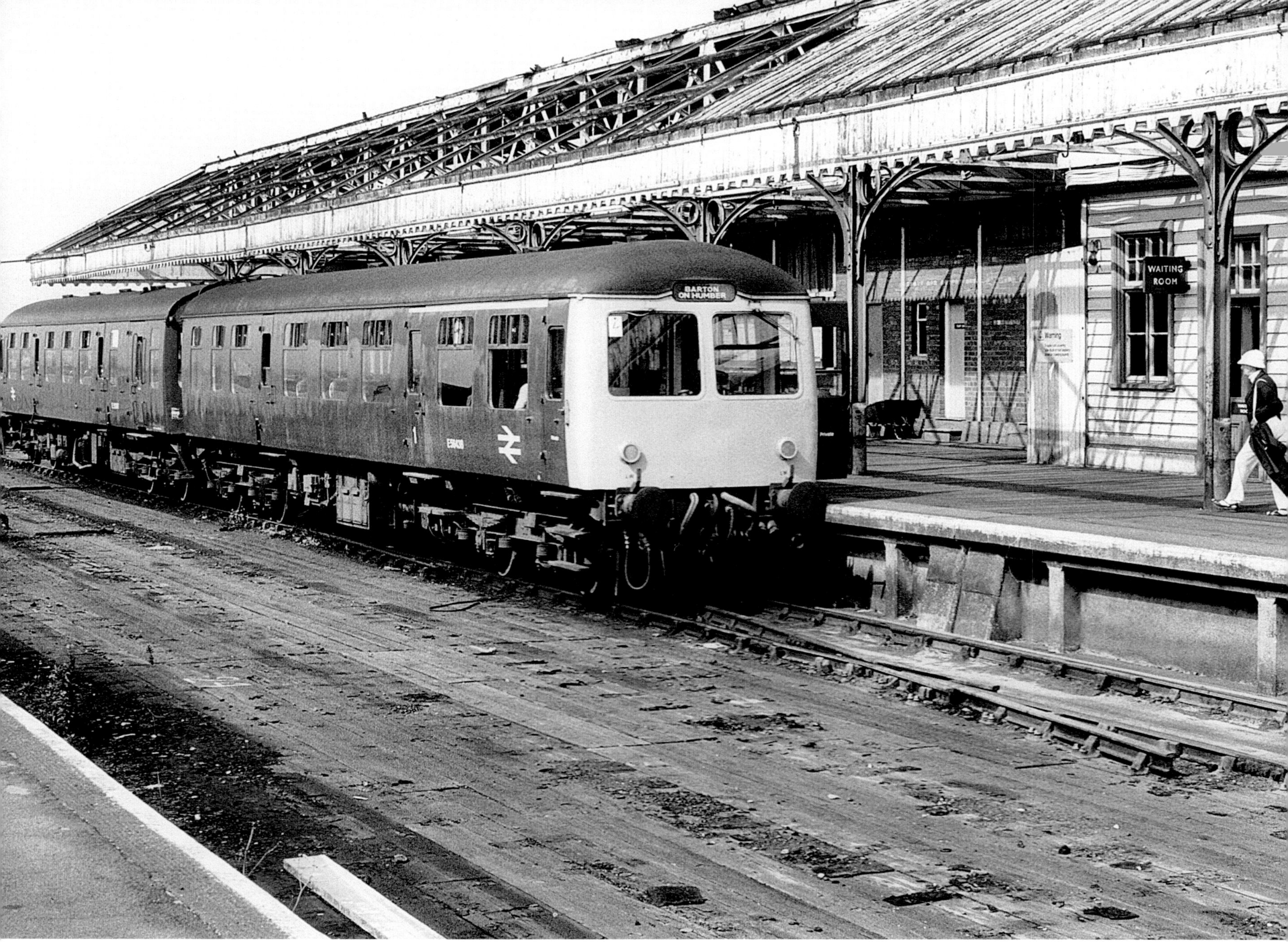

Where's the Roof Gone? New Holland Pier, August 1980.
The canopy glass-roof section has disappeared; it must have blown away in the high winds. The station extended out into the Humber Estuary and, looking at the state of it, I am surprised more of it had not ended up in the water – a terrific end-of-the-line station, which was sadly soon-to-be closed. The Sealink Hull–New Holland ferry it served would become redundant as soon as the Humber Bridge was opened. The Class 105 DMU is waiting to depart for the next leg of its journey, to New Holland and Barton-upon-Humber.

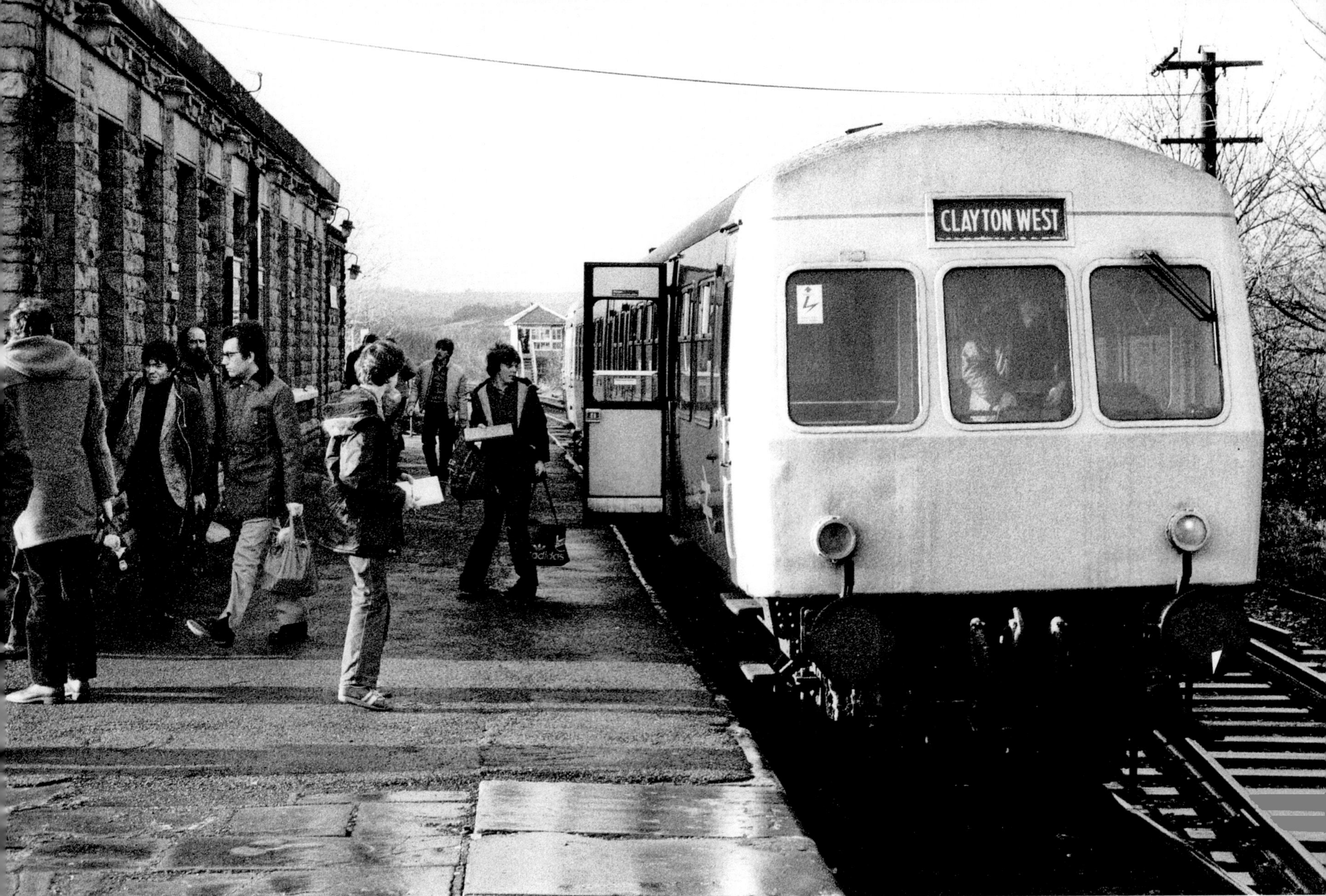

Mining Town Terminus, Clayton West, February 1981.
I was surprised that the line from and to Clayton West hadn't closed by the end of the 1960s or early '70s, being a low passenger volume branch line to a small town. Plus, the branch was only 4 miles long, with one intermediate station at Skelmanthorpe. Not a sure-fire money-spinner. These traits usually guaranteed making it on to Beeching's hit list. The line survived thanks to plenty of rail-borne coal traffic from the adjacent colliery and a subsidy from West Yorkshire County Council. Unfortunately, it finally closed to passengers on 2 January 1983. Freight traffic came to an end during October of the same year; the tracks were lifted three years later. During the 1990s it gradually blossomed into a superb 15in-gauge line, extending from Clayton West to Shelley. The station at Clayton West and its yard has been transformed into the smart headquarters of the Kirklees Light Railway. It includes comprehensive visitor facilities and a loco shed; it is well worth a visit and a ride on the trains.

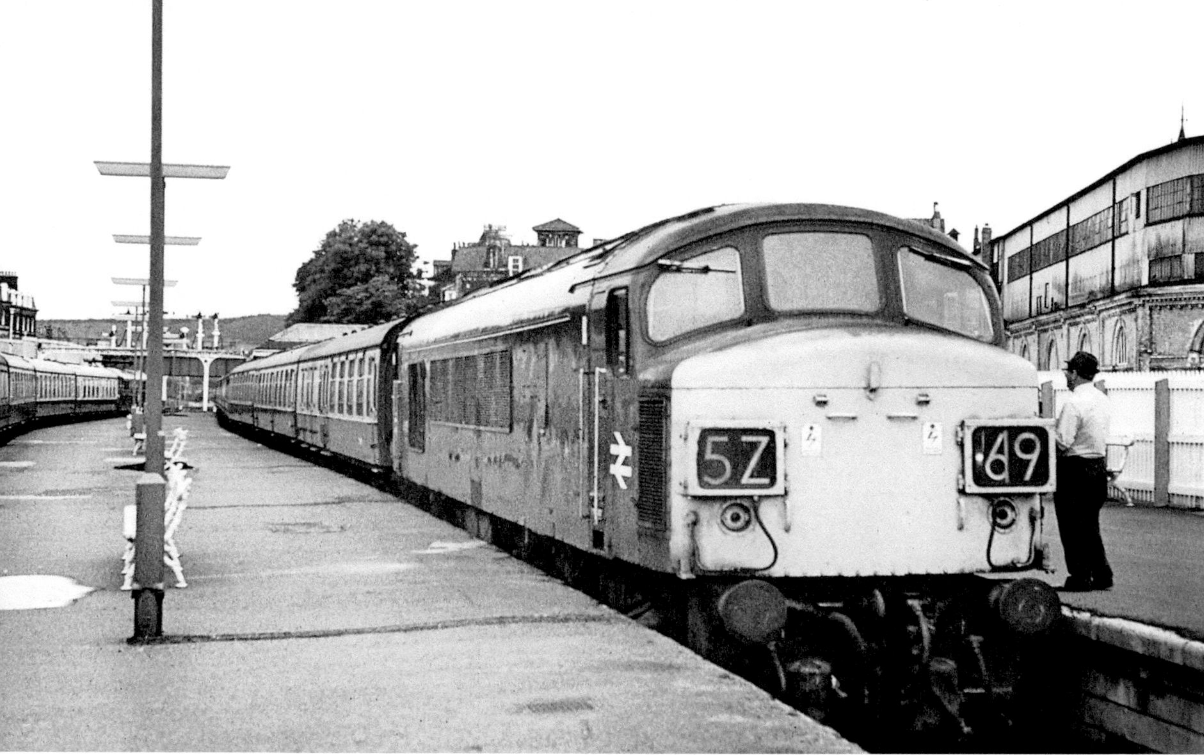

Peak Season, Scarborough, July 1975.
During the 1970 and '80s, Scarborough generated lots of loco-hauled traffic. Both scheduled and excursion trains. Because of this the station had two Class 03 shunters to draw back the empty coaching stock to enable incoming locos to be released from the seashore end of the station. In this shot a Class 45 has recently arrived with an excursion from the East Midlands. On the adjacent platform is a Class 31 excursion. The 31 has already been released and is at the head of its train, which will return day-trippers to Banbury.

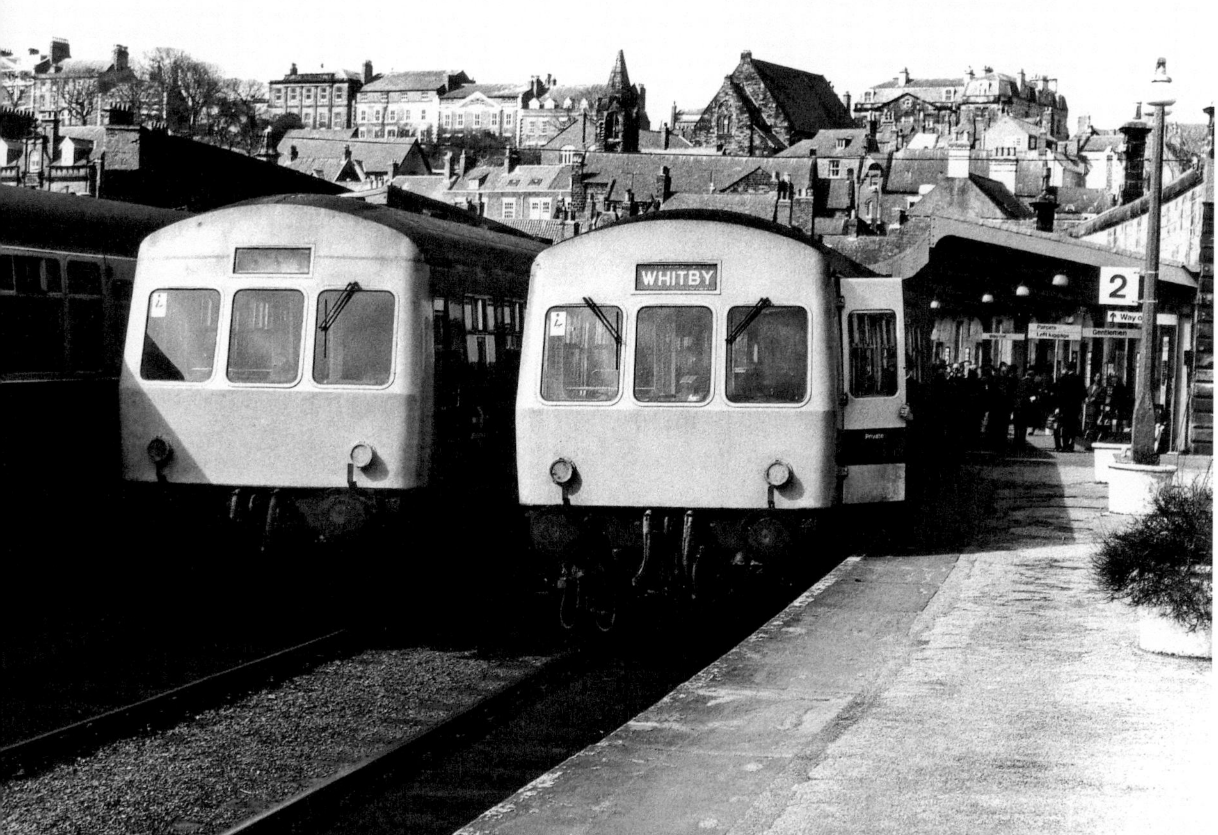

Fish and Chips are a Must, Whitby, August 1975.
Surely everybody has fish and chips when they do a day trip to Whitby? Hot, with plenty of salt and vinegar. My mouth is watering as I type this caption. Back in the 1970s the terminus station at Whitby was quite sizeable, with four platforms and storage sidings. It was well equipped to handle plenty of trains. On the afternoon I took this shot there was a Class 40-hauled excursion on Platform 1. It is alongside the two Class 101 DMUs seen in the photograph. Fortunately, it has not been totally decimated like many end-of-the-line stations. It did lose Platforms 3 and 4 to a supermarket development and for a time had only one rail-served platform (Platform 1). The North Yorkshire Moors Railway has turned round its fortunes. By August 2014 they had reinstated track to Platform 2, allowing it to be regularly used by their trains, which serve Pickering.

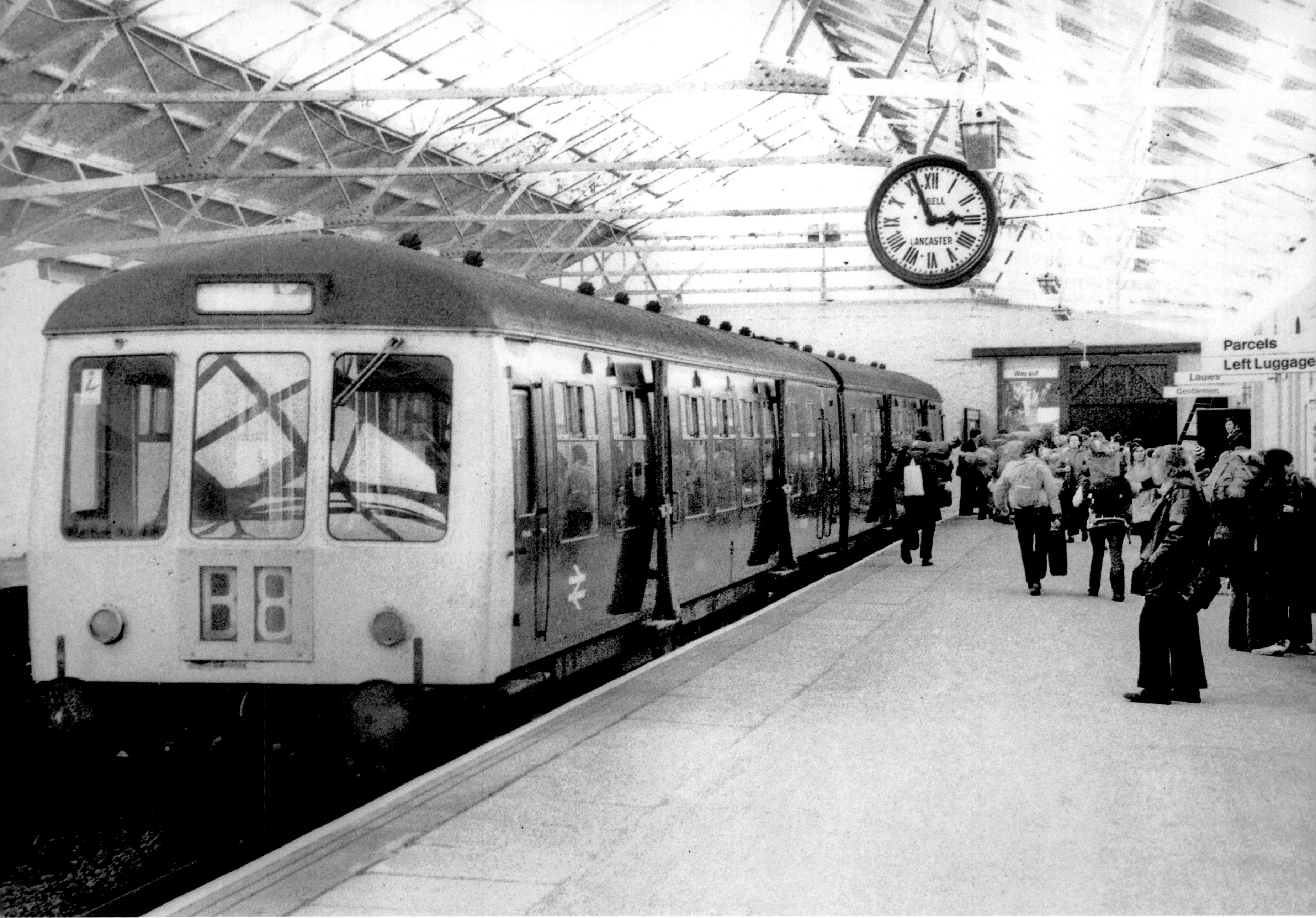

Gateway to the Lakes, Windermere, Easter 1973.
The solidly built station at Windermere once boasted four platforms beneath its overall roof. Not long before I took this photograph the three tracks had been taken out of use and the line was reduced to one-train operation. Excursions and loco-hauled trains could no longer be accommodated. I think the cut back was too harsh, bearing in mind Windermere is such a popular destination. Sadly the cut backs didn't stop there. Instead of the station regaining track and facilities, it was partially demolished. In its place stands a supermarket, which incorporates its facade and canopy. The replacement station is located close to the supermarket, making it handy for rail-borne shoppers. In this shot the Class 108 DMU has just arrived from Oxenholme. It was full of backpackers – you can see them disappearing out of the station.

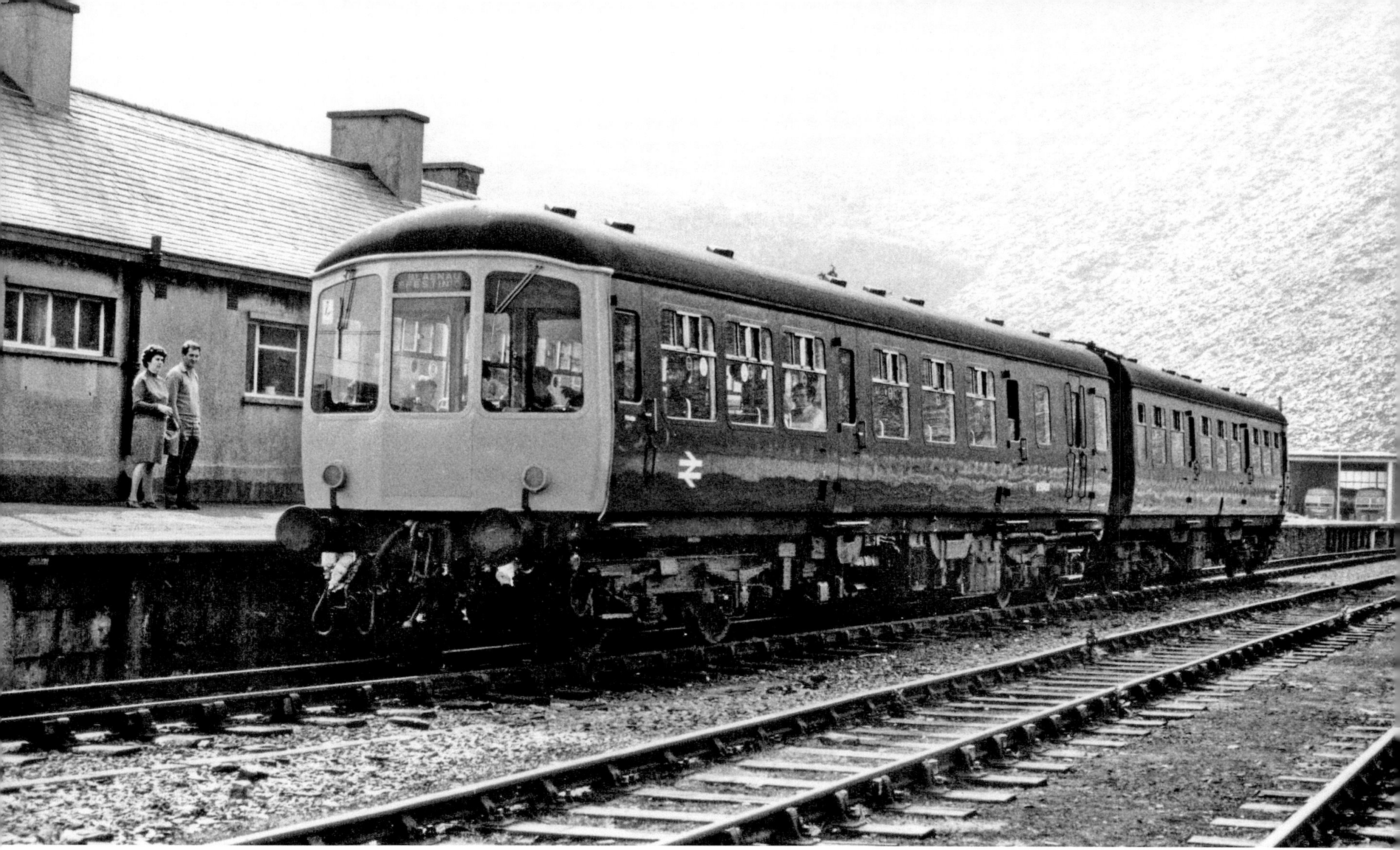

Beneath a Slate Mountain, Blaenau Ffestiniog, 30 May 1977.
Class 103 *Park Royal* DMU has recently arrived at Blaenau Ffestiniog from Llandudno on 30 May 1977, via the Conway Valley Line. The 103s were built at the Crossley Motors works in Stockport, where they also built buses. That is probably why some of their interior fittings were reminiscent of the Crossley buses that ran in my locality. This type of DMU is amongst my favourite first-generation examples, although I do like them all. The station was located some distance away from the town's centre. It was previously known as Blaenau Ffestiniog North and was part of the LNWR/LMS empire. There was another station in the town, the ex-GWR Central station, which closed at the beginning of 1960. In theory the location of the photograph is the end of the Conway Valley Line, but it wasn't. The building of Trawsfynydd power station between 1958 and 1965 led to the extension of the route through the old Central station to gain access to the site. This was for construction items and, later, nuclear flask shipment. Bearing this in mind, you would have thought that the ex-GWR station would have been reopened. Passenger trains running into the centre of the town had to wait until 1982, when the Ffestiniog Railway arrived, after the full reopening of their line to Porthmadog. A new joint station was opened to serve BR and the Ffestiniog Railway. When this happened the station was the new end of the line, extended rather than truncated – the latter being what we had become accustomed to. The station shown in this photograph was closed as a result, which was a shame because I liked its austere look in the shadow of the massive slate mountain. Check out the old Crosville buses in the adjacent garage.

Carcasses, Reddish, June 1980.
The end of the Woodhead route and its electric locos was imminent when I took this photograph at Reddish Depot during June 1980. In order to keep locos running, withdrawn locos were cannibalised. The grounded bodies of 76050 and 76057 have lost their bogies for stock, along with many other important bits of hardware. Seven years earlier I photographed 76057 rumbling through Godley station with a steel train (see p. 76); here it is only fit for the scrap man's oxyacetylene torch. They marked a sad and premature end to the LNER-inspired modern electric railway across the Pennines. I can't help but think if it had lasted a few more years it would now be a well-used and vital part of the modern rail network.

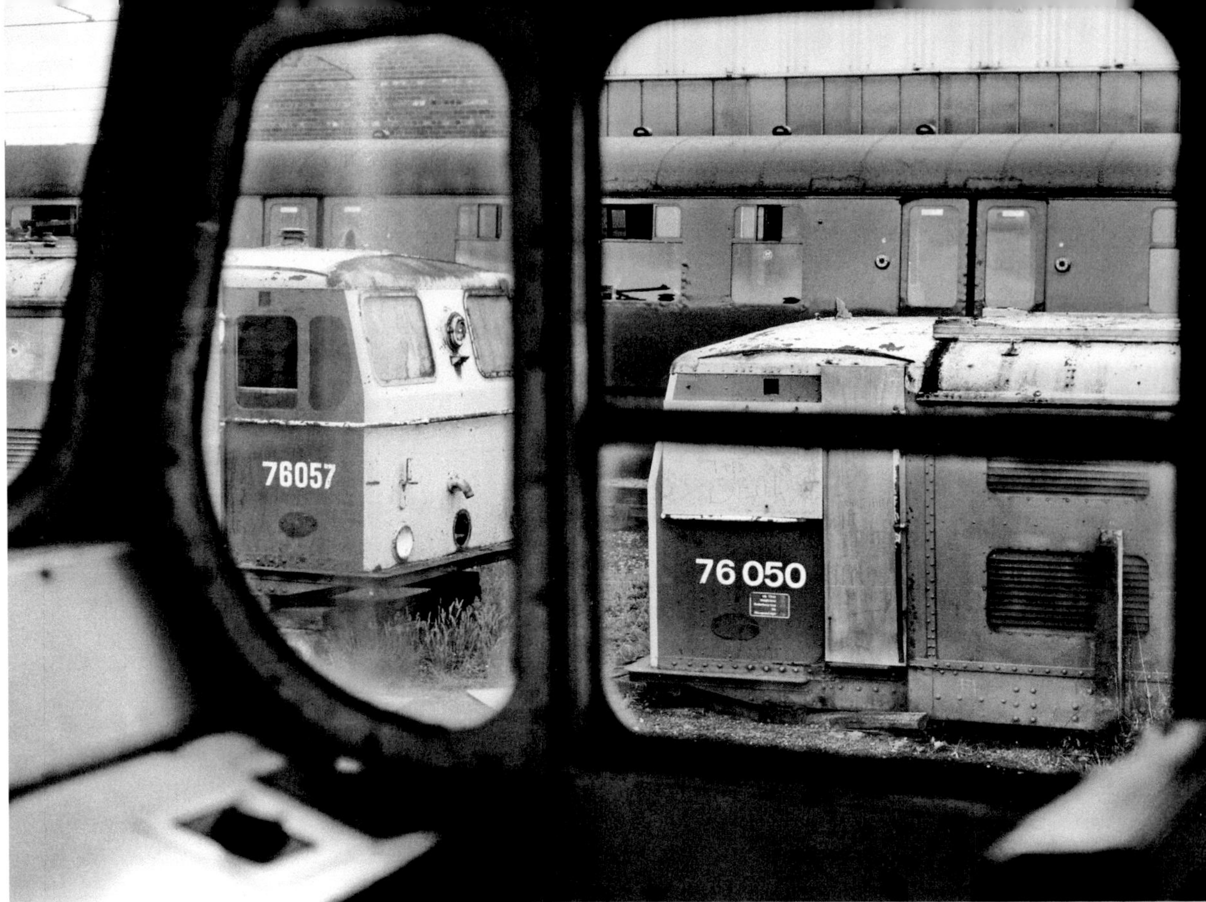

'Skin Head' has Hit the Buffers, Reddish, December 1975.
'Skin Head' Class 24 24020/5020 has reached the end of the line at Reddish Depot. It had been withdrawn during the summer and would linger at the depot, along with the equally forlorn 24005, 24021 and 24024, until February 1977. They were then hauled away to Swindon works for breaking up. They lasted until April 1977. The locos only had sixteen years in BR service. I guess changing rail traffic meant their medium power wasn't up to the job of hauling modern trains. They were of course ideal for lighter-weight old-fashioned small wagon freight trains; unfortunately for the Class 24 by then they were becoming far less plentiful. A rather nice-looking loco, which reminded me of summer holidays in North Wales, where they were once commonplace.

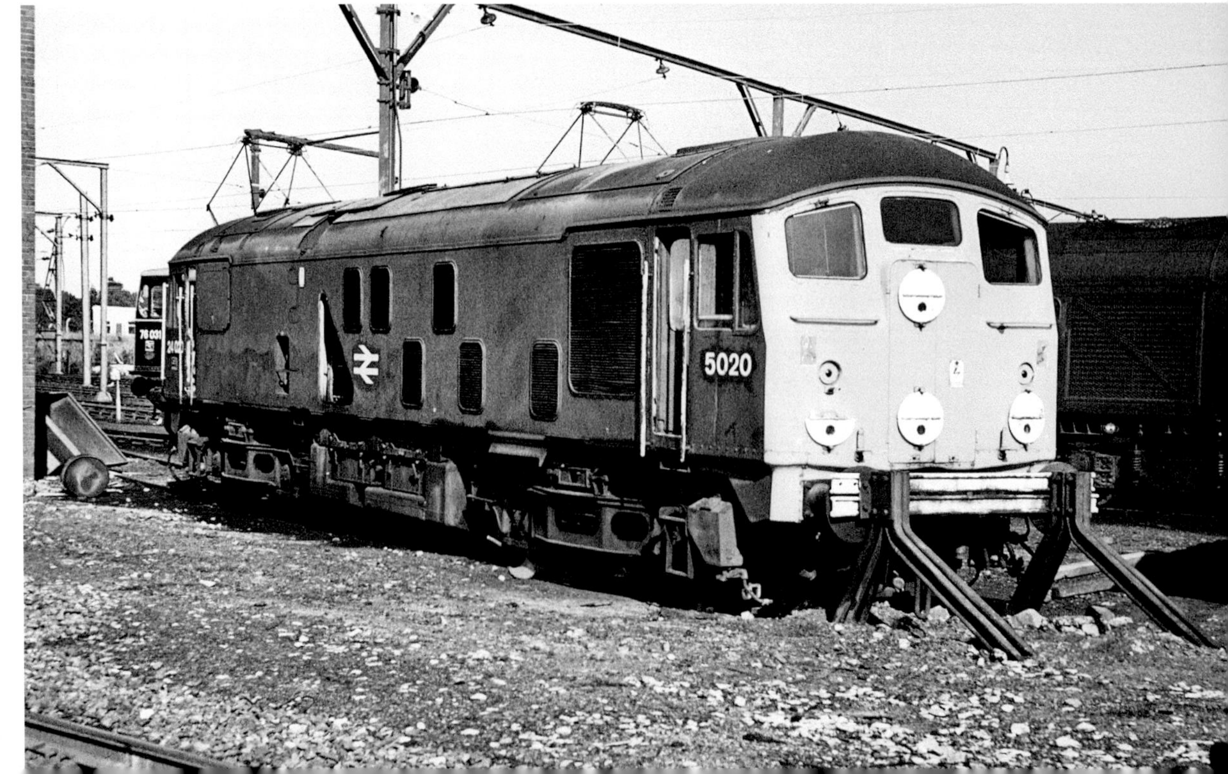

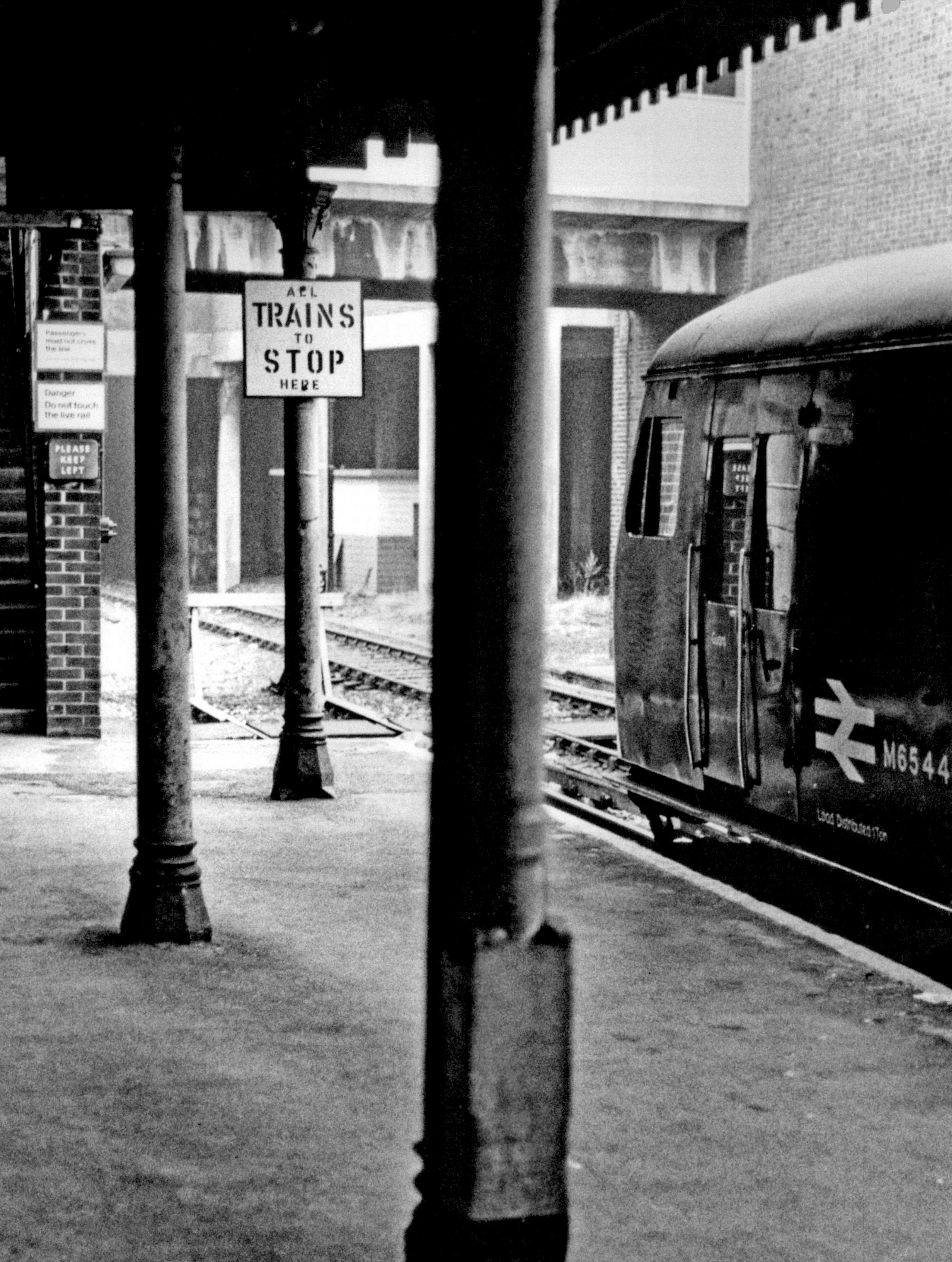

'All Trains to Stop Here', Bury Bolton Street, winter 1979.
This shot of a Class 504 EMU at Bolton Street station, taken during the winter of 1979, epitomises the rundown and hopeless nature of many parts of BR's network at the time. It really is the end of the line for the passenger service from Manchester Victoria. Soon the services would transfer to the brand-new Bury Interchange and the station would close. Until 1980 freight trains did still pass through bound for the coal terminal at Rawtenstall, so it wasn't actually the end of the line. The coal trains gained access to Bury using the freight-only line through Heywood, rather than the third-rail electric route via Radcliffe. After the coal trains ended, the Heywood route was truncated at the Standard Railway Wagon works. Now the East Lancashire Railway is flourishing using both the Heywood Line and route from Bury to Rawtenstall. A must-visit, time and time again, preserved railway. Bury Bolton Street has been fully restored and is a delight to experience.

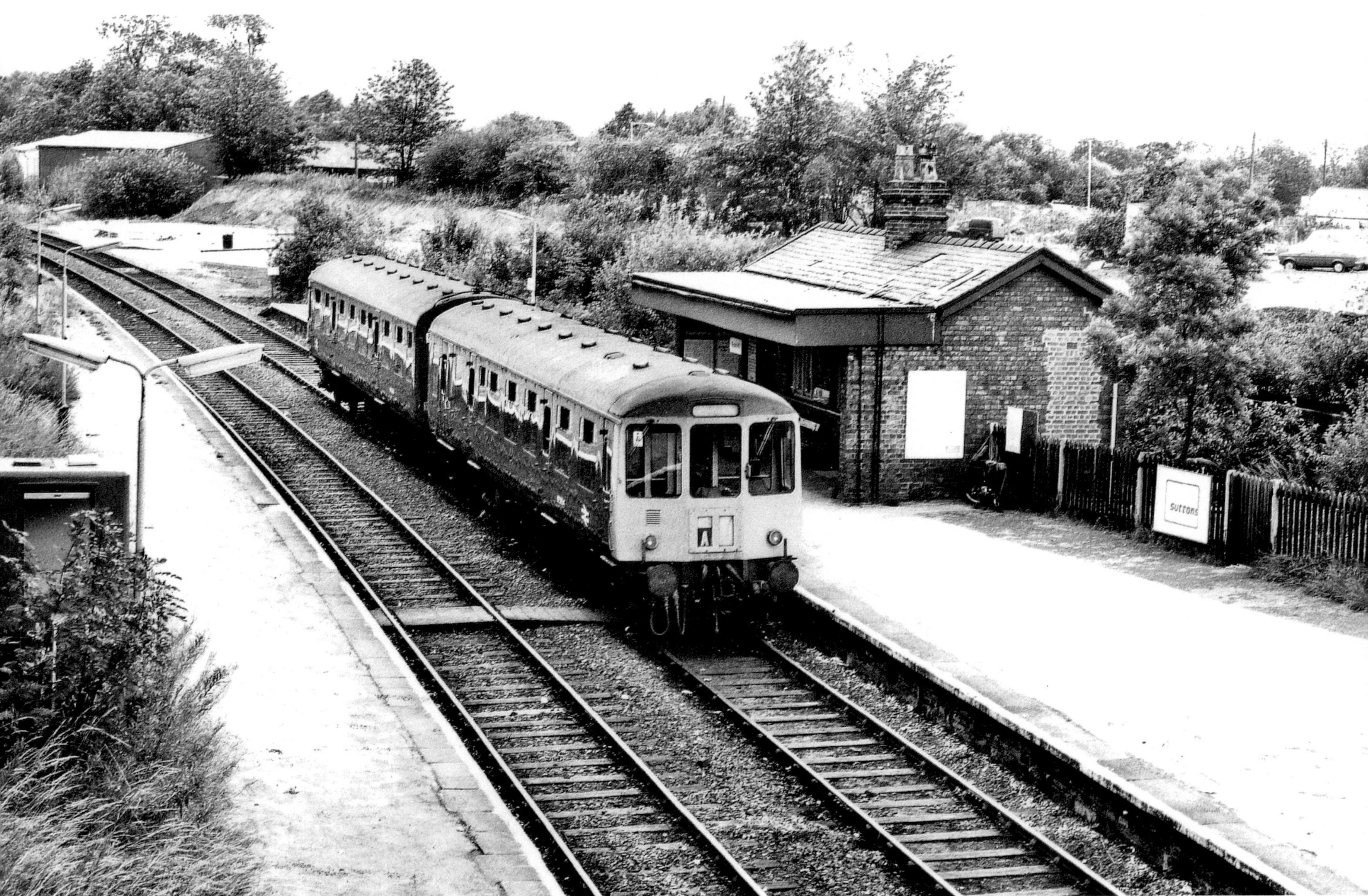

Double Track Deception, Rose Hill, summer 1975.
At first glance, and maybe after many glances, this Class 104 is calling at an intermediate station on a twin-track cross-country rail route. There is plenty of evidence to confirm this. It is, however, the terminus of the truncated route from Macclesfield to Manchester via Bollington. The through route was closed at the beginning of 1970, leaving just the stub from Marple Junction. The redundant track bed beyond Rose Hill is now the 'Middlewood Way'. The line to the left has long since gone and vegetation has taken over; there is now no doubt that it is an end-of-the-line station. It survived because of its high volume of passengers, which is still the case.

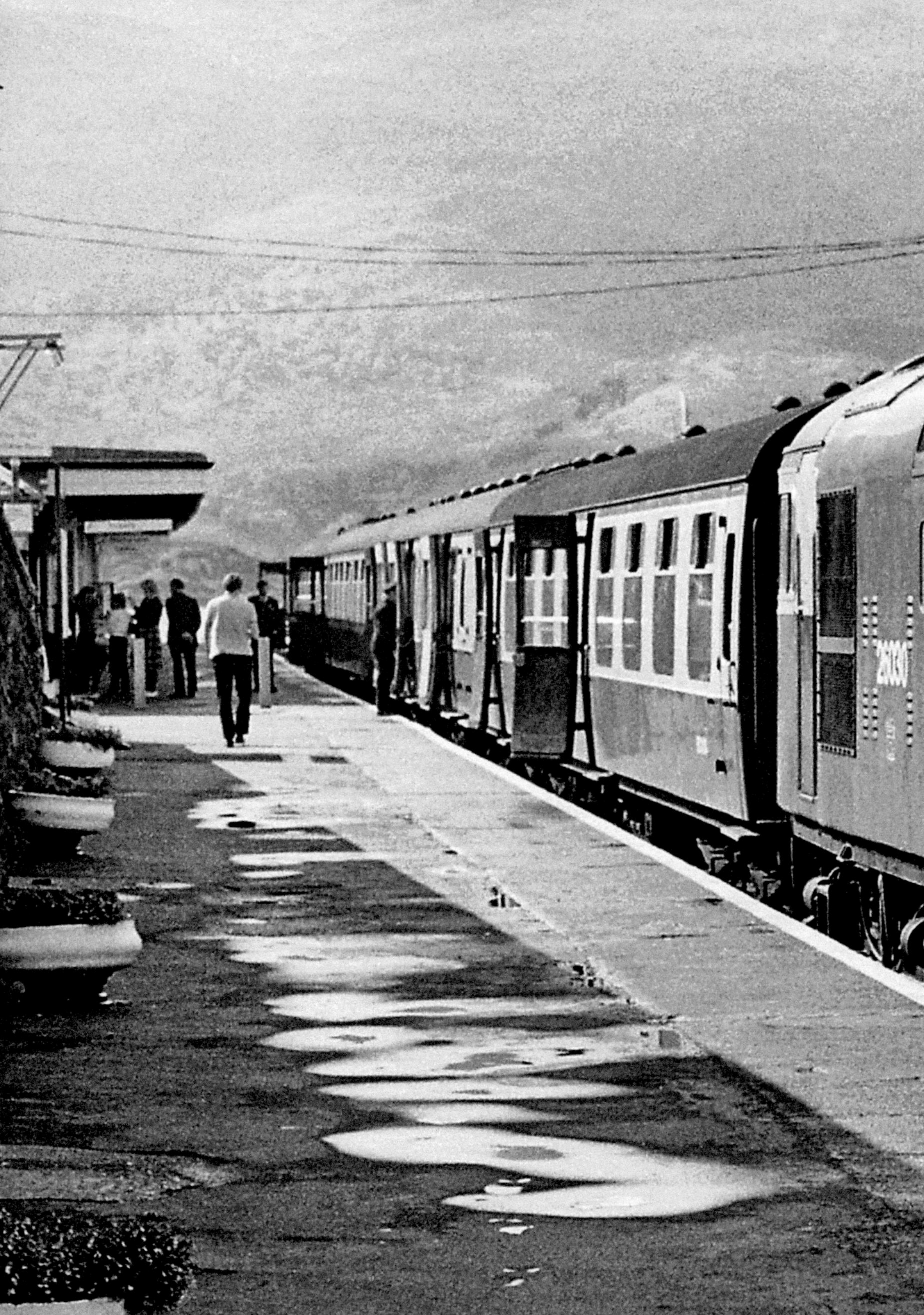

The Rain has Stopped, Kyle of Lochalsh, summer 1981.
It has not long since stopped raining and the morning sun is drying the station platform. 26030 has just run round its train after arriving with the first service of the day from Inverness. This brilliant end-of-the-line station facilitated a quick route to Skye via the close-at-hand ferry, now superseded by the Skye Bridge. It is a terrific station and line, which I have promised my partner, Sheila, we will one day sample together. Thank goodness it survived the Beeching cuts; it is now set to be with us for a long time to come. If only it still had Class 26s hauling its trains.

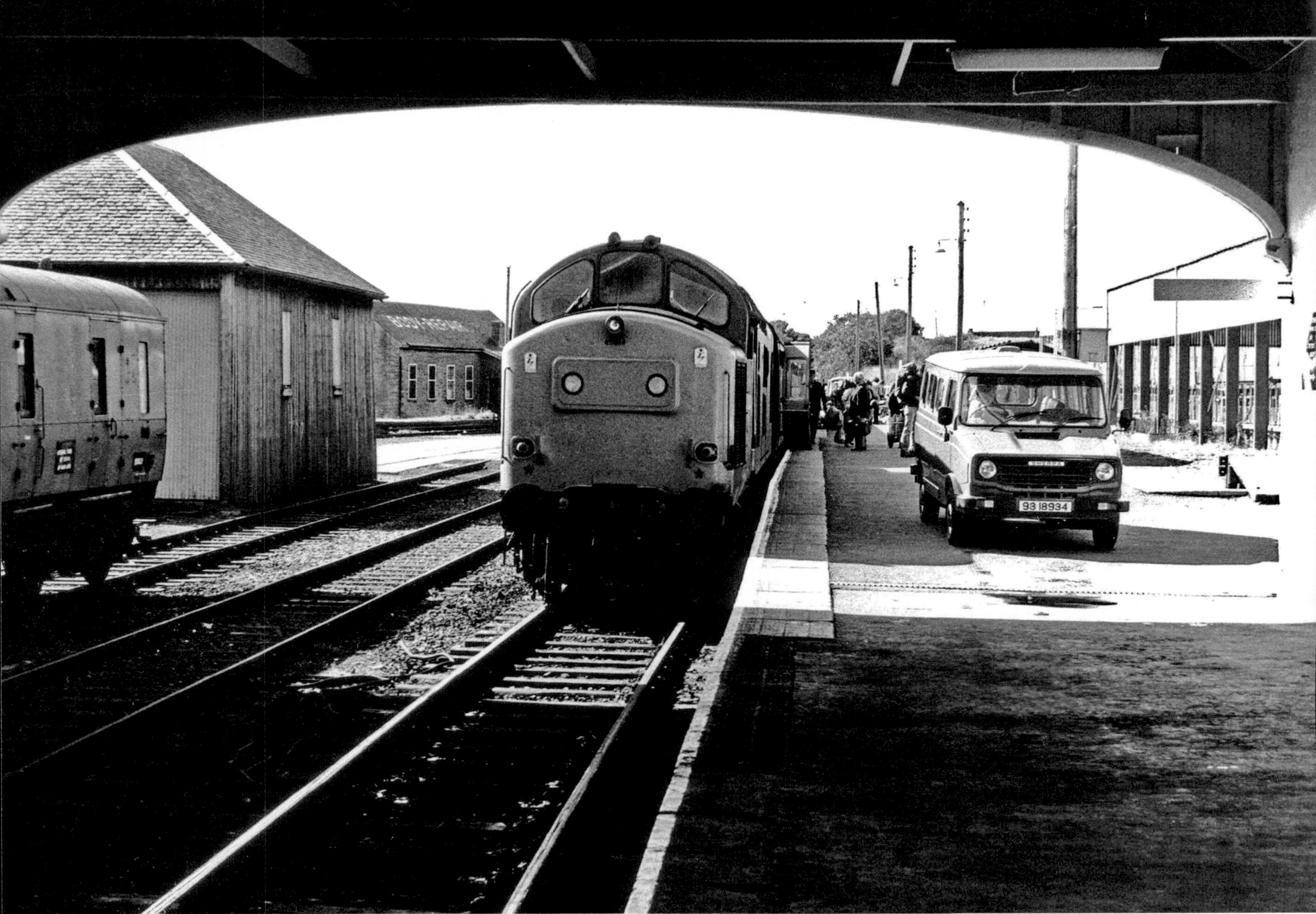

The Far North, Thurso, August 1982.
This is handy steam-heat-boiler-fitted and air/vacuum-braked Inverness-based 37260, previously allocated to London's Stratford Depot, just arriving at Thurso from the Highland capital. Waiting in the terminus station's approach road is a bus, which would take most of the passengers to the P&O Orkney ferry terminal at Stromness. I was amongst them; it would be my first trip to Orkney, but not my last. 37260 was named *Radio Highland*; on 7 July 1984; unfortunately it caught fire during 1989. The damage sustained was too great to allow a viable repair to be undertaken. It was finally cut up by MC Metals at Springburn yard on 25 August 1991. If it had survived, its handy on-board equipment would have made it a versatile loco for any preserved railway. Alternatively, like quite a few of its classmates, it might still be hauling trains on the modern railway network. They have far from reached the end of the line.